Under Pressure

Higher Education Research in the 21st Century Series

Series Editors

Pedro Teixeira (*CIPES and University of Porto, Portugal*)
Jussi Välimaa (*University of Jyväskylä, Finland*)

International Editorial Advisory Board

Mari Elken (*University of Oslo, Norway*)
Gaële Goastellec (*University of Lausanne, Switzerland*)
Manja Klemenčič (*Harvard University, USA*)
Simon Marginson (*University College London, United Kingdom*)
Emanuela Reale (*Institute for Research on Firm and Growth CERIS – CNR Rome, Italy*)
Creso Sá (*University of Toronto, Canada*)

VOLUME 11

The titles published in this series are listed at *brill.com/cher*

Under Pressure

Higher Education Institutions Coping with Multiple Challenges

Edited by

Pedro N. Teixeira, Amélia Veiga,
Maria J. Rosa and António Magalhães

BRILL
SENSE

LEIDEN | BOSTON

All chapters in this book have undergone peer review.

The Library of Congress Cataloging-in-Publication Data is available online at http://catalog.loc.gov
LC record available at https://lccn.loc.gov/2019014394

ISSN 2542-8837
ISBN 978-90-04-39846-7 (paperback)
ISBN 978-90-04-39847-4 (hardback)
ISBN 978-90-04-39848-1 (e-book)

Copyright 2019 by Koninklijke Brill NV, Leiden, The Netherlands.
Koninklijke Brill NV incorporates the imprints Brill, Brill Hes & De Graaf, Brill Nijhoff, Brill Rodopi, Brill Sense, Hotei Publishing, mentis Verlag, Verlag Ferdinand Schöningh and Wilhelm Fink Verlag.
All rights reserved. No part of this publication may be reproduced, translated, stored in a retrieval system, or transmitted in any form or by any means, electronic, mechanical, photocopying, recording or otherwise, without prior written permission from the publisher.
Authorization to photocopy items for internal or personal use is granted by Koninklijke Brill NV provided that the appropriate fees are paid directly to The Copyright Clearance Center, 222 Rosewood Drive, Suite 910, Danvers, MA 01923, USA. Fees are subject to change.

This book is printed on acid-free paper and produced in a sustainable manner.

CONTENTS

Acknowledgements — vii

List of Figures and Tables — ix

Notes on Contributors — xiii

Part 1: Introduction

1. Higher Education Institutions Dealing With Multiple Challenges — 3
   Pedro Teixeira, António Magalhães, Amélia Veiga and Maria J. Rosa

Part 2: Setting the Stage

2. Higher Education and Science in the Age of Trump, Brexit and Le Pen — 17
   Simon Marginson

3. Adaptive University Structures: From Theory to Practice and Back — 37
   Barbara Sporn

4. Governance and Management – Challenges of Today, Adapting to the Times — 55
   S. Feyo de Azevedo

Part 3: Changes and Challenges in Governance and Management

5. Human Resource Development for Junior Researchers in Germany: Stocktaking and Prospects — 65
   René Krempkow and Mathias Winde

6. Shadows of Hierarchy: Managerial-Administrative Relationships within Universities under Pressure — 77
   Ton Kallenberg

7. Higher Education Institutions Responding to Issues: Gender-Based Violence on Campus — 91
   Melindy Brown, James Williams and David Kane

Part 4: Quality Management and the Relevance of Strategy

8. Strategic Quality Management – A Contribution to Autonomy: The Example of TU Darmstadt, Germany — 113
   Tina Klug

CONTENTS

9. Innovativeness of Higher Education Institutions: Preconditions for the Development of Co-Operative Innovations   125
  Cindy Konen

10. Internal Quality Assurance: A Political Process Challenging Academics' Professionalism?   147
  Maria J. Manatos, Sónia Cardoso, Maria J. Rosa and Teresa Carvalho

Part 5: Students and the Effectiveness of Learning

11. Grades as a Measure of Students' Learning Outcome   173
  Magnus Strand Hauge

12. The Emerging Differential Tuition Era among U.S. Public Universites   191
  Gregory C. Wolniak, Casey E. George and Glen R. Nelson

Part 6: The Role of Higher Education in Regional Innovation

13. The Institutional Environment and Organisational Challenges of Universities' Regional Engagement   217
  Verena Radinger-Peer

14. Universities' Role in Regional Innovation Reconsidered: Looking at the Bottom of the Iceberg   235
  Jürgen Janger

ACKNOWLEDGEMENTS

We would like to thank the University of Porto for hosting the 2017 EAIR Forum and offering such a great environment for fruitful discussions and exchange.

The research underlying the theme of the conference and the book has been supported by Project UID/CED/00757/2013 funded by FCT – Fundação para a Ciência e a Tecnologia (Portugal).

FIGURES AND TABLES

FIGURES

2.1.	Comparative tertiary-level participation on the basis of the UNESCO gross enrolment ratio and the Clancy index, OECD countries, 2013	19
2.2.	Level of education and interpersonal trust, OECD countries, 2015. Q. 'Do you trust other people?' Proportion (%) answering 'yes'	21
2.3.	Level of education and political connectedness, OECD countries, 2015. Q. 'Do you believe you have a say in government?' Proportion (%) answering 'yes'	22
2.4.	Investment in R&D as a proportion (%) of GDP, United States, United Kingdom, Germany, China, South Korea, India: 1991–2015. There are series breaks for India, with no data for 2012–2014 inclusive	24
2.5.	Annual number of published science papers, United States, China, Germany, United Kingdom, South Korea: 2003–2016	26
3.1.	Adaptive university structures (Sporn, 1999)	38
3.2.	WU history: Becoming an entrepreneurial university	42
5.1.	Career goals of junior researchers in ten years' time (in %)	69
5.2.	Personnel categories for junior researchers and tenure opportunity (in %, multiple responses)	70
6.1.	Four types in the managerial-administrative relationships	85
8.1.	Institutional evaluation procedure at TU Darmstadt 2017	119
8.2.	Current state of objectives implemented at TU Darmstadt,	120
9.1.	Part capabilities of manifestation from Teece (2007) and Faix (2017)	132
9.2.	Model of the innovativeness of HEIs	134
9.3.	Expectancy theory adjusted for HEIs	137
10.1.	Perceptions of academics regarding the drivers for the creation or edification of internal QA practices	153
10.2.	Perceptions of academics regarding the cultures promoted by internal QA	154
10.3.	Academics' perceptions regarding internal QA effects	155
10.4.	Academics perceptions regarding autonomy and professionalism	160
11.1.	Schematic presentation of the regression models	179
12.1.	Patterns of institutional adoption of differential tuition policies, 1991–92 to 2015–16	204

FIGURES AND TABLES

14.1.	A conceptual model for the role of universities in innovative activity	241
14.2.	An iceberg model of universities' impact on regional innovation	245

TABLES

2.1.	Expansion in the number of world universities publishing more than 10,000, 500 and 1,200 journal papers over four years, 2006–2009 to 2013–2016	23
2.2.	Leading universities in (1) Physical Sciences and Engineering and (2) Mathematics and Complex Computing, based on published papers in the top 10 per cent of their field by citation rate: 2012–2015 papers	27
5.1.	Personnel development for junior researchers in Germany over time (values in %)	66
5.2.	Percentage of people with permanent employment contracts at universities	73
9.1.	Statistical key figures of HEIs	127
10.1.	Sample's characterisation	152
10.2.	Academics' perceptions of internal QA according to gender (results of Mann-Whitney tests)	156
10.3.	Academics' perceptions of QA according to the higher education sector (results of Mann-Whitney tests)	157
10.4	Academics' perceptions of QA according to the performance of management functions (results of Mann-Whitney tests)	158
10.5.	Academics' perceptions of QA according to tenure/non-tenure (results of Mann-Whitney tests)	158
10.6.	Academics' perceptions of internal QA according to involvement in decision making processes (results of Kruskal-Wallis tests)	159
10.7.	Correlations between QA drivers and the variables reflecting autonomy and professionalism (Spearman correlation coefficients)	162
10.8.	Correlations between QA cultures and the variables reflecting autonomy and professionalism (Spearman correlation coefficients)	163
10.9.	Correlations between QA effects and the variables reflecting autonomy and professionalism (Spearman correlation coefficients)	164
11.1.	Correlation between different types of learning outcomes and grades in HE	177
11.2.	The adjusted r^2 of the models shown in Figure 11.1	181
11.3.	Regression models 4a, 5a, 7a and 5b – results	182
11.4.	Institutional effects on HE grades and change in institutional effects from model 4a to model 7a	186
12.1.	Institutions adopting DT policies by year	200

12.2.	Sample means by institutional differential tuition status, 1991–92 to 2015–16	205
12.3.	Estimated odds ratios of differential tuition adoption	207
12.4.	Estimated hazard rate of differential tuition adoption	208
13.1.	Analysis of the institutional framework and mechanisms as well as organisational change processes of selected models of university engagement. (N = normative nature, C-C = cultural cognitive nature, R = regulative nature)	223
14.1.	Various ways of how university outputs can become relevant for regional innovation	239

NOTES ON CONTRIBUTORS

Melindy Brown is a Lecturer in Criminology at Birmingham City University. In addition to her role as a lecturer, Melindy is completing her PhD, focusing on the support within the community for released prisoners whose substance misuse has played a factor in their offence. Melindy's research mainly focuses on substance misuse, desistance and the probation service. However, she has been involved in many projects regarding gender-based violence, particularly within a Higher Education Setting, including her Master's thesis titled 'Women and Their Sense of Safety on Campus'.

Sónia Cardoso is a researcher both at the Portuguese Agency for Assessment and Accreditation of Higher Education (A3ES) and at the Centre for Research in Higher Education Policies (CIPES). She completed her PhD in Social Sciences under the topic of Quality Assurance in Higher Education. Her main research interests and publications, in reference journals and books, are within the fields of higher education policies, quality assurance, and institutions and institutional actors' relation with quality assurance. She is a member of CHER.

Teresa Carvalho is an Associate Professor at the University of Aveiro. She is a senior researcher at CIPES (Center for Research in Higher Education Policies) and the Director of the PhD program in Public Policies at the University of Aveiro. She is a member of the ESA (European Sociological Association) Executive Committee, as chair of the RN-Council, for 2017–2019. Develops research in public reforms and has a special interest in issues related with the role of professionals in formulating and implementing public policies. The main focus of her current research is the relation between managerialism and academic professionalism with an emphasis on gender issues. She has developed research and published her work in *New Public Management*; sociology of professions, gender and academic careers in several journals and books.

Sebastião Feyo de Azevedo was born in Porto, Portugal, in 1951. He holds a PhD in Chemical Engineering from the University of Wales (1982). In the recent past he was: Rector of the University of Porto (June 2014–June 2018); Dean of Engineering; Vice-president of ENAEE-European Network for Accreditation of Engineering Education; Chairman of the Working Party on Education of the European Federation of Chemical Engineering. On the 9th of February, 2018, he was awarded the Honorary Doctorate by the Ivane Javakhishvili Tbilisi State University, Georgia. He is the recipient of the Dieter Behrens Award, 2013, highest distinction of the European Federation of Chemical Engineering.

NOTES ON CONTRIBUTORS

Casey E. George, PhD, is an Assistant Professor of Higher Education Administration and the Assistant Director for the Center for Economic Education at the University of Louisville. Her research efforts are focused on examining postsecondary access and equity for traditionally marginalized populations, with primary attention given to how institutional programs and policies affect students' access and experiences. Her work has been published in *American Educational Research Journal*, *Teachers College Record*, *Studies in Higher Education*, and the *Journal of Student Financial Aid*.

Magnus Strand Hauge is a senior adviser at the Norwegian Agency for Quality Assurance in Education (NOKUT) where he primarily works with quality enhancement activities as student surveys and indicators on quality in higher education and vocational education. He has previously worked with quality assurance of higher education. He holds BA and MPhil degrees in political science from University of Oslo, Norway.

Jürgen Janger works as a senior researcher and deputy director at the Austrian Institute of Economic research (WIFO) in Vienna. His main research interests are in the economics of science and innovation where he works on innovation measurement frameworks, determinants of job choice in academia, the attractiveness of academic jobs in a cross-country comparative perspective as well as on impact pathways for university-created knowledge.

Ton Kallenberg (1960) studied pedagogical sciences at Leiden University and has defended his PhD thesis at Tilburg University. From the 80s he fulfilled several functions on educational management at Leiden University and the Erasmus University Rotterdam. Since January 2014 he is Director Education and Student Affairs at the faculty Humanities of Leiden University. His research and publications are focussing on leadership and (middle) management in higher education; on didactics in higher education and on teacher education programs.

David Kane is Senior Research Fellow at Birmingham City University, UK. David has been a full-time researcher at Birmingham City University since joining the Social Research and Evaluation Unit (SREU) in September 2004. During this time, David has been an active participant in SREU projects including their work relating to social exclusion in the community at large, exploring aspects of prisoner health, offender support and supporting vulnerable people. David is also engaged in SREU's Higher Education research, particularly aspects of student experience. He has given papers at many EAIR conferences and acted as a track chair when BCU hosted EAIR in 2016. In his spare time(!), David plays guitar, writes songs and escapes the city on his motorcycle.

Tina Klug is Director of Quality Management and Governing Bodies Department at TU Darmstadt. Before she started at TU Darmstadt in 2009, she was working

NOTES ON CONTRIBUTORS

in international non-profit and research management outside the university. Her background is economy and sociology, her key activities and interests are evaluation, quality management, organizational development, management of governing bodies and university politics.

Cindy Konen studied business administration in Dortmund (Germany). After her degree, she was an organisational developer at a state bank as well as in the HEI-sector. Currently, she works at the University of Applied Sciences in Dortmund as a scientific assistant for innovation management of Higher Education Institutions, is a lecturer for business administration and is doing her PhD at the Europa-University Flensburg.

René Krempkow holds a doctoral degree in sociology of education and currently works at Humboldt-University of Berlin. René focuses on research and consulting in the field of Higher Education Management and Higher Education Research. Former stations of his work were Stifterverband Berlin, Institute for Research Information and Quality Assurance Berlin, HIS-Institute for Higher Education Development Hannover (HIS-HE), Free University of Berlin, University of Freiburg and Dresden University of Technology.

António M. Magalhães is Associate Professor at the Faculty of Psychology and Educational Sciences of the University of Porto where he acts as Head of the Department of Education Sciences. He is also Senior Researcher at the Centre for Research in Higher Education Policies (CIPES) and member of its Directive Board. His field of expertise lies on education policy analysis with a focus on higher education policies and also researches on methods of policy analysis. He has coordinated and participated in research projects in these areas and has been publishing in these areas both in Portugal and abroad.

Maria J. Manatos holds a doctoral degree in Management from the ISEG Lisboa School of Economics and Management, Universidade de Lisboa. She is a researcher at the Centre for Research in Higher Education Policies (CIPES). Her main research topics are quality management in higher education institutions. She has published her work in higher education and quality management journals.

Simon Marginson is Professor of Higher Education at the University of Oxford, Director of the ESRC Centre for Global Higher Education in the UK, and Editor-in-Chief of the journal Higher Education. His is also a Lead Research at the Higher School of Economics in Moscow and was the Clark Kerr Lecturer on Higher Education at the University of California in 2014. He focuses on global and international aspects of higher education, system design, and higher education and social inequality.

NOTES ON CONTRIBUTORS

Glen R. Nelson is the Vice President for Finance and Business Affairs at Idaho State University. He is a higher education practitioner having served in senior leadership roles at several public universities and systems, frequently speaking on topics relevant to university business officers, and was selected as a Fulbright Specialist Roster Candidate. His research focuses on the impact of policy decisions on the educational choices made by students from low-income backgrounds and has been featured in *The Chronicle of Higher Education* and on MSNBC. He brings a practice-based perspective to the topic and is a collaborator with Drs. Gregory Wolniak and Casey George on the "Affordability and Transparency Initiative".

Verena Radinger-Peer holds a doctor's degree from the University of Natural Resource and Life Sciences Vienna (BOKU) in regional development and planning. As FWF-Hertha Firnberg Grant holder at the Institute for Sustainable Economic Development her focus lies on various topics regarding the role of universities for regional development. Her research entails the investigation of effects of decentralized location patterns, migration behaviour of graduates, knowledge transfer and cooperation activities (spin-off foundations, R&D cooperation) and more adaptive roles universities may play for socio-institutional change and regional development (third mission, sustainable development). In recent studies, her work has focused on the role of universities within regional sustainability transitions.

Maria J. Rosa is an Assistant Professor at the Department of Economics, Management, Industrial Engineering and Tourism at the University of Aveiro. She is also a senior researcher at the Center for Research in Higher Education Policies – CIPES. Her main research topic is quality management at both higher education systems and institutions levels. She has coordinated and participated in research projects in this area and has published her work in higher education and quality management journals and books. She is a member of CHER and of EAIR.

Barbara Sporn is Professor and Director of the Institute for Higher Education Management at WU Vienna University of Economics and Business. She served as Vice-Rector for Research, International Affairs and External Relations at WU from 2002 to 2015. Professor Sporn's experience includes in-depth knowledge of internationalization, research management, and development of universities as well as business school. Her research concentrates on issues of university management, institutional adaptation, and changing environments for universities from an international and comparative perspective. More recently, she has been interested in business modelling and innovation for universities as well as the building of science and excellence clusters of higher education.

Pedro N. Teixeira is Associate Professor at the Faculty of Economics of the University of Porto (Portugal) and Director of CIPES (Center for Research in Higher

NOTES ON CONTRIBUTORS

Education Policies). He is also Special Adviser to the President of Portugal on Higher Education and Science. His main research interests are on the Economics of Education and the History of Economics. He has published several journal articles in higher education and economics journals and has edited several collective volumes.

Amélia Veiga is Assistant Professor at the Faculty of Psychology and Education Sciences at the University of Porto, Portugal, and researcher at the Centre for Research and Intervention in Education (CIIE) and at the Centre for Research in Higher Education Policies (CIPES). Her academic interests focus on education policy analysis, namely on the Bologna process and higher education governance in areas such as internationalisation, globalisation and quality assurance. She has been involved in national and international projects. She has written book chapters and coedited books and published articles on European integration and higher education governance in key journals such as Higher Education, Studies in Higher Education and Higher Education Quarterly.

James Williams is Senior Research Fellow at Birmingham City University, UK. He is best known for his work on student feedback mechanisms as part of the quality improvement process in higher education and has published extensively in the area. Dr Williams is Associate Editor of the international journal *Quality in Higher Education* and regularly contributes to various forums in this field.

Mathias Winde heads the activities in "Higher Education Policy" at the Stifterverband's capital office. He conducts research on personnel development, competence requirements of companies and cooperation between companies and universities. He previously worked as a researcher in the fields of education, science and innovation at the Institut der deutschen Wirtschaft in Cologne.

Gregory C. Wolniak is Associate Professor of higher education at the University of Georgia's Institute of Higher Education. Wolniak's research focuses on how socioeconomic trajectories are affected by experiences in college, educational choices, and institutional environments, and the degree to which learning and developmental gains made during college translate to post-college outcomes. He frequently publishes research on the career and economic influences of college, and recently, in collaboration with Drs. George and Nelson, launched the "Affordability and Transparency Initiative" aimed at improving the ways higher education institutions communicate their tuition and cost information to the public. His work has been featured in recent articles appearing in *The Atlantic, The Chronicle of Higher Education, The Conversation, Inside Higher Education,* and *MarketWatch*. In addition, Wolniak is co-author of *How College Affects Students: 21st Century Evidence that Higher Education Works* (2016, Wiley/Jossey-Bass).

PART 1
INTRODUCTION

PEDRO TEIXEIRA, ANTÓNIO MAGALHÃES, AMÉLIA VEIGA
AND MARIA J. ROSA

1. HIGHER EDUCATION INSTITUTIONS DEALING WITH MULTIPLE CHALLENGES

INTRODUCTION

A core position in the knowledge economy policies has been ascribed to higher education (Grubb & Lazerson, 2004; Etzkowitz, 2008). This has further enhanced the complexity of the environment within which HEIs (higher education institutions) operate. Systems and institutions deal with a wide range of pressures stemming from the State, the corporate world, the society at large and other political interests (Weisbrod et al., 2008; Marginson & Considine, 2000). Additionally, there are those arising from the constituencies of HEIs (academics, students and non-academics).

HEIs as 'autonomous agents' are subject to demands underlining the need for accountability and awareness to local, regional, national and supranational agendas (Neave, 2013; Stensaker & Harvey, 2011). Institutions are expected to cope with these pressures by developing strategies involving quality management, performance and assessment, innovation, while reconfiguring the relationships between research, teaching and learning, and service to society (Bok, 2003).

Within this landscape, the core business of HEIs is being reshaped and challenging institutions' internal life to strategically respond to the reconfiguration of education, research and service to society. At the core of how institutions are responding to multiple challenges triggered by their ever-changing environment, topics such as governance and management, strategies and strategizing, budget control, performance and assessment, quality management, local and regional innovation come to the fore front (Shattock, 2006; Huisman, 2009).

In this book we aim to analyse how HEIs and their staff are coping with the multiple challenges confronting higher educational globally and how the policy initiatives of the last decade have shaped those institutional responses. We will pay particular attention to four dimensions of change that seem to us as key elements in higher education transformation: governance, quality assurance, performance and assessment, and the role of professionals. The chapters included in this volume contribute to illustrate that these various dimensions of change are significantly intertwined and that the effectiveness of policy initiatives regarding each of these aspects requires an integrated approach and needs to take into account the interplay of the aforementioned dimensions within HEIs, building upon previous collective work along these lines of research (see Sarrico et al., 2016).

A LANDSCAPE OF COMPLEX INSTITUTIONAL TRANSFORMATIONS

Higher education is undergoing a major transformation (Musselin & Teixeira, 2013). As this sector has continued to expand, governments' responses have been to seek structural changes (Taylor et al., 2008). These changes have had a major impact on the external and internal regulation of HEIs, namely by stressing its economic dimensions and the potential of HEIs to contribute to individual and socio-economic goals (Teixeira, 2007, 2014). This shifting view about institutions and their primary purposes has led to a need to rethink and adapt the contextual framework in which these organizations operate. Hence, we have seen a reconfiguration of the sector along market rules (Teixeira et al., 2004; Teixeira & Dill, 2011). Higher education has now moved from an expanding sector to a mature industry (Teixeira, 2011) and governments and societies have become more demanding. Previous research showed that this had important consequences in higher education, notably through a much more explicit participation of external stakeholders in formal and informal mechanisms of governance (Middlehurst & Teixeira, 2012). Moreover, the pervasive managerial and economic dimensions of institutions have been promoting the influence of management (Magalhães et al., 2016).

The emergence of these new managerial ideas has contributed to put the focus on universities to change their 'traditional' nature (Amaral et al., 2003). Having to take into account the interests of a variety of stakeholders, and to deal with growing international competition, HEIs had to rethink their forms of organisation, governance and management, putting a new emphasis on the implementation of effective co-ordination and control systems. These mechanisms are to be directed to improve organisational performance (Clark, 1998) and respond to societal changes while promoting effective and innovative institutional management (Shattock, 2006; Middlehurst & Teixeira, 2012).

In many HEIs the strategic power of the governance structure was enhanced in detriment of collegial bodies' power (Veiga et al., 2015; Magalhães et al., 2013a, 2013b; Santiago et al., 2015). The right to self-governance attributed to HEIs is counter-balanced by what has been called 'grid of visibilities' (Rose, 1996), namely quality assurance processes and structures. To this, one can add the growing pluralisation of governing and governance's social regulatory technologies. The shift from collegial governance to management concepts, structures and methods has enabled HEIs to act more strategically. However, the emphasis on institutional autonomy does not correspond to the retraction of state regulatory power. The transformation of the regulation relationships between the state and institutions has replaced a priori control, via inputs (e.g., funding), by a posteriori control, referred to institutions' output (Neave, 2012). This has induced the elaboration of instruments based on performance indicators that are spreading in many higher education systems (Melo et al., 2010; Teixeira et al., 2017).

The institutional adaptation to this new context has been moulded by a change from a cycle of trust and confidence in institutions to a cycle of suspicion (Amaral & Rosa, 2010). This has been visible in the rise of a series of accountability instruments such as the movement towards accreditation that has been observed in recent years (Schwarz & Westerheijden, 2004). However, and more recently, a quality enhancement approach has also come into the fore, which is based on the idea that the responsibility for quality and its assurance should lie with HEIs (Rosa & Amaral, 2014). Consequently, it is possible to observe a trend towards the implementation of internal quality management systems in HEIs, in line with the Standards and guidelines for quality assurance in the European Higher Education Area (ESG) (Manatos et al., 2015). Increasingly, HEIs have to respond not just on the quality of their education provision, but also to a variety of aspects of their performance (Sarrico, 2010). Despite the fact that performance is increasingly measured, there is scarce evidence that it is leading to changes in behaviour and performance (Melo & Sarrico, 2015). Moreover, that is done as a collection of disjoint parallel systems that increase bureaucracy, workload and erode the goodwill of staff. This leads us to conclude that performance management in universities is something that is not just a technical problem, but increasingly an organisational one, where the issues of values and governance structures take prominence (Sarrico et al., 2010).

The question of how academics and non-academics are responding to this newly created environment is a matter requiring increasing attention. This interest is particularly evidenced in the reflection over the effects of the aforementioned changes in governance and in the assumption of a management culture over academics' identities and professionalisation processes (Santiago & Carvalho, 2016). Concerning administrative and management staff, theoretical reflection and empirical analysis are yet to be developed, since this group tends to be interpreted as a residual category (Watson, 2009; Meek et al., 2010).

This volume aims to contribute to the understanding of the effects of national and supra-national political coordination of research, innovation, education and service to society in HEIs and to assess their response to the challenges posed to the production and circulation of knowledge in major areas of change in HE such as governance, quality, performance in the various missions (teaching and learning, research, and service to society) and the role of the different internal and external stakeholders. The novelty brought about by this perspective is filling the gap on the knowledge about how, at the institutional level, these areas interact and influence each other, and how global, national and institutional policy coordination play a role in the articulation of effective and innovative forms of institutional management (Sarrico et al., 2016).

The chapters included in this volume constitute a selection of some of the best papers presented at the 2017 EAIR Forum, under the theme "Under Pressure? Higher Education Institutions Coping with Multiple Challenges". The Forum addressed these topics by convening approaches to the understanding of the interactions between policy drivers and institutional practices. The Forum attracted more than 300 researchers from around the world that contributed to the discussions based on research in the field of higher education, institutional research and case studies on that theme, as well as policy-based accounts. The themes covered a variety of issues such as the following ones:

- Governance and Management. Chairs: Amélia Veiga, CIIE, CIPES & University of Porto and Rosalind Pritchard, University of Ulster;
- Quality Management. Chairs: Patricia Moura e Sá, University of Coimbra & Antigoni Papadimitriou, John Hopkins University;
- Strategy and Strategizing. Chair: Pedro Saraiva, University of Coimbra;
- Teaching and Learning. Chair: Helena Araújo, Isabel Menezes, and Carlinda Leite, CIIE & University of Porto;
- Regional Innovation. Chair: Carlos Rodrigues, GOVCOPP and University of Aveiro;
- Funding. Chair: Ben Jongbloed and Hans Vossensteyn, CHEPS and the University of Twente, The Netherlands;
- Professionals. Chair: Teresa Carvalho, CIPES and University of Aveiro;
- Performance and Assessment. Chairs: Hugo Figueiredo and Ana Melo, CIPES and University of Aveiro.

After the conference we have made a selection of papers presented at the conference according to certain major topics that we considered could contribute to a better understanding of some implications of the interacting effects of the aforementioned institutional changes and transformations. Hence, we will start by a series of contributions from the keynote speakers invited for the conference that aimed at setting the policy and institutional landscape for those transformations. We then move to a series of chapters that look at changes in governance and management and the way these impact in several institutional areas of activity, from human resources management to personal tensions. The following group of chapters pursue this attention to management, but focusing more on issues of quality and strategy, reflecting the way these issues have gained importance following the strengthening of institutional autonomy and decision-making, but also the increasing and diverse pressures from various external forces. This strengthening of institutions' autonomy has also been followed by growing pressures of accountability and effectiveness, notably in the way HEIs address their traditional missions such as education and learning. Thus, in recent years we have seen a growing attention to issues such as teaching and learning, students' satisfaction and the management of the relationship with that estate, which constitutes the underlying theme of the third group of chapters included in this volume. Another major demand posed to institutions in their relationship with internal and external stakeholders refers to its contribution to their local communities and the extent of which HEIs are capable of responding to local economic and social needs. Thus, in the final group of chapters selected to be included in this volume we look at the role of HEIs to the local economic and social development. We will now proceed to a more detailed presentation of the specific contents of this volume by introducing briefly each of the chapters.

CONTENTS OF THE VOLUME

The first group pf chapters included in this volume correspond to the keynote lectures that framed each of the days of discussion during the conference. In his contribution, Simon Marginson introduces some of the major background trends that are shaping contemporary higher education and the context in which HEIs face multiple challenges. He starts by noting the rapid growth in higher education and in scientific activities and the fact that these have become global trends, beyond the so-called Western countries, spreading to a large number of middle income countries, from Eastern Europe and Latin America to parts of the Middle East/North Africa and Central Asia, and much of East and South East Asia. Nonetheless, he points out that the key problem, corroding both democratic politics and the role of higher education, is the acceleration of economic inequality and the social and political disquiet that it is creating. These forces create a major threat to many higher education values, but also an opportunity for higher education to reassert its centrality in society, notably through by strengthening its commitment to reflection, critical thinking, and social progress.

This concern with the social responsibility of HEIs is picked-up by Barbara Sporn in the following chapter. Based on her combined and rich experience as higher education researcher and as Vice-Rector at the WU Vienna University of Economics and Business (between 2002 and 2015), she reflects about the role of universities in society. Thus, in her chapter, she uses her book "Adaptive University Structures" to compare past and present research and focuses on the topic of adaptation and environmental vulnerability. She underlines the continued need to understand university steering as self-reliant, adaptive, entrepreneurial, or innovative and that universities are still in the process of finding the right balance between demand and response. This is further triggered by stark societal developments like digitalization, immigration and integration, and inequality, major societal trends that had been discussed in Marginson's chapter.

Finally, in his chapter Sebastião Feyo de Azevedo oursues further this issue of adaptive Universities by focusing on issues of governance and management. Feyo de Azevedo points out that, as other disciplines have highlighted, it is not the strongest but the most flexible and adaptive individuals and institutions that thrive. As the authors of the two previous chapters had pointed out, he considers that Universities represent (or should represent) major instruments for changes in society, notably through their capacity to anticipate and to model the future. Nonetheless, they are complex organizations and that places a heavy burden upon management to create the conditions for such high-level communities to accomplish the relevant scientific, social, cultural and economic goals that are part of their mission.

The second group of chapters focuses on the Changes and Challenges in Governance and Management. In the first chapter of this part, René Krempkow and Mathias Winde analyses Human Resources development for junior researchers in Germany. Personnel development, understood as the systematic promotion of an employee's aptitudes and abilities in preparation for future activities, is still rare for academic personnel at German HEIs. Nonetheless, in recent years, structures have been established at HEIs that, as a core element, have adopted measures for professional guidance and skills development. Using a survey on the personnel development of junior researchers developed in 2015, he presents some key results from 150 academic institutions in Germany. In the first part of the chapter he focuses on which developments in the past ten years have comparable indicators in HEIs, and in the second part he focuses on a small area of personnel development, namely on the extent to which personnel structures and arrangements related to tenure-track and the establishment of permanent positions in HEIs are available and planned for the next three years. The results show that human resource development for junior researchers in Germany has generally made significant progress over the past decade, although there is even more potential for development.

Then, Ton Kallenberg discusses the managerial-administrative relationships under pressure. Under the influence of the so-called 'New Public Management' (NPM), the focus has been on issues such as cost-cutting, transparency in resource distribution and increasing performance management, which has led to greater interaction and tensions between the academic and management estates. The manner in and the extent to which the faculty managers and senior administrators cooperate with each other is not only important for the functioning of the separate domains of academics and administrators, but also for the institutional organization as a whole. Thus, it is important to gain insight about the managerial-administrative relationships within the faculties, their degree of cooperation and the factors that may help or hinder that interaction. In order to obtain a better understanding of these relationships and factors, he has conducted a series of interviews with faculty managers and senior administrators within several faculties and universities in the Netherlands centred on their mutual relationships, the way in which they cooperate and their views about managing faculty developments. The focus of the analysis is therefore on the managerial-administrative relationship itself rather than on its effects on the processes in the organization.

Finally, Melindy Brown, David Kane and James Williams look at how HEI's may respond to certain issues, namely to gender-based violence on campus. Gender-based violence against students has been highlighted as one of the crises currently confronting universities and an issue that requires concerted action. Although the scale of the problem is still unclear, media attention and subsequent research has tended to focus on traditional universities, students and higher education culture. Modern higher education is characterised by diversity, especially in the demographics of the student body, thus, it is important to explore the extent to which the common depiction of this problem applies to a broad range of students. Although there is evidence that university senior management teams are beginning to take the matter seriously, to date, there has been little work with university students and staff that examines their perceptions about the problem in the university context. In this chapter the authors explore students and staff perceptions in a modern inner-city university with a diverse student body to analyse the institutional dynamics associated to the responses to controversial issues.

The fourth part focuses on issues on Quality Management and the Relevance of Strategy. In the first chapter of this part, Tina Klug discusses to what extent strategic quality management may be a contribution to institutional autonomy. According to her analysis, one important aspect is the connection between quality management and strategy and that autonomy can benefit from quality management that both integrates the institutions' core activities and is closely linked with strategic management. In addition, she shows how an integrated approach to quality management promotes autonomy by discussing those topics in the European higher education context. Her analysis about the instruments that support the connection between quality management and strategy making are introduced and discussed with reference to TU Darmstadt in Germany. Based on these practice examples, she aims at pointing out how the instruments presented contribute to appropriate governance to underpin the university's autonomy. The analysis presented in her chapter shows that it is very important to adopt an integrated approach to quality management that includes not only studying but also other core areas of HEI such as research, promotion of early careers, structure and administration, and that is closely linked with strategy making. She argues that, though this integrated perspective is already being practised in the evaluation mechanisms in place in various European countries, this is less the case in other countries, such as Germany, where quality management is still largely focused on the field of studying.

In the following chapter, Cindy Konen analyses the innovative ability of HEIs, namely by discussing the preconditions for the development of cooperative innovations. Like in many countries, the classical understanding of the role of HEIs in Germany has been subjected to profound change and HEIs are becoming increasingly an actor in the economic competition and are thus expected to contribute their resources, knowledge and competencies to create co-operative innovations with enterprises. The changed expectations from politics and society are, for example, expressed by the increasing importance of the third mission, a financing structure which is increasingly changing in the direction of higher third-party interests, or, more recently, the federal and state government initiative "Innovative higher education system (Innovative Hochschule)". However, it is increasingly driven by the higher education system itself. This changed expectation does not replace the classic tasks of German HEIs of basic research and teaching, rather needs to be understood as an additional task which superimposes the original pillars. Thus, her chapter tries to show how can HEIs organise their internal institutional factors to increase their innovativeness and thereby (successfully) generate co-operative innovations.

In the last chapter of this part, Maria João Manatos, Sónia Cardoso, Teresa Carvalho, and Maria J. Rosa discuss to what extent is quality assurance 'threatening' academic professionalism by looking at the perceptions of Portuguese academics about these issues. At a national level, supra-institutional QA schemes have been developed and implemented and accreditation has arisen as a mechanism par excellence for the assessment and assurance of higher education quality. More recently, the emphasis has been put on the development by institutions of internal QA systems (or on the formalisation of the existing internal QA practices) and on ensuring that both the accreditation of the study programmes and the certification of the internal QA systems is achieved. The increasing establishment of the logic of accountability and of the QA idea in HEIs has led to different degrees of acceptance and support by academics, which largely depend on how they perceive QA in higher education. Thus, in their chapter they discuss to what extent is internal QA being perceived by academics as a political process and, as such, able to challenge their professionalism. Their aim is to understand 'how' academics perceive internal QA drivers, cultures and effects, and whether academics' perceptions differ according to some of their characteristics. Moreover, their study intends to understand whether a greater political perception of internal QA is related with a greater perception of a challenge to academic autonomy and professionalism.

The fifth part of this volume focuses on Students and the Effectiveness of Learning. In the first chapter of this part, Magnus Hauge looks at grades as predictors of student performance. His analysis looks at the experience of Norway that, in 2003, introduced a new national grading scale in higher education. One of the features of the new national grading scale was that it would make comparisons across different subject fields, and between study programmes, easier. It was also supposed to be a useful tool for employers when considering applicants for a job. In his chapter, an attempt is made to use data from the Norwegian National Student Survey to make an indicator measuring the value-added component from a HEI on their students' learning outcome. Using data from this source makes it possible to use new control variables that can potentially remove at least some of the institutional bias in grading. Although students' learning outcome is often measured by using grades, other indicators should also be considered, especially considering the lack of comparability of grades across institutions and subject fields. Besides higher education grades as measure for the learning outcome, which is the main focus of the study, the student survey also includes variables on the students' self-reported learning outcomes. An attempt is also made at substituting higher education grades for self-reported learning outcomes as a measure for learning outcome.

Then, Gregory C. Wolniak, Casey George and Glen Nelson analyse college costs and the challenge faced by HEIs in an era of differentiated tuition practices in the U.S.' system of higher education. In recent years, the implementation of differential tuition policies by postsecondary institutions has become a prevalent strategy in many systems in hopes of increasing revenue or to offset instructional costs in some areas of study, increasingly being the subject of debate at public colleges and universities across the country. While forms of differentiating tuition have a long history in U.S. public higher education in relation to whether or not students attend college in their home state (where "in-state" enrolment accompanies lower tuition and "out-of-state" enrolment accompanies higher tuition), their focus with the present study is on a more recent and more nuanced form of tuition differentiation;

that which is based on the major area of study and/or year of enrolment, which are increasingly the subject of debate at public colleges and universities in the U.S. and the European contexts. Taken together, pricing fields of study differently may lead to unintended consequences in terms of how differential tuition influences students' higher education decision-making and may potentially further marginalize disadvantaged groups of college students. Against this backdrop, they sought to take an important step towards improving understandings of differentiated tuition policies in the U.S. and advancing research on college tuition rates and affordability.

The last part of this volume looks at the Role of Higher Education in Regional Innovation. In the first chapter of this part, Verena Radinger-Peer analyses the role of universities as regional development agents and discusses the organizational and institutional challenges of regional engagement. Apart from their contribution to regional innovation, attention is increasingly directed towards the wider contribution of universities to regional, cultural and community development, often referred to as the third mission of HEIs, a loose and complex concept. Thus, several concepts have been proposed to encompass these realities such as "the civic university", "the engaged university" or "the sustainable university", which attempt to grasp this broader and more adaptive role of universities in regional development. This chapter aims to contribute to the "how" of universities' regional engagement, therewith enfolding the institutional and organizational challenges and change processes which accompany universities' regional engagement activities. The analysis is largely based in the case study of the Johannes Kepler University Linz in Austria, though its findings aim to place it into a broader context.

In the last chapter of this volume, Jürgen Janger reconsiders universities' role in regional innovation, pointing out that policies towards regional innovation have recently been driven by the concept of the entrepreneurial university, encouraging universities to contribute to innovation through licensing of patents or academic spin-offs. Based on a conceptual model of universities' role in innovative activity and a review of the evidence, he argues that a focus on increasing universities' contribution to regional innovation through licensing of technologies or creating spin-offs is an approach that tends to overlook the main traditional contribution of universities to regional innovation. He considers that commercialisation of research results through licensing patents or creating spin-offs firms is just one way among many for universities to affect regional innovation and that success in commercialisation depends to some extent on the quality of the institutions in performing its traditional missions of research and teaching. Accordingly, in his chapter he proposes a conceptual model of the potential contributions of universities to regional innovation processes to establish the various potential ways of engagement or interaction between universities and regional innovation actors, followed by a review of the empirical literature on which university contributions firms actually rely most on. He then uses his results to discuss whether recent regional innovation initiatives overly stress universities' third mission as a driver of regional innovation performance, neglecting the first and second mission of universities also in terms of funding and hence putting pressure on universities' efforts to increase research and teaching quality.

Overall, we believe this volume presents a stimulating and careful set of analyses about the multiple and complex challenges faced by HEIs worldwide and the way different systems and HEIs are addressing the effects of those transformations. They also underline the importance of developing a more integrated analysis of those various changes. We hope that the conference and this volume will contribute to encourage higher education researchers to pursue further those relevant research themes within various national and institutional contexts.

REFERENCES

Amaral, A., & Magalhães, A. (2003). The triple crisis of the university and its reinvention. *Higher Education Policy, 16*(2), 239–253.

Amaral, A., Meek, V. L., & Larsen, I. M. (Eds.). (2003). *The higher education managerial revolution?* Dordrecht: Kluwer Academic Publishers.

Bok, D. (2003). *Universities in the marketplace: The commercialization of higher education*. Princeton, NJ: Princeton University Press.

Carvalho, T., & Santiago, R. (2010). Still academics after all. *Higher Education Policy, 23*, 397–411.

Etzkowitz, H. (2008). *The triple helix: University-industry-government innovation in action*. New York, NY: Routledge.

Grubb, W. N., & Lazerson, M. (2004). *The education gospel: The economic power of schooling*. Cambridge, MA: Harvard University Press.

Huisman, J. (Ed.). (2009). *International perspectives on the governance of higher education: Alternative frameworks for coordination*. London: Routledge.

Magalhães, A., Veiga, A., Amaral, A., Sousa, S., & Ribeiro, F. (2013a). Governance of governance in higher education: Practices and lessons drawn from the portuguese case. *Higher Education Quarterly, 67*(3), 295–311.

Magalhães, A., Veiga, A., Sousa, S., Ribeiro, F., & Amaral, A. (2013b). Governance and institutional autonomy: Governing and governance in portuguese higher education. *Higher Education Policy, 26*(2), 243–262.

Magalhães, A., Veiga, A., & Videira, P. (2017). Hard and soft managerialism in portuguese higher education governance. In R. Deem & H. Eggins (Eds.), *The university as a critical institution?* (pp. 39–53). Rotterdam, The Netherlands: Sense Publishers.

Manatos, M. J., Rosa, M. J., & Sarrico, C. S. (2015). The importance and degree of implementation of the European standards and guidelines for internal quality assurance in universities: The views of portuguese academics. *Tertiary Education and Management, 21*(3), 245–261.

Marginson, S., & Considine, M. (2000). *The enterprise university*. Melbourne: Cambridge University Press.

Meek, L., Goedegebuure, L., Santiago, R., & Carvalho, T. (Eds.). (2011). *Changing deans. Higher education middle management in international comparative perspectives*. Dordrecht: Springer.

Melo, A. I., & Sarrico, C. S. (2015). Performance management systems and their influence on the governance structures of Portuguese universities: A case study. In I. M. Welpe, J. Wollersheim, S. Ringelhan, & M. Osterloh (Eds.), *Incentives and performance* (pp. 81–97). Cham: Springer International Publishing Switzerland.

Melo, A. I., Sarrico, C. S., & Radnor, Z. (2010). The influence of performance management systems on key actors in universities: The case of an English university. *Public Management Review, 12*(2), 233–254.

Middlehurst, R., & Teixeira, P. (2012). Governance within the EHEA: Dynamic trends, common challenges and national particularities. In A. Curaj, P. Scott, L. Vlasceanu, & L. Wilson (Eds.), *European higher education at the crossroads: Between the Bologna process and national reforms* (Part 2: Governance, financing, mission diversification and futures of higher education) (pp. 527–551). London: Springer.

Musselin, C., & Teixeira, P. (Eds.). (2013). *Policy design and implementation in higher education*. Dordrecht: Springer.

Neave, G. (2012). *The evaluative state, institutional autonomy and re-engineering higher education in Western Europe: The prince and his pleasure* (Issues in higher education). London & New York, NY: Palgrave MacMillan.

Rosa, M. J., & Amaral, A. (Eds.). *Quality assurance and higher education: Contemporary debates*. Basingstoke: Palgrave MacMillan.

Santiago, R., & Carvalho, T. (2016). The 'dark side' of the moon: The 'non-teaching' structures in the Portuguese HEIs. In C. Sarrico, P. Teixeira, A. Magalhães, A. Veiga, M. J. Rosa, & T. Carvalho (Eds.), *Global challenges, national initiatives, and institutional responses – The transformation of higher education* (pp. 55–76). Rotterdam, The Netherlands: Sense Publishers.

Santiago, R., Carvalho, T., & Cardoso, S. (2015). Portuguese academics perceptions on HEIs governance and management: A generational perspective. *Special Issue – Generational Change and Academic Work of Studies in Higher Education, 40*(8), 1471–1484.

Sarrico, C., Teixeira, P., Magalhães, A., Veiga, A., Rosa, M., & Carvalho, T. (Eds.). (2016). *Global challenges, national initiatives, and institutional responses – The transformation of higher education*. Rotterdam, The Netherlands: Sense Publishers.

Sarrico, C. S., Rosa, M. J., Teixeira, P. N., & Cardoso, M. F. (2010). Assessing quality and evaluating performance in higher education: Worlds apart or complementary views? *Minerva, 48*, 35–54.

Sarrico, C. S., Teixeira, P., Rosa, M. J., & Cardoso, M. F. (2009). Subject-mix and performance in Portuguese universities. *European Journal of Operational Research, 197*(1), 287–295.

Shattock, M. (2006). *Managing good governance in higher education*. Maidenhead: Open University Press.

Taylor, J. S., Ferreira, J., Machado, M. L., & Santiago, R. (Eds.). (2008). *The non-university higher education in Europe*. Dordrech: Springer.

Teixeira, P., & Dill, D. (Eds.). (2011). *Public vices, private virtues? Assessing the effects of marketization in higher education*. Rotterdam, The Netherlands: Sense Publishers.

Teixeira, P., Jongbloed, B., Dill, D., & Amaral, A. (Eds.). (2004). *Markets in higher education: Rhetoric or reality?* Dordrecht: Kluwer Academic Publishers.

Veiga, A., Magalhães, A., & Amaral, A. (2015). From collegial governance to boardism: Reconfiguring governance in higher education. In J. Huisman, H. de Boer, D. Dill, & M. Souto-Otero (Eds.), *The Palgrave international handbook of higher education policy and governance* (pp. 398–416). London: Palgrave Macmillan.

Weisbrod, B., Pallou, B., & Asch, E. (2008). *Mission and money: Understanding the university*. Cambridge: Cambridge University Press.

Westerheijden, D. F., Stensaker, B., & Rosa, M. J. (Eds.). (2007). *Quality assurance in higher education: Trends in regulation, translation and transformation*. Dordrecht: Springer.

PART 2
SETTING THE STAGE

SIMON MARGINSON

2. HIGHER EDUCATION AND SCIENCE IN THE AGE OF TRUMP, BREXIT AND LE PEN

INTRODUCTION

Both the number of students in higher education and scientific output are expanding rapidly, driven by globalisation, world-wide modernisation and massification. High participation higher education and national research capacity are becoming much more widely distributed. In most countries, and nearly every world region, tertiary participation is growing rapidly or is at near saturation levels as it is in much of Europe and North America. Despite Brexit combined science and education in Europe are moving forward. In East Asia the volume of students and the volume of scientific activity both now exceed Europe and in the leading East Asian universities research quality in the physical science-based disciplines is at North American levels.

Yet this remarkable fluorescence of universities and colleges is taking place under tighter funding conditions in most countries, and in a more unstable political environment, with the strident assertion of national identities and interests within the global setting. Nativism and global/national tensions cut across the ordinary operations of cosmopolitan research universities. Nativist populism, which exploits economic inequality without solving it, and exacerbates conflicts on migration while undermining the multilateral forums where they can be addressed, undermines the Enlightenment narrative at the base of the modern university – the notion of shared individual and social formation via higher education and rational public discourse.

The chapter is a quick tour across this large general terrain and provides a background setting for the other more specific chapters in the book. It includes data on developments in national higher education systems and the global patterns and connections across and between them and reflects on both the growing centrality of universities and science and the new ambiguities and perils that they face.

The chapter looks first at the expansion in higher educated populations in many countries (second section), and then the growth of research volume and the number of research-intensive World-Class Universities (WCUs) and the dispersion of research capacity among more countries (third section). Then it looks at the geo-political shifts in higher education, with the lifting of capacity in the middle-income countries and the rise of East Asia, especially China, Singapore and South Korea (fourth section). The fifth section discusses the changing character of economic globalisation, the increase in global/national tensions in some countries, and the growing inequality of incomes in the majority of countries, an inequality in which higher education has become implicated. The sixth section comments on the populist exploitation of these factors, including the positioning of universities as part of the problem, and the way the division between the higher educated and others played out in Brexit and the rise of Trump – despite the fact that higher education is not the main driver of income distribution, and the mobility of international students (or any other migration) is not the maker of inequality or poverty. A brief conclusion (seventh section) follows.

THE GROWTH OF PARTICIPATION

Between 1971 and 1995 the worldwide Gross Enrolment Ratio (GER) at tertiary level rose slowly from 10 to 15 per cent of the school leaver age cohort, with a more substantial increase in the richest region, North America and Western Europe, from 31 to 59 per cent. After that enrolments began to increase much faster than GDP and on a worldwide basis. Between 1995 and 2014 the worldwide GER rose by an average of one per cent a year, from 15 to 35 per cent – note that four fifths of tertiary students are in degree programmes – and approached 80 per cent in North America and Western Europe. In a small number of countries, led by South Korea, the GER topped 90 per cent and tertiary education was becoming universal (UNESCO, 2018).

The GER exaggerates enrolments in some countries. The calculation includes migrants and mature students not part of the foundational age cohort. However, there is no doubt about the trend. By 2013, 56 national systems had participation rates of 50 per cent and another 56 were at 15–50 per cent, with only 42 of the poorest national systems, unable to sustain the infrastructure of tertiary education or a fast growing middle class with educational aspirations, at below 15 per cent. The GER has increased rapidly in all but the poorest one quarter of countries, and in every world region except Central Asia where it has stayed at about 25 per cent since the early 1990s. Even in Sub-Saharan Africa, Pakistan and Bangladesh, where the GER is very low at 10 per cent or less, it is increasingly rapidly from its low base. In Latin America the GER has reached 50 per cent, Eastern Europe has almost caught up to Western Europe, and in all countries in East Asia apart from China it now exceeds 50 per cent. In China, India and Indonesia, three of the four most populous countries (the other is the US), the GER is climbing rapidly (UNESCO, 2018).

Within the near universal trend, there is significant in-country variation in total participation, and in the social, in-country regional, ethnic and gender mix of participation both overall and in the different fields of study. The institutional configuration of participation also varies – in some countries the majority of the age group are enrolled in research universities, in others research universities serve a much smaller elite. These variations are to be expected. Just as there can be more than one form of modernisation (as the rise of East Asia, combining long historical Confucian culture with Western forms, makes clear), so also the observable universal patterns associated with modernity, including the emergence and rapid growth of higher education systems, are articulated through the full range of national histories, traditions, cultures, and political economy and politics. Figure 2.1 compares OECD nations' participation using two measures, the GER and University College Dublin scholar Patrick Clancy's index, which combines the average rate of entry with other factors including completion and the inclusion of students from historically under-represented social groups. The graph shows that there is significant variation within OECD on both indicators and also variation in the gap between the indicators. In 18 countries the system is noticeably stronger in its raw performance at entry than on the full range of participation indicators (Clancy & Marginson, 2018).

Even where the GER or the Clancy index are the same, this conceals other variations. Though the term 'participation' and standardised data fosters a sense of equivalence, neither the quality nor the quantity of tertiary education are constant, between or within countries. Not all teachers are trained. Not all curricula are knowledge-intensive. Not all programmes are transformative. Resources are often weak. Growth is often accompanied by declining funding per student. Some institutions, credentials and earning programmes are more empowering than others.

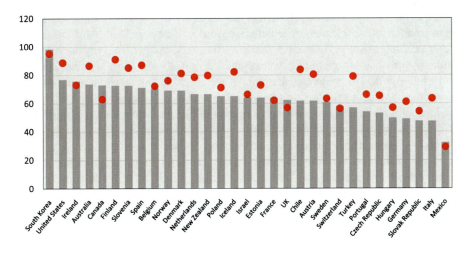

Figure 2.1. Comparative tertiary-level participation on the basis of the UNESCO gross enrolment ratio and the Clancy index, OECD countries, 2013. (Source: Clancy & Marginson, 2018, table 2.7)

Nevertheless, taken on an average basis and on the systemic and world scales, the binary of participation/non-participation remains crucial. All else being equal, those outside higher education are much less likely to become immersed in knowledge-intensive learning than those within it. With the advance of the GER it is clear that the world is becoming more educated, and at a rapid rate.

In a study of High Participation Systems of Higher Education, released in October 2018, Brendan Cantwell, Anna Smolentseva and I find that growth in higher education enrolments is not driven primarily by economic demand for human capital, though it is associated with the spread of higher educated labour to a larger proportion of the workforce. Tertiary education is expanding rapidly in countries with very different rates of GDP growth and diverse industry configurations. The only countries where participation remains low are those that are still predominantly Neolithic. Growth appears most closely associated with modern urbanisation and can be mapped against the growth of the urban middle classes (for this see Kharas, 2017). Higher education is provided in cities. Cities funnel mass family aspirations for higher education. Urban populations put pressure on governments to expand opportunities and governments of all political types seem to comply. Governments never reduce participation rates, or if they do so it is not for long, though they may hold down funding for participation. The medium-term outcome is always an expansion of the role of higher/tertiary education (Cantwell et al., 2018, chapter 1).

In assessing the meanings of this remarkable expansion it is essential to look outside the bounded world of higher education to the larger world beyond. Yes, it means more work in higher education, greater responsibilities, greater resource needs, larger and more professional administration and often more corporate governance, bigger classes, more heterogeneous student populations and continuing outreach to extend participation, larger institutions, greater diversity within them and within their programmes, sometimes but not always more diverse kinds of institution, often more diverse and innovative curricula and teaching methods, new systems of student selection and so on. Growth and massification transform higher education as Martin Trow famously argued (1973). But while we mostly focus on what massification means within higher education, its larger social meanings are, arguably, more important and should be more widely discussed. From the social viewpoint this is a very positive development. Not only does massification signify the widening of opportunity – though this is not in itself sufficient to create greater equality it is an expansion of human rights – massification on the present worldwide scale is a tremendous uplift in individual and collective human capability. We are seeing the emergence of more educated and knowledgeable human societies at a level that previous generations could not have imagined. Underneath the shallow talk about graduate employability and unemployment that is what is really happening.

We see in this the fulfilment on a democratic scale – albeit partial and distorted, uneven and incomplete as it is in many respects– of the Kantian notion of Bildung, which is education's mission of forming people as critically-minded self-fulfilling actors and public persons, steeped in social communications and lifelong learning and prepared so as to contribute to the continuing betterment of society as a whole (Kivela, 2012, p. 59). It is a lofty ideal but not an empty one. It is the idea of the Enlightenment that underpinned the Humboldtian approach in Germany and via the American university has been taken into the DNA of universities across the world.

Higher education matters above all because of two functions. First, it reproduces, creates and systematizes codified knowledge. It is not the only social institution where this happens but the most important. Second, it changes people – and changes

HIGHER EDUCATION AND SCIENCE

people by immersing them in complex transformative knowledge while at the same time immersing them within common social codes and systems. It forms people as more competent in communication and cooperation, more tolerant of difference and diversity, less nativist. On average it brings to people higher levels of confidence and agency freedom, a more advanced capacity for proactive, will-directed behaviour. They live longer, are more healthy and manage money better (McMahon, 2009). All else being equal, and on the basis of averages, graduates are more international in outlook compared to non graduates and have a greater capacity for personal mobility both social and geographic. And higher education does all this on a scale far greater than imagined by Kant, Rousseau and von Humboldt.

In successive editions of Education at a Glance the OECD has released data showing that higher education augments a broad range of individual attributes, not only earnings power and employment rate but capabilities in social relations. For example, the 2012 OECD survey of adult skills showed that capability in information technology – electronic sociability – was closely associated with level of education achieved (OECD, 2015, pp. 46–47). Figures 2.2 and 2.3 contain two further examples.

As Figure 2.2 indicates, the 2012 OECD survey also reported that people's willingness to trust each other increases with the level of education. People with tertiary education were more likely to trust others than those with just upper secondary or lower secondary education, a finding that held after statistically accounting for differences in gender, age and income. While the level of solidaristic interpersonal trust in many countries was low in this survey, in the Nordic countries it reaches close to 50 per cent among the tertiary educated (p. 163).

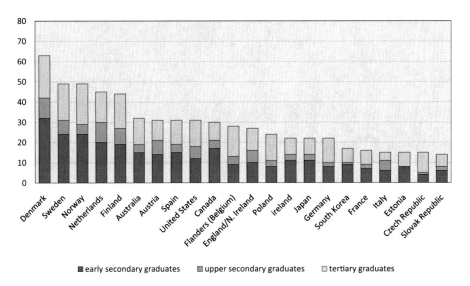

Figure 2.2. Level of education and interpersonal trust, OECD countries, 2015. Q. 'Do you trust other people?' Proportion (%) answering 'yes' (Source: OECD, 2015, p. 163)

On the question of whether people feel they have an effective connection to the political system, Figure 2.3 shows that the sense of political connection was twice as high among the tertiary educated as those with only lower secondary education. Again, the common thread in both Figures 2.2 and 2.3 is that the tertiary educated have greater social capacity, relational confidence and sense of personal agency.

The OECD's Perspectives on Global Development 2017: International migration in a shifting world (2016) contains research data comparing the respective tendencies to migrate across borders of persons with, and without, university degrees. Among those without degrees the tendency to move across borders was correlated to income. As income rises people had more scope for mobility. The capacity for mobility appears to be economically determined. However, among those with university degrees the pattern was different. First, at a given level of income, those with degrees were much more mobile than those without. In other words, higher education helped to democratise mobility (provided higher education itself was accessed). Second, for those with degrees, as income rises, above a modest threshold of income there was little change in potential mobility. That is, the propensity to move became income inelastic. Strikingly, this suggests that because higher education helps graduates to achieve greater personal agency, it weakens the limits created by economic determination and class.

Degree level education constitutes greater personal agency, freedom, in its own right. In that respect it builds democratic capability in the larger sense, everywhere, and this happens regardless of the changing opportunity structures of the labour

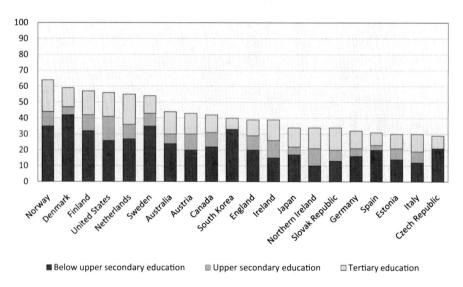

Figure 2.3. Level of education and political connectedness, OECD countries, 2015. Q. 'Do you believe you have a say in government?' Proportion (%) answering 'yes'. (Source: OECD, 2015, p. 164)

markets and whether the particular political regime in the country is subject to electoral contestation or not. This contribution to personal agency (Marginson, 2018a) is made by higher education, across the world, to more people every year.

Despite the many issues facing people within higher education – despite all the legitimate concerns about the growing and destructive effects of competition in higher education, inequality, performance-management, attenuated provision and standards, and the evacuation of academic governance, to name only some – this great expansion of the social effects of higher education must be seen as positive.

RESEARCH SCIENCE

Between 2006 and 2016 the total world number of science papers as measured by UNESCO increased from 1,567,422 to 2,295,608 (NSB, 2018, table A5-27). The expanding role of research science is driven by several factors – the growing emphasis on innovation in the advice of international agencies and in national economic policies; the growing industry demand in knowledge-intensive sectors, though this demand is uneven by country; the competitive pressures generated by global rankings, which are more universal and have directly stimulated enhanced R&D investments in countries such as Germany, France, Russia, Saudi Arabia, South Korea and Japan where government has implemented WCU programmes.

Table 2.1. Expansion in the number of world universities publishing more than 10,000, 500 and 1,200 journal papers over four years, 2006–2009 to 2013–2016

Number of universities publishing more than:	2006–2009	2007–2010	2008–2011	2009–2012	2010–2013	2011–2014	2012–2015	2013–2016
10,000 papers	25	26	31	34	39	46	50	58
5,000 papers	122	128	135	143	154	171	190	209
1,200 papers	594	629	657	682	712	743	780	827

Source: Leiden University (2018)

In 2016, 35 countries produced more than 10,000 papers, including emerging research systems in Iran, Malaysia, Egypt and Romania. There have been spectacular increases in science paper output in countries like Iran (15.1 per cent annual growth in the years 2006–2016), India (11.1 per cent), China (8.4 per cent) and Brazil (6.6 per cent) where research funding has risen sharply (NSB, 2018, table A5-22).

One way of illustrating the growth of research science and its impact in the higher education sector is to trace the expanding number of universities at a given level of output of science papers. Table 2.1 does this. The Leiden University data show that in the four years 2006–2009 there were 25 universities that produced more than 10,000 science papers. Only seven years later the number of universities had risen to 58. There were also sharp increases at lower size levels (Leiden University, 2018).

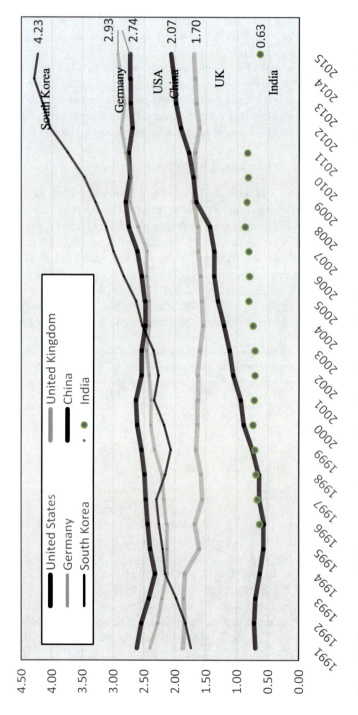

Figure 2.4. Investment in R&D as a proportion (%) of GDP, United States, United Kingdom, Germany, China, South Korea, India: 1991–2015. There are series breaks for India, with no data for 2012–2014 inclusive. (Data drawn from NSB, 2018, table A4-12)

It is significant that in most countries the main part of the growth of science is taking place in large multi-disciplinary 'multiversities' not in specialist disciplinary universities, government laboratories or industry, notwithstanding (or perhaps because of) the multi-purpose character of the multiversity form (Cantwell, Marginson, & Smolentseva, 2018, chapter 4). It often suits industry to draw on the subsidised research capacity of universities and the public goods they produce, rather than funding the whole process on a private basis. This valorisation of a substantial body of basic, academically controlled research sustains the university form. In other words, in the outcome the growth of science is both nurtured by and reinforcing of semi-autonomous universities in this era. It can be argued that for all its flaws, including the Anglo-American cultural and structural biases built into the notion, the 'World-Class University' norm has strengthened the overall social weight of higher education (though it is less clear that it benefits the great majority of higher education institutions that are not research intensive). Continually advanced by the leading research-intensive universities that benefit from it, the growth of science provides the strongest continuing mainstream argument for both the economic utility of the goods universities produce, and the public funding they receive. It is more difficult to defend the public funding per student for teaching purposes.

GEO-POLITICAL SHIFTS IN HIGHER EDUCATION

Figure 2.4 traces the pattern of national investment in R&D in seven large and important national research systems in the period 1991 t0 2015. What stands out is first, the common trend to increase over time except in the UK, and second, the changing balance between the world regions. While the level of GDP share rose slowly in the United States and Germany it doubled in South Korea and multiplied by four times in China. The total investment in R&D in East Asia now exceeds that of North America –China alone is catching the United States – and is well ahead of the UK and Europe combined (NSB, 2018, table A4-12). This is a sign of China's mergence as the largest economy and second strongest global power after the US.

There is a parallel shift in the geopolitical balance of tertiary enrolments. With the majority of the world's population located in Asia the rapid expansion of participation in China, Indonesia and India means that it is inevitable that the majority of the world's students and graduates – including PhD trained graduates – will also come from East Asia. In China the GER has lifted from 2 per cent to more than 40 per cent in one generation. China now has the largest student population in the world. Participation is growing rapidly also in India, pushing towards 30 per cent, though most students are enrolled in small poor quality private colleges. However, it is in research that the changing geo-political balance shows directly.

The shift in the balance of R&D investment is associated with the shift in favour of East Asia in its share of world scientific output (NSB, 2018, table A5-27). Figure 2.5 shows that while in 2003 English language science paper output in China was at one quarter of the United States level, by 2016 China had caught up with the US.

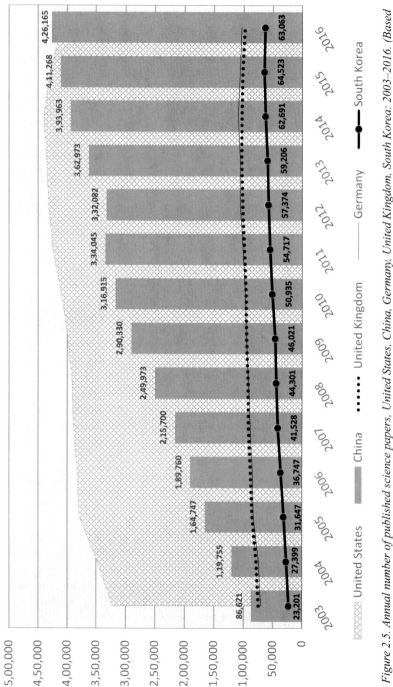

Figure 2.5. Annual number of published science papers, United States, China, Germany, United Kingdom, South Korea: 2003–2016. (Based on data from NSB, 2018, appendix table 5-27. Inclusion of papers for the most recent years 2015 and 2016 appears incomplete. It is likely in future compilations the number of papers for those years will increase for all countries)

While the quantitative expansion of East Asian science is a trend that is becoming well known, what is less well known is that the quality of East Asian science, as measured by citation rates, has also markedly improved, especially in some fields.

In China, Taiwan, Singapore, South Korea and Japan the main priorities for governmental research investment have been the physical sciences STEM disciplines: physics, chemistry, engineering, mathematics and complex computing. These fields underpin strategic national development in areas such as communications systems, transport, urbanization and advanced manufacturing. Research in these fields also feeds into cyber-security and military requirements. In these disciplines, the top East Asian universities in China and Singapore are now performing not just at European levels but at American levels.

Table 2.2 lists the strongest universities in the production of leading research papers published in the 2012–2015 period, papers positioned in the top 10 per cent of their field of study by citation rate, in the physical sciences STEM disciplines. China

Table 2.2. Leading universities in (1) Physical Sciences and Engineering and (2) Mathematics and Complex Computing, based on published papers in the top 10 per cent of their field by citation rate: 2012–2015 papers

	University	System	Top 10% papers in Physical Sciences & Engin.		University	System	Top 10% papers in Maths & Complex Comput.
1	UC Berkeley	USA	1176	1	Tsinghua U	CHINA	367
2	Massachusetts IT	USA	1175	2	Nanyang TU	SING.	259
3	Tsinghua U	CHINA	1054	3	Zhejiang U	CHINA	256
4	Stanford U	USA	976	4	Huazhong USA	CHINA	250
5	Nanyang TU	SING.	931	5	Massachusetts IT	USA	245
6	Harvard U	USA	875	6	Harbin IT	CHINA	236
7	Zhejiang U	CHINA	857	7	NU Singapore	SING.	226
8	U Cambridge	UK	801	8	Stanford U	USA	208
9	NU Singapore	SING.	749	9	Xidian U	CHINA	205
10	U S & T	CHINA	720	10	Shanghai Jiao T U	CHINA	196
11	ETH Zurich	SWITZ.	678	11	City U Hong Kong	HK SAR	188
12	U Tokyo	JAPAN	649	12	U Texas, Austin	USA	187
13	Shanghai JT U	CHINA	638	13	South East U	CHINA	184
14	Peking U	CHINA	636	14	UC Berkeley	USA	184
15	Caltech	USA	635	15	Beihang U	CHINA	177

Source: Leiden University (2018) data

had more than half of the world's top 15 universities in research on Mathematics and Complex Computing. Tsinghua was well ahead of all others, with Singapore's Nanyang in fifth place. In the larger Physical Sciences and Engineering cluster, Berkeley and MIT are one and two but China had five of the top 15 universities, the same as the United States. Note that the two Singapore universities were each in the top 15 in both discipline clusters; and when the two columns are added up, Tsinghua just shades MIT as the world's leading university in the production of top 10 per cent papers in the physical sciences, engineering, mathematics and computing.

The rise of China in the physical sciences STEM cluster concerns some in the United States, but there has been no decline in the quality of US research in these fields. Rather there has been an expansion and pluralisation of global capacity; and because research is inherently collaborative (a large number of joint US-China papers are produced each year), everyone gains from the entry of new talent into the global science system. What is surprising is that it has happened so quickly.

Here the East Asian miracle should be kept in perspective. Regional universities in China and the other East Asian countries are weaker in biological and life sciences than in the physical sciences/engineering, and much weaker in medicine, psychology and the social sciences. The humanities are also comparatively neglected. From the viewpoint of the Kantian or Humboldtian university, the achievement is unbalanced.

GLOBAL/NATIONAL TENSIONS AND SOCIAL INEQUALITY

It is evident from the above data that the rise and spread of science and higher education have a profound social, economic and political momentum. Yet the growth of participation and research activity are taking place amid an increasingly difficult set of conditions, especially in Europe and English-speaking countries, conditions not generated by universities and colleges but in which they have become implicated. These conditions cross and are partly shaped by the global/national boundary.

First, while economic globalisation has been associated with the process of worldwide modernisation, narrowing the gaps between countries (Milanovic, 2011), in the context of neoliberal deregulation and low tax policies designed to attract mobile capital to national economies, economic globalisation has become increasingly regressive in its economic effects within countries. At the same time the momentum of economic globalisation has faltered. Perhaps it has diminishing returns in a nation-bound world, except in countries expanding their share of global economic activity. For these reasons together, the World Trade Organisation (WTO) policy form of economic globalisation has lost some support, and generated growing resistance in North America and Europe – though not in emerging Asia where growth rates are high and the expansion of the middle class compensates for the tendency of economic globalisation and national deregulation to foster greater inequalities.

Second, in many countries, in some political quarters, the economic tensions on the global/national boundary have been translated into opposition to all forms of globalisation, including people mobility and cultural globalisation. The resulting global/national tension in turn significantly affects higher education and research. Indeed, as with economic inequality, higher education (especially the research-intensive universities which are highly globalised) becomes seen as a causal factor, as a source of global pressures and tensions that is fostering globalised elites.

The present era of communicative globalisation dates from the beginning of the 1990s. The advent of the Internet facilitated the spread of networked activity in real time in production, trade, finance, science and many other spheres. For a time, economic globalisation and cultural globalisation – the spread of world markets and of networked communications and homogeneous products and practices, supported by growing people movement – seem to all move together. But a split has now developed between trends in the economic sphere and in the cultural sphere.

Global integration in communication and culture continues to roll out, as does the world system of academic knowledge in research. Though this tends to suppress national-cultural differences and marginalise work in languages other than English, it must be said that those substantial problems have not retarded the globalisation of knowledge. Rather, there has emerged an uneasy coexistence between on one hand the increasingly global sciences, on the other hand the more nation-centred (and under-funded) humanities plus some social sciences and professional disciplines.

However, economic globalisation has run into difficulties. Two features of 1990s globalisation, the growing weight of multinationals and the formation of world markets in a liberal trading environment, have faltered. This predates the Trump presidency, dating rather from the recession in the Atlantic countries in 2008–2010. In January 2017 The Economist published an article on 'The retreat of the global company'. Between 2012 and 2017 multinational profits declined by 25 per cent. Returns to capital were at the lowest level since the 1990s. More sophisticated local firms, drawing on production, management and marketing techniques pioneered by multinationals, had narrowed the efficiency gap and were better at nuancing products for local tastes. Of the 500 largest firms, in eight out of ten industry sectors multinationals were expanding sales more slowly than domestic peers. In six sectors multinationals had lower returns to equity. Multinationals had little more to gain from tax breaks. Offshore relocation and long cross-border supply chains were vulnerable to political intervention by national governments. The share of exports accounted for by cross-border supply chains was no longer increasing and flows of foreign direct investment had declined sharply since the recession. The Economist found that among listed firms the share of global profits going to multinationals had fallen from 35 to 30 per cent since 2007 (The Economist, 2017).

Rodrick (2017, p. 27) finds that when the deregulation of trade approaches its limit, 'the ratio of political/distributive costs to economic gains is particularly unfavourable'. The efficiency gains with each reduction are progressively smaller, and the number of losers created by liberalisation increases, for example workers displaced by the offshoring of production, workers whose wages are reduced under pressure of foreign competition. This in turn exacerbates the tendency to growing income inequality that has been typical of nearly all OECD countries since the 1980s.

In the United States in 2010, the top 1 per cent of income receivers took in 20 per cent of all income, the same share as the bottom 50 per cent. In Europe the top 1 per cent received 10 per cent of all income and the bottom 50 per cent received 25 per cent of income. Fostered by the deregulation of wages in the workplace, the boom in managerial salaries, the declining returns to low wage jobs and tax reforms favouring the wealthy, income inequality in the US is now at the highest level on record, though inequality of wealth has not yet return to nineteenth century levels (Piketty, 2014; Saez, 2013). In contrast, in Nordic countries and some other parts of Europe, social protections, wage setting and tax policy all act together to cushion the tendencies to inequality in free trade and other market transactions. 'Flat' and well resourced, inclusive higher education systems help to sustain the social consensus on equality (Marginson, 2018b), though by themselves cannot secure greater income equality. Everywhere global financial and trading economies tend to inequality; and a new wave of automation now threatens to further hollow out the middle class.

Together these tendencies mean that some capitalists and many workers, especially in the United States with its weak social protections and high private cost of health care, no longer support high economic globalisation in the 1990s form of free and open exchange. While for many people in higher education it may seem that globalisation is heading in the right direction –continuing momentum for cultural globalisation is now coupled with a check to the neoliberal enthusiasm for economic deregulation with its ever-growing inequality –it is not so simple. The wavering of world economic integration has facilitated nation-bound state agendas and the rise of nativism in the popular arena, weakened the pooling of sovereignty and the modest trends to regional and global governance of the 1990s/2000s and contributed to the fracturing of a sense of common global interest (combined action on climate change is now more elusive), and spilled over into resistance to all other forms of closer global integration, demographic and cultural as well as economic. Perhaps this shows that in building a sense of common interest, the world relied too much on capitalist economies and in Europe a combined currency and not enough on political processes, but that is the world that the present generation has inherited.

Global interest and nation-bound interest do not always coincide. Across North America and most of Europe significant part of both national elites and electorates no longer have a stake in international openness and cooperation. This has facilitated the politics of anti-migration, which has become the primary springboard for the rise of the populist-nativist political right. People mobility in all forms, especially long-term migration, is on the fault-line between national and global. This fault-line is always problematic because there is an unresolvable tension between the right to cross-border mobility, to go anywhere, and the right to national border control. In Europe this tension is exacerbated by a Middle East in flames and regional conflict, environmental collapse and the absence or break-down of viable state structures in parts of Africa, and by urban terrorism and the politics of security. The United States has a long border with a Mexico in which the state is failing, poverty seems endemic and much of the north of the country is wracked by drug violence.

What are the specific implications for the positioning of higher education? There are two. First, higher education is seen to be implicated – and especially in high inequality countries, is actually implicated – in the growing income inequality. Second, higher education, positioned as a cosmopolitan anti-nativist sector, is under growing suspicion while also being increasingly retarded by anti-migration policies.

On the first point, higher education is itself partly to blame for the perception that it 'causes' social inequality. Not only do both policy and universities celebrate the maximisation of graduate returns (and hence the maximisation of the gap with non-graduates), most people see higher education as responsible for graduate outcomes and this inexorably this includes both the inequalities between different graduates and those between graduates and non graduates. By embracing the human capital myth, which has been a prime rationale for public and private investment in higher education, the sector has actively propagated the notion that it determines not only opportunity but employability and salary levels. Performance measures like the UK Teaching Excellence Framework, which ranks universities on the basis of graduate returns, lock higher education closer to those expectations. Yet higher education is only one part of the cluster of influences on incomes and not the most important. Social research places growing emphasis on family background as a determinant of graduate outcomes (Belfield et al., 2017); and as Piketty (2014) notes, both wage determination and tax policy outweigh human capital investment.

The advance of massification ought to dispel the notion that higher education is necessarily an elite forming sector –when half the population is enrolled in higher education they are scarcely heading for membership of the top 1 per cent of income earners that are the main beneficiaries of this political economy – but the myth dies hard. One reason is that it remains partly true for the upper echelons of higher education systems, especially in countries where incomes are especially stratified, matching the vertical hierarchy of higher education institutions. Higher education, or part of it, is most culpable in inequality where graduates from socially exclusive top universities are able to gain substantial traction simply from the institutional brand.

On the second point, there have always been issues in higher education at the global/national border. One example is that many national systems are closed or partly closed to foreign academic appointments, particularly permanent positions. Countries in Europe vary markedly in their degree of openness and closure to merit-based mobility. But global/national problems are now multiplying as nations become more restrictive of visas for short-term visitors, students and work-based migrants.

Donald Trump's ban on entrants from part of North Africa and the Middle East is one example. Another is UK international student policy (HEC, 2018). In commercialising international education the UK created a major export industry, one that also provides for global mobility and generates other public good benefits through diverse engagement in more multicultural universities. However, migration resistance in the UK electorate forced the government to promise a major reduction in net migration. This was difficult to achieve. International students are temporary rather than permanent migrants, but are included in the net migration count, and the

Prime Minister left them in the count because they are the easiest category to cut. In 2016 the government promised a 30–40 per cent reduction in non-EU international student numbers. While the reduction was not implemented, visa policy has been managed so as to hold constant or slightly reduce non-EU student, both reducing demand from South Asian families and breaking the education/work nexus in disciplines where internship or work experience are required. The UK government's lack of support for international education is costly in terms of UK export earnings, illustrating the point that in this era nativism and migration resistance can be stronger political forces than standard economic rationales. Though the UK is losing export market share, and sooner or later that will trigger a change in the government's position, as of mid 2018 there is little evident support in the political mainstream for the lifting of the curbs on international education.

Note that these two positioning effects can be combined. Higher education can become seen as both the handmaiden of inequality, the tool of the elite; and as a Pandora's Box of invasive foreigners and alien influences. The danger for higher education, of all kinds, elite and non-elite (but especially for the global research universities) is that it becomes positioned as a socially elite and cosmopolitan globalist sector that is necessarily ranged against egalitarian native identity. And in the rise of populist politics of the alt-right Trump-Brexit kind, this has happened.

NATIVIST-POPULISM AND HIGHER EDUCATION

Amid conditions of fragmented globalisation and growing inequality the new politics emerged, the nativist-populist politics of the Brexit campaign, Donald Trump and Marine Le Pen, and Hungary, Italy, Austria, Netherlands, parts of Germany and so on. The rise of nativist right-wing populism is not a bizarre aberration. It connects to the deep-seated global/national tensions and (especially) the tensions generated by inequality and frustrated economic and social aspirations. Nations, economies and education promise. Yet wealth and even opportunities seem increasingly confined.

The new politics raises many concerns. One is the funding of national electoral campaigns by off-shore corporations with deep pockets, and cyber-intervention by foreign governments. Another is the subversion of democracy by data mining companies that use the store of data on each person's likes, desires and fears, and social media techniques for individualising messages, so that voter can be manipulated by pressing exactly the right emotional buttons. More generally, there is the increasing preponderance on both political Right and political Left of sectional identity politics and the weakening of a sense of the common interest. But for higher education the new nativist-populist politics has posed two more direct challenges.

One challenge is the positioning, in both the 2016 Brexit campaign and the 2016 US presidential election, of higher education exactly as suggested above – as a socially elite and cosmopolitan globalist sector that is necessarily ranged against egalitarian native identity. This threatens to undermine the democratic mission of the sector and could even set in train a halt to the growth of aspirations, the motor of expansion.

The other challenge is the attacks on science and expert judgment, and the degrading of public discourse itself, which threatens to undermine the Enlightenment ideal that is foundational to the contemporary university and especially to its public role.

Here the problem for higher education is not solely reducible to political rhetoric or communication strategy. More fundamentally, it lies also in the binary character of the education/non-education distinction, which was a political problem that was waiting to be exploited. This problem, not anticipated by Martin Trow, is inherent in expansion itself. Paradoxically, education/non-education distinction becomes more rather than less pejorative as participation advances. As higher education expands the line between participation and non-participation (which as noted is also a line between mobile cosmopolitan agency and bounded agency) becomes increasingly regressive for those who are non-participants. Those without a degree are worse off in a society in which 60 per cent have tertiary qualifications than a society in which only 20 per cent are qualified and a degree is not yet indispensable for full social status. Why then should today's non-graduates love higher education? In their private domains the common public benefits are not very apparent, while at the same time they are excluded from many of the jobs on offer, and from social status itself. Politicians like Trump who debunk higher education, degrees and knowledge find willing listeners. So did the Brexit campaigners and so does Orban in Hungary.

In the Presidential election, the best predictors of how people would vote were not income or class, they were ethnicity ('race'), whether they lived in large cities, in which case they voted for Clinton; or in small towns and rural areas, in which case they voted for Trump, and educational level – whether or not they attended college (Silver, 2016). Trump openly celebrated the 'uneducated' in his campaign. Likewise in the case of Brexit. The predictors of voting behaviour were first, whether people lived in large cities, where the clear majority voted for the EU, or small towns and rural areas, which mostly supported Brexit; and second, whether they had degrees. These factors are related. Like global connections, degree holders tend to concentrate in cities and are comfortable with migrants and mobility. In the UK, 26 per cent of degree holders supported Brexit, but 78 per cent of people without qualifications. Young people, the most educated generation in UK history, more at ease with migration and multiple identities than any predecessor generation, voted overwhelmingly to remain. The least educated and least cosmopolitan age cohort, those aged over 65 years, voted in massive numbers to leave (Swales, 2016, p. 8).

Trump's attacks on climate science and on the conduct of political discussion at Berkeley and other public universities are signs of a broader hostility to the sector. However, the deepest challenge lies in the transformative effects of the particular form of nativist populism that has evolved, the effects of the reality show discourse in negating public rationality with its the notion of open debate grounded in reason and evidence that provides university-based expertise with its forms of public action. As John Harris remarks in The Guardian, here Trump builds on the fact that the United States has experienced forty years of relentless inequality. With the faltering of the meritocratic dream in a highly unequal society, in which university-based culture and science, like well-paid secure employment, appear increasingly beyond the reach of many, expectations are low. Reality television outshines the Kantian public ideal.

> 'In that context, even if he achieves next to nothing, the spectacle of a president endlessly provoking the liberal establishment, speaking to the prejudices of his electoral base, and putting on the mother of all political shows, has an undeniable appeal. And if everything is a circus, who cares about the bread? ... Social media are dissolving the connection between everyday experience and political argument to the point that the latter often seems to take place in its own self-sealed universe, purely as an ever more hysterical kind of entertainment. And from that, no end of awful political consequences could follow ... We have a whole lexicon – rhetoric, presentation, 'spin' – for the supposedly ephemeral aspects of politics, as if beneath them lurks the noble stuff to which we can somehow return. But what if it has gone, and there is no way of getting it back?' (Harris, 2017)

This underlines the importance of the universities as a public sphere in the sense discussed by Calhoun (1992) and Pusser (2006) – not only as the source of new knowledge but as stewards of the conditions of the Enlightenment rationality itself.

CONCLUSION

Higher education and science are growing on a worldwide basis with unprecedented momentum. This is uplifting individual and collective capabilities, immersed in complex knowledges, on a major scale. This will transform future society. These tendencies are near universal and a great strength of this period is that advanced education is no longer largely confined to Europe, North America and Japan. Educated capability and evidence-based science are spreading to a large number of middle income countries, from Eastern Europe and Latin America to parts of the Middle East/North Africa and Central Asia, and much of East and South East Asia. The lurch into nativist populism, with its unanticipated potentials to destabilise the popular enthusiasm for higher education and foster scepticism about science and truth-based public discourse is more localised to North America and Europe but given the continuing importance of those countries, in politics and culture as well as economics, the new mood has larger than regional effects.

Arguably, the key problem, corroding both democratic politics and the role of higher education, is the acceleration of economic inequality with no end in sight. Economic inequality also generates political inequality and subordination. Plutocratic control of the economy has been translated into the money control of Congress in the US (Stiglitz, 2013; Mettler, 2014) and the financing of the manipulated Brexit vote. Equally, money power has the capacity to reposition the universities; and their elite cultural claim leaves them always vulnerable – unless their openness, their egalitarian mission, is self-evident. Here the vulnerability of higher education and science varies by country. That egalitarian mission is self-evident in the Nordic countries, but less so in France and the Anglo-American world.

How could record levels of inequality in the US and increasingly in the UK not have a profound political effect, catching universities and science it the net? A large layer of people has been excluded from the possibility of individual or family betterment. The call to aspirations has diminishing returns. Scapegoating is inevitable. In the manner of nativist politics, in which all questions at bottom are reduced to the us/them framing of identity that sustains the populist coalition and becomes an end in itself, the explanatory narratives have no necessary relation to reality. But it is rampant economic and social inequality that ultimately sustains nativist populism and anti-migration politics and threatens to position higher education, especially research universities, on the wrong side of history.

How then does higher education find itself on the right side? There is much at stake. The institutional guarantors of public rationality are the liberal media and the large multi-disciplinary universities, that harbour both specialised and generic public intellectuals. With the media positioned and self-positioned as just another body of opinion (fake news) more than a reputable source of evidence-based truth, and often placed on the defensive, it falls to knowledge-intensive science and to the pluralist universities, with their long commitment to Kantian rationality, to take forward and make real the high democratic mission that is implied in their growing social role.

REFERENCES

Belfield, C., Britton, J., Dearden, L., & van der Erve, L. (2017). *Higher education funding in England: Past, present and options for the future*. London: Institute for Fiscal Studies. Retrieved from https://www.ifs.org.uk/publications/9334

Calhoun, C. (1992). Introduction. In C. Calhoun (Ed.), *Habermas and the public sphere* (pp. 1–48). Cambridge, MA: The MIT Press.

Cantwell, B., Marginson, S., & Smolentseva, A. (Eds.). (2018). *High participation systems of higher education*. Oxford: Oxford University Press.

Clancy, P., & Marginson, S. (2018). Comparative data on high participation systems. In B. Cantwell, S. Marginson, & A. Smolentseva (Eds.), *High participation systems of higher education* (pp. 39–67). Oxford: Oxford University Press.

Harris, J. (2017, August). Liberals can't hope to beat Trump until they truly understand him. *The Guardian*, p. 30. Retrieved from https://www.theguardian.com/commentisfree/2017/aug/30/liberals-donald-trump-rightwing-populists

Higher Education Commission. (2018). *Report of inquiry into education exports*. London.

Kharas, H. (2017, February). The unprecedented expansion of the global middle class: An update. *Global economy and development* (Working Paper 100). Washington, DC: Brookings Institution.

Kivela, A. (2012). From Immanuel Kant to Johann Gottlieb Fichte – Concept of education and German idealism. In P. Siljander, A. Kivela, & A. Sutinen (Eds.), *Theories of bildung and growth: Connections and controversies between continental educational thinking and American pragmatism* (pp. 59–86). Rotterdam, The Netherlands: Sense Publishers.

Leiden University. (2017). *CWTS leiden ranking 2017. Centre for science and technology studies, CWTS*. Retrieved from http://www.leidenranking.com

Marginson, S. (2018a). *Higher education as self-formation. Inaugural professorial lecture at the UCL institute of education*. Retrieved from https://www.ucl-ioe-press.com/books/higher-education-and-lifelong-learning/higher-education-as-a-process-of-self-formation/

Marginson, S. (2018b). Equity. In B. Cantwell, S. Marginson, & A. Smolentseva (Eds.), *High participation systems of higher education* (pp. 151–183). Oxford: Oxford University Press.

McMahon, W. (2009). *Higher learning greater good*. Baltimore, MD: The Johns Hopkins University Press.

Mettler, S. (2014). *Degrees of inequality: How the politics of higher education sabotaged the American dream*. New York, NY: Basic Books.

Milanovic, B. (2011). *The haves and the have nots: A brief and idiosyncratic history of global inequality*. New York, NY: Basic Books.

National Science Board (NSB). (2018). *Science and engineering indicators 2018*. Retrieved from https://www.nsf.gov/statistics/2018/nsb20181/assets/nsb20181.pdf

Organization for Economic Cooperation and Development (OECD). (2015). *Education at a glance 2015*. Paris: OECD.

Organization for Economic Cooperation and Development (OECD). (2016). *Perspectives on global development 2017: International migration in a shifting world*. Paris: OECD.

Piketty, T. (2014). *Capital in the twenty-first century*. Cambridge, MA: Belknap Harvard University Press.

Pusser, B. (2006). Reconsidering higher education and the public good. In W. Tierney (Ed.), *governance and the public good* (pp. 11–28). Albany, NY: SUNY Press.

Rodrik, D. (2017). *Populism and the economics of globalization*. In F. John (Ed.), F. Kennedy School of Government Cambridge, MA: Harvard University. Retrieved from https://drodrik.scholar.harvard.edu/files/dani-rodrik/files/populism_and_the_economics_of_globalization.pdf

Saez, E. (2013). *Striking it richer. The evolution of top incomes in the United States*. Berkeley, CA: University of California, Berkeley, Department of Economics. Retrieved from http://eml.berkeley.edu/~saez/saez-UStopincomes-2012.pdf

Silver, N. (2016). *Education, not income, predicted who would vote for Trump* (Five Thirty Eight). Retrieved from http://fivethirtyeight.com/features/education-not-income-predicted-who-would-vote-for-trump/

Stiglitz, J. (2013). *The price of inequality*. London: Penguin.

Swales, K. (2016). *Understanding the leave vote*. London: Nat Cen and the UK in a Changing Europe. Retrieved from http://natcen.ac.uk/our-reseach/research/understanding-the-leave-vote/

The Economist. (2017, January 28). *The retreat of the global company*.

Trow, M. (1973). *Problems in the transition from elite to mass higher education*. Berkeley, CA: Carnegie Commission on Higher Education.

United Nations Educational, Social and Cultural Organization (UNESCO). (2018). *UNESCO institute for statistics data on education*. Retrieved from http://data.uis.unesco.org/

BARBARA SPORN

3. ADAPTIVE UNIVERSITY STRUCTURES

From Theory to Practice and Back

INTRODUCTION

The world of universities today can be described as complex and full of rapid changes. Technology, immigration, poverty and budget constraints are some of the most pressing issues institutions of higher education are facing. Often institutional responses do not seem to fit pressing demands and institutions are struggling to develop adequate answers that are satisfactory to the different stakeholders.

Previous research (Clark, 1998, 2004; Tierney, 1998; Dill, 1999; Etkowitz et al., 2000; Sporn, 1999; Leih & Teece, 2016) has looked into the relationship between universities and their environment and more importantly to successful institutional adaptation. Through this, a couple of key factors were found that play an important role in the process. Most prominently, Burton Clark investigated in his seminal book on the entrepreneurial university those elements: entrepreneurial culture, diversified funding, enhanced academic heartland, strengthened steering core, and extended developmental periphery. In this chapter, I will come back to these elements and compare them to today's situation.

PREVIOUS RESEARCH ON ADAPTIVE UNIVERSITIES

In my book published some twenty years ago, studies of universities in Europe and the US compared different approaches of responses to environmental challenges. Adaptation was the key theoretical lens to analyze this relationship. The following definition was used:

> Organizational adaptation requires structural modifications or alterations in order to respond to changes in the external environment. There is a constant search for equilibrium between the organization and its environment. Adaptation refers to the process of responding to some discontinuity or lack of fit that arises between the organization and its environment. (citing Cameron 1984 in Sporn 1999, pp. 74–75)

Based on this definition the research investigated how institutions – through their governance, management, and leadership – change their university structure as a response to environmental forces. A key element in the conceptualization was the notion of crises or opportunity that created the impetus for change to both the institutional and societal environment.

Six cases were produced: the University of Michigan (US), New York University (US), University of California at Berkeley (US); Universität St. Gallen (Switzerland), Universita Bocconi (Italy), and WU Vienna University of Economics and Business (Austria) with the following results (i.e., factors positively influencing adaptation):

- Shared governance, i.e., collegial decision-making structures
- Committed leadership, i.e., ability to understand environmental forces and react to them
- Professional management, i.e., agile administration able to implement changes
- Clear mission; i.e., a coherent sense of direction and purpose
- Differentiated structure, i.e., structural arrangements with different functions flexibly responding to environmental demands
- Entrepreneurial culture, i.e., value of trial and error and the sense of viewing environment as an opportunity

These results were aligned with results from other authors at the time (especially Clark, 1998 and 2004). They showed that the environment is a source of change for all universities. The type of adaptation depends largely and the six factors above. Their combination can form a very strong and innovative new arrangement. It can also lead to a more reactive less opportunity driven approach (see Figure 3.1).

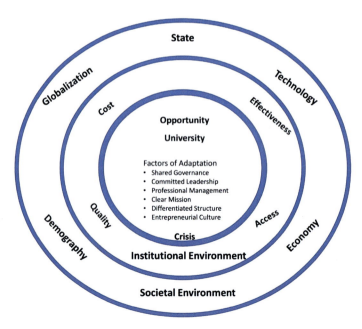

Figure 3.1. Adaptive university structures (Sporn, 1999)

PRACTICE WHAT YOU PREACH: WU AS AN ADAPTIVE CASE

The previous research was published some 20 years ago and it seemed appropriate to revisit the results. The goal has been to find out if the factors are still valid or if other areas need to be considered when looking at change and adaptation in universities. Given my institutional background and experience, it made sense to use WU Vienna University of Economics and Business as a case.

The role of ViceRector for Research, International Affairs and External Relations enabled me to combine both and to offer an in-depth view of WU: This institution has gone through quite substantial changes because of a complete reform of the legal basis. The University Act 2002 changed all elements of public university organization from scratch.

The WU Vienna University of Economics and Business was founded in 1898 as the College of Commerce at the time. It grew into a university until 1971 and offers a whole range of programs since then. Student numbers have been sharply increasing. Within the last 50 years, the numbers rose from some 8,000 to 22,000 by 2018. Programs are all "business related" and range from bachelor and master to PhD programs. The university has a yearly budget of some 110 million Euro, 2,000 employees of which roughly 100 are full professors. WU enjoys complete institutional autonomy and is funded some 90% by the state. Steering is managed through three-year performance contracts and yearly reports, a newly established university board, and legal amendments.

THE ENTREPRENEURIAL UNIVERSITY: THE CASE OF AUSTRIA

In 2002, the Austrian parliament passed a new university law (UG, 2002, University Act, 2002) which should change institutions of higher education in its totality. Universities had altogether two years to implement all requirements. This led to huge changes in all Austrian institutions.

The new law UOG 2002 had three building blocks, i.e., autonomy, global budgets, contracts. It is fair to say that this reform was the result of a decade-long debate fueled by new public management and the wish to get away with steering through direct orders (Ferlie et al., 2008; Enders et al., 2011; Bleikle et al., 2011).

Autonomy – in the view of the UG 2002 – is granted to universities to a very large extend in four areas. Public universities in Austria from 2004 onwards have enjoyed organizational autonomy. This means universities can freely define their structure and processes. The only restriction is the institutional tradition and the need to coordinate at the same time. The number of faculties or departments, the interdisciplinary research institutes, the creation of competence areas can be decided freely. Only required structural elements are a Rector's Council, a Senate, a University Board, and an administrative structure.

Personal autonomy follows the same pattern and the consequences for those seeking employment at an Austrian public university since then have been drastic. With the new legal basis, the government abolished the status of civil servant at universities. No longer did the possibility exist to get benefits from that status but staff was employed based on a regular (private) contract with the university. The universities in return have been empowered to hire personnel on individual contracts and on all ranks. Competitive salaries, flexible arrangements, and diverse contracts became possible and enhanced universities to recruit internationally and from industry.

Program autonomy lends itself to the fact that institutions could introduce new programs of all sorts without seeking public approval. This meant that universities decided individually about the introduction of a three-tier-system (i.e., Bologna system), the types of programs offered, and the degree of specialization. The state only defined the terms of student access – if controlled or not – and the amount of tuition fees. By now, Austrian public universities charge no tuition fees for regular programs and student access is free except for a few disciplines of higher demand (including medicine, business, psychology, biology, architecture, etc.).

Financial autonomy lies at the heart of the above-mentioned areas of autonomy. Universities receive a lump sum budget for three years and have been able to allocate it to whatever area desired. Hence, universities moved to cost control and financial management through a balance sheet, investment areas, personnel budgets, etc. and could shift finances as need be. Only exception of this is real estate where the state through a state-controlled agency controls all university property and buildings.

This autonomous university status together with a three-year global budget requires university leadership to ensure strategic decision. At the same time, steering and control through state authorities has been reduced. A key instrument was created to address the issue (based on the idea of new public management): contracts (Höllinger & Titscher, 2004). Accordingly, since 2004 universities have been steered through performance contracts on all levels. They exist between the ministry and the institutions, between the rectorate and the board, and between the rectorate and the departments or academic units.

In order to form contracts universities have been required to develop strategies in the form of a so-called Development Plan. This is the key strategic document for each public university that contains the strategic direction, the programs offered, the represented disciplines, and the faculty positions. It sets out the strategy regarding research and internationalization and is accompanied by an organization plan defining the basic university structure.

Above that, the UG 2002 installed a university board overseeing the major areas of activities of universities. It has a supervisory function and consists of members nominated by the university senate and by the government. Major decisions include the appointment of the rector, the approval of the budget, the performance contracts, the organization and development plan.

Key Challenges of Austrian Higher Education Reform

The change process triggered by UG 2002 led to a completely revised organization and strategy for WU by 2004. WU overall interpreted the new law as an opportunity to create a revised identity as an autonomous institution and initiated an opportunity driven change process. The new leadership team – the Rector's Council – redefined its role more in the direction of strategic vision and was able to convince the community to move along with it. An entrepreneurial approach for all activities was created with the motivation to implement innovation in all areas affected. The result was a new view of WU that was stakeholder and performance driven. Four areas of expertise were developed out of a very differentiated and complicated structure (see Figure 3.2): the undergraduate school; the graduate school; the executive academy; and the expert centers.

Taken all these massive changes into the account it was possible to create a sense of benefit and a successful decade of implementations started. Not without some key challenges.

In this lengthy process, *seven key challenges* appeared. The first and most important one regards the need and wish to become *autonomous*. The tradition of WU was always linked to its public status and the relationship with the ministry. All of the sudden, the university had to independently find its vision for the future, define its character, and develop a strategy. The strategic development was the result of a highly participative process that involved all key stakeholders and many consultants. Under the title ALFA – autonomy in programs, research and administration – WU was able to create a sense of change. It was not without costs of coordination and time stretch that this came about.

A second challenge regards the area of *leadership*. The new law shifted power substantially around in the institution. The state delegated its power to the Rector's Council and that way created a new power center within the university. For control purposes, the newly established University Board has to approve the rector, strategy and budget as its major responsibilities. Nominations to the Board are rather political as the University Senate and the government can nominate equal number of members. Most importantly, the Senate lost its power as the major center of control. Its role was reduced to one of competence-based responsibility, i.e., today it decides on all "academic" issues like programs and student affairs, faculty search, and research matters. In other areas like personnel, finances, strategy, etc. it only has to be notified. The challenge has been to continue the tradition of trust and collaboration of a shared governance system with the WU faculty and at the same time initiate all major and necessary changes.

A third challenge concerns *contract* management. A new philosophy was established with the implementation of UG 2002. Institutions had to go through planning cycles in order to define their mid-term priorities, their needs and expected outcomes. This was true both for the whole WU but also for all Administrative Units and Departments as well as Research Centers. It took a longer planning to establish the competence of developing a contract that can be renewed in any given period. For the institutional contracts, it was essential to name priorities and to define respective faculty lines.

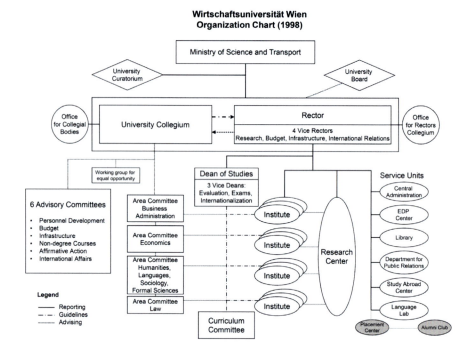

Figure 3.2. WU history: Becoming an entrepreneurial university

Fourthly, in the area of *personnel* the changes have been substantial. All new administrative and academic employees were no longer civil servants but university employees with private contracts. Reduced job security, better employment conditions regarding salary, and more outcome base expectations were widely discussed. Especially for university professors the situation needed some time of adjustment as some newly hired colleagues expected to be treated based on the old legal status. Combined with it where questions like retirement as emeritus, pension regulations, and presence at the university. For WU, this area was only relevant for a certain period. Within 10 years, more than 60% of the faculty retired and new colleagues were hired internationally who have been used to the new system of all-in individual and negotiable contracts.

Funding is the fifth area of change. WU was used to a line budget that needed to be negotiated with the ministry directly. With UG 2002, WU received a global budget for three years with unrestricted budget responsibility and spending discretion. It implied that financial planning was key and WU decided to implement a new accounting system. This challenged many colleagues as performance got measured and more transparent. The cost of programs was a key building stone for program planning. The expertise for finance had to develop as well. Financial accountants, tax experts, and controllers were employed. The clash of cultures between the academic and the administrative world became even more apparent.

The sixth area of change regards the WU *programs*. With the new law, the university was able to change all programs to the Bologna structure. A three-tier system developed in order to enhance the internationalization of WU. The university also used this to innovate its programs with a completely new philosophy. A large general bachelor program and law degree were followed by specialized master degrees. On top of that came doctoral and PhD programs. The challenge has been to redesign courses, pedagogy and long-held teaching traditions. Through the collegial change process that involved all major stakeholders faculty support was guaranteed.

Overall, it would be fair to say that the challenges WU was facing turned into an opportunity that helped to completely renew WU. The University changed from a decentralized and loosely coupled institution to be more integrated and differentiated at the same time. Departments formed grouping related fields in one area. They have become the major academic unit at WU delivering courses at all levels and for all programs and doing research for the academic community as well as for industry. Additionally, WU decided to offer further education in the form of WU's Executive Academy and to disseminate research expertise. Different management processes were established for different offers regionally and internationally.

Personal Experiences as a Vice-Rector

For this analysis, it is essential to share some personal experiences and insights as well. The author has been part of the change process for 13 years in different functions. First, as Vice-Rector for International Affairs (from 2002–2004) a new strategy was formulated which aimed at positioning WU within the international community of business universities and schools. Second, additional responsibilities were added to the portfolio, i.e., Research and External Relations (2004–2015). A fundraising campaign and research measures like new funding schemes, a research strategy, and support services were developed. Altogether, the personal reflection regards some key areas: autonomy, governance, leadership, change, management, and quality improvement.

Autonomy refers to the process of the university gaining increased institutional power to decide on key issues ranging from organization to financial matters. With this new freedom, the Rector's Council became more important and professionalized. At the same time, the individual freedom of employees (especially those of professors) was limited. In a change process of this magnitude, it is important to integrate all stakeholders and be aware of the friction between individual and institutional autonomy. Most faculty would feel impeded by new requirements of reporting, ranking, output and quality management. A fine balance between the areas needed to develop to implement necessary changes.

Shared governance is another area that I found of pivotal importance in a university change process. In order to implement a new structure, organization, and strategy within a university it seems necessary to develop a comprehensive process that involves all major stakeholders. Especially with the new governance structure, the challenges have been very clear. The principle of delegation led to the fact that key groups have not been fully represented. They needed to delegate power to certain trusted colleagues. As a consequence, certain groups were left behind while a certain "power" house developed.

Another area of personal experience is the necessity of *committed leadership*. Successful decisions are made with a clear understanding of the future. The university community should share this vision as much as possible. For the period of change, a strong vision provided identification: "becoming an internationally reputed institution". This certainly served as a driver for change but was not suited for all. Again, it is important in a change process to realize how different groups are involved in strategic planning and implementation.

Related to this point, is the notion that the vision for change is an *ongoing piecemeal process*. There are constant and ongoing adjustments and developments that need to be taken into account. The institution needs to develop a change mindset rather than viewing change as an outcome. If enough institutional members believe in the need of constant development and change success will follow. At the same time, there was a sense of burden, a claim to relax from change and to move into a steady state mode. Institutions need phases of (radical) change followed by periods of slower alterations.

Professional management is a necessity when becoming an entrepreneurial university. As was demonstrated by scholars (Rhoades & Sporn, 2002), the number of administrative staff has been increasing steadily while the number of faculty have been more or less stable. Hence, a new administrative cadre developed of qualified professionals supporting core processes. These new "third space" professionals" (Whitchurch, 2008) have been well trained and qualified to run the institution professionally. The clash of values and culture has become even stronger as administration and academy became more professionally managed.

Along the same line, constant *quality* improvement has established itself as good university practice. It is hard to find a well-known university without an office or manager responsible for quality management. It is needed for the area of teaching, research and external relations of all sorts. Students require universities to design programs and courses following a certain quality standard. Research needs a lot of attention on quality. For external relations with regard to rankings, accreditations and international collaborations it is of key importance to follow certain patterns of quality control. Academic values and standards often run opposite to those of quality management. Hence, it needs careful management as well.

BACK TO THEORY AND RESEARCH

After this depiction of WU as a case for an entrepreneurial university showing the need to adapt to changing environments and depicting required adjustments, let us now turn back to theory and research. For this, I look at the higher education environment today in Europe, present some facts, and revisit seminal work in the area.

The Environment for Higher Education in Europe Today

Many analysts have presented the very dynamic environment for institutions of higher education today especially in Europe but also elsewhere in the world. These trends can be summarized into two major streams, i.e., *expansion and globalization*. Expansion refers to the process of widening access for many different groups of society (Trow, 2000). In times of mass higher education, different formats and degrees are offered ranging from traditional bachelor programs to specialized online courses. Especially in Europe where most systems and institutions receive public funding, expansion becomes rather expensive. Consequently, public budgets for higher education have been increasing and at the same time, public spending became more visible. State officials and governments have started to require universities to report more on their outputs – be it graduates or research publications. The legitimacy of institutions depends on this and it puts pressure on universities to respond. It leads to a call for accountability and eventually impact. Through demonstrating their performance, universities comply and implement a variety of impact measures (Meyer & Sporn, 2018). Examples of this trend towards impact are manifold, i.e., showing the importance of providing value to society through educational services be it in research or teaching programs. They range from rankings and accreditations, the role of CSR in university policy to entrepreneurship education.

A second major environment development is globalization. Goods, services, and people can travel freely to find an adequate job and market. The same dynamic is in place for education. As the world of work has internationalized the universities have globalized substantially. This led to more competition not only nationally but also internationally. The number of institutions of higher education has increased swiftly and students are more educated to make their best choice for education. Competition is part of this dynamic and leads to more differentiation in function and forms. Today, we can see online universities, vertically and horizontally specialized institutions (colleges, and graduate schools, technical universities), hybrid models (university colleges, corporate universities), as well as new models (flipped university, community and network approaches). Examples are the University of Phoenix, Hult University, or a new creation "Station1" – a nonprofit organization dedicated to education founded by a former Dean of MIT (see www.station1.org).

Some Facts on Higher Education

There is ample evidence of this development of expansion and globalization (see e.g. IAU, WHED World Higher Education Database 2016, Eurostat). There are some 24,000 institutions of higher education worldwide. About half offer law, economics and social sciences. These are the areas were most employment opportunities arises. Universities and colleges often specialize in these fields.

Regarding access there has been an increased participation rate within the OECD countries. On average, the participation of the respective cohort of 18 to 24 year olds is 50 to 60%. With this high amount, universities and colleges are major players in society.

On the output side, employment numbers show the importance of a higher education degree dramatically. On an OECD average, graduates with a tertiary degree have 85% employment followed by 75% with a secondary degree and only 55% with a lower degree. Hence, it is still fair to say that it makes a difference to get a college or university degree.

Revisit Clark's Self-Reliant University

The renowned higher education researcher Burton Clark continued his work on the entrepreneurial university and published a second – follow-up – book looking at sustained change in universities (Clark, 2004). He investigated new cases around the world to deepen our understanding of the entrepreneurial university. By amplifying variations in university entrepreneurialism, he developed cases in Africa (Uganda), Latin America (Chile), Australia (Monash University) and the US (Stanford University, MIT, University of Michigan, UCLA, Georgia Institute of Technology). As a result, Clark promoted the self-reliant university as a model.

Clark suggests five *elements* for sustained change (and success of universities): aligning the strengthened steering core; forming an extended developmental periphery; many sources of financial support; entrepreneurialism in heartland departments; institution-wide entrepreneurial culture (Clark, 2004). First, the professional management needs to be integrated with the academic side of the institution. Faculty participation in major councils is a critical component.

Second, there are basic forms of the extended developmental periphery addressing environmental expectations that need to be implemented (e.g., interdisciplinary research centers, teaching outreach programs). Third, the diversified funding base is a key factor in sustaining change in universities. Not through commercialization but through a broad portfolio of income sources, universities become self-reliant to fund their strategies. Fourth, the academic departments (i.e., university heartlands) form a building block for sustained change. Attractive places for students, faculty, and external partners represent an entrepreneurial attitude and dynamic places within the institution. Fifth, an institution-wide entrepreneurial culture can form and influence the value system of the university. The run for prestige and recognition in modern universities today calls for entrepreneurial ideas that will lead to a prime position in the educational market.

Additionally, it is necessary to look at *process* as well. Clark presents three dynamics through which sustained change can happen. On the one hand, reinforcing interaction is a key element in the process. The institution needs to provide enough opportunities to interact and exchange views on the issues involved. Decisions and agreements need to be in line with the envisioned future that can enhance a change-oriented culture. Then a sense of perpetual momentum needs to be in place in order to support the self-reliant university, i.e., the notion of ongoing adjustments, negotiations, interactions, environmental scanning, etc. Only through this, can an institutional dynamic stay alive. On the other hand, the institution needs to develop an ambitious collegial volition. Clark makes a very strong argument that only an 'ambitious volition help propel the institution forward to a transformed character'. He goes on saying that inertia in traditional universities has many rationales, beginning with the avoidance of hard choices' (Clark, p 94). In the end, it needs two miracles (p. 95):

> One is to *get started*, facing down the fear of failure before beginning. Many universities will simply not try to start down the new road. It is risky: a hallowed institution may be laid low. The other miracle is *sustaining* a virtuous circle of successful accomplishments over a decade or more, facing down the multitude of conserving tendencies in organizations – especially universities – and among organized sponsors – especially ministries – that bring change to a halt. At the heart of each miracle lies willful agency. It is not the demands of the day in themselves that drive a university to change, we now know, but rather the many specific responses to those demands, in the form of emergent acts of will that are summoned from within.

With this beautiful citation, the whole 'story of change' or 'moments of truth' can be summarized. It is not one act, it is not one person, and it is not one reason for change to happen. It is necessary to create an ambition that is shared by the university community. Then this ambition will need ownership, carrying as well as delivering. Lastly, it is only from within that the drive of change can originate. The transformation will lead to the self-reliant university.

The Economist Perspective: Governance and Performance

The Harvard economist Philip Aghion and colleagues from European think tanks offer a completely different departure point (Aghion et al., 2008, 2010). They looked at governance and performance of universities in Europe compared to institutions worldwide. The goal has been to find indicators that will enhance performance (measured by the position in the Shanghai Ranking).

In this research, a large database on rankings was used to investigate the system and institutional characteristics of high performing research universities. The hypothesis tested if institutions are more productive when they are autonomous and face competition. Survey data showed the level of autonomy and competition for European and US universities. In summary:

> the results "show that there are strong positive correlations between these indices and multiple measures of university output. To obtain causal evidence, we investigate exogenous shocks to US universities' expenditures over three decades. These shocks arise through the political appointment process, which we use to generate instrumental variables. We find that an exogenous increase in a university's expenditure generates more output, measured by either patents or publications, if the university is more autonomous and faces more competition. Exploiting variation over time in the 'stakes' of competitions for US federal research grants, we also find that universities generate more output for a given expenditure when research competitions are at high stakes. We draw lessons, arguing that European universities could benefit from a combination of greater autonomy and greater accountability. Greater accountability might come through increased reliance on competitive grants, enhanced competition for students and faculty (promoted by reforms that increase mobility), and yardstick competitions (which often take the form of assessment exercises). (Aghion et al., 2010, p. 1)

Aghion and colleagues argue that a combination of better (competitive) funding and increased autonomy will lead to higher performing universities in Europe. There are two elements to this. First, universities need to have the power to decide upon their curriculum and especially faculty hiring. To negotiate wages and work packages is a key element to attract the best faculty in the world. Second, more competition and funding are of key importance, i.e., research grants, foundations and external sources. Grants require accountable results and special reporting, e.g., universities need to show output and through this have a stronger focus on their research performance.

Above that, competition in Europe would require more mobility. Mobile students and faculty will chose institutions based on certain performance indicators those places that best fit their needs. Hence, Aghion et al. (2010) recommend:

> Our evidence leads us to recommend higher education reforms in Europe, at both the national and EU levels, that combine higher autonomy with higher accountability through greater reliance on competitive grants, enhanced

mobility of students and faculty, and yardstick competition exercises such as assessment programmes. (p. 10)

Compared to Clark's sociological approach, this is a rather different departure point. The economist see markets and institutional responses as the key building blocks of performance. It becomes evident that universities change their behavior in more competitive circumstances. Leadership and governance are much more geared towards outputs and competitive funding calls for accountability. Mobility adds to the fact that institutions (and faculty or students) start to compare institutional characteristics and performance. In this sense, transparency adds dynamic to the process and changes competitive behavior.

OECD and the Entrepreneurial University

In recent years, the OECD – more specifically their higher education group – added more to this topic by creating a platform for entrepreneurial universities. The EU Commission and the OECD funded the development of a tool under the heading of HEInnovate some four years ago (see https://heinnovate.eu/en). Online case studies and trainings help institutions to assess their innovative and entrepreneurial capacity. Over 100 participants registered in three years. Here is the mission of HEInnovate (online statement from July 10, 2018):

> HEInnovate is a self-assessment tool for Higher Education Institutions who wish to explore their innovative potential. It guides you through a process of identification, prioritisation and action planning in eight key areas. HEInnovate also diagnoses areas of strengths and weaknesses, opens up discussion and debate on the entrepreneurial/innovative nature of your institution and it allows you to compare and contrast evolution over time. You can have instant access to your results, learning materials and a pool of experts. The European Commission and the OECD have joined forces in the development of HEInnovate. It is free, confidential and open to anyone to use. HEInnovate can be used by all types of higher education institutions. This website offers more than just an interactive tool; it also contains case studies, user stories and supporting material to help you to design solutions tailored to your needs.

The tool includes some seven indicators that serve as building blocks for innovative universities:

1. Leadership and governance
2. Organizational capacity: funding, people, incentives
3. Entrepreneurial teaching and learning
4. Preparing and supporting entrepreneurs
5. Knowledge exchange and collaboration
6. The Internationalized Institution
7. Measuring impact

Leadership capacity coupled with an efficient governance system plays a key role in setting up innovation. Capacity building is the second area where higher education institutions need to invest. This capacity builds on three pillars. The funding must be sufficient and flexible enough to finance innovation. Faculty and staff should be open to innovation; an entrepreneurial spirit is needed. Incentives must be in place – both intrinsic and extrinsic – to support grassroot and bottom-up initiatives. Teaching and learning are entrepreneurial activities showing how faculty work with students in a creative and effective way. The economy worldwide is changing so enhancing entrepreneurship needs to be part of any innovative institution of higher education. The right preparation and the support of upcoming talent is key in the process. Knowledge production followed by exchange and collaboration across institutional boundaries supports cross-fertilization and interdisciplinary problem solving. Different institutional types can work together innovatively. Internationalization, the network of partners and clear visibility play a key role for universities. Institutional positioning, ranking and accreditation as well as network formation need to be integrated in a strategic way in an innovative higher education institution. Measuring impact has become a prime expectation of universities. It needs to be clear how research and teaching influence local, regional and national societies and economies. The innovative university will gain legitimacy by demonstrating impact.

CRITICS

The entrepreneurial university concept has been widely received by the higher education community. As this chapter showed, many recommendations developed in order to make universities better perform in a increasingly competitive higher education market. At the same time, there are a number of critics that need to be presented.

Often authors describe entrepreneurialism as a version of new public management and academic capitalism. (e.g., Ferlie, Musselin, & Andressani, 2008; de Boer, Enders, & Schimank, 2007; Slaughter & Leslie, 1997). They warn to see universities as managed organizations, programs as products and students as customers. Research is mainly serving an implementation purpose especially in applied fields like STEM.

Added to that is the problem of increased competition fired up by rankings. Higher education has become a reputational good mainly concerned with market positioning. Program design, student selection and faculty expectations are driven by the view of performance to achieve good ranking results.

This leads to the danger of commercialization of universities evidenced through a couple of trends. Governance moved from collegial to managerial. Many committees and even senates became smaller or even unimportant. Decisions are taken less by collegial bodies but by leadership positions. Faculty are no longer the key and sole contributor to quality of the core function, i.e., research and teaching (through the establishment of technology transfer centers, or learning labs) (Rhoades & Sporn, 2002). In the area of research, Mode 2 (Nowotny et al., 2003) gains importance as well. Emphasis is on the applicability of research (impact) and competitive funding mechanisms for research. The importance of the STEM area in many universities is a vital sign of this development and represent a threat to traditional disciplines like the humanities.

Although there is a fair amount of critics, there are enough good examples that show that universities need to constantly adapt and change in order to stay legitimate (Gumport & Sporn, 1999). They can do this with a view on entrepreneurialism that features a sense of opportunity, the emphasis on collegial values and participation, a clear commitment to professional management, a respect for autonomy of academic units and a focus on impact.

Recent Patterns of Development in Higher Education

Recent developments point in the direction of innovation and entrepreneurialism in higher education institutions. There is a move from an adaptive to a more entrepreneurial model with changing governance structures. Institutions find new ways to organize and to respond to environmental challenges. It is less a view of threats and more a view on opportunities that is driving change. The governance supports this development.

Universities are viewed more and more as organizations rather than as institutions. Consequently, more concepts from organization research and management are applied to universities including strategic planning, leadership, vision and mission, accountability and impact (Musselin, 2007) Legitimacy will increase and the set-up of a governance structure gains importance (Gumport, 2000).

Academic values of discovery and dissemination tend to be replaced by entrepreneurial values (Christensen & Eyring, 2011). It is driven by the idea that problem solving is more part of the research function. Faculty members are expected to produce answers to pressing questions of society.

Steering is moved away from the academy and the state to the market (Bok, 2009; Marginson, 2006). The rules of demand and response are a guiding principle to design research and teaching in universities. The market is a key player in defining services and the efficiency and effectiveness is measured in those terms.

As a result, institutional diversity is replaced by profiles and reputation. As universities are becoming more alike, other forms of differentiation play a role. Institutional profiles containing clear definitions of areas of strengths and attractiveness are used. The positioning in the education and research market is a clear consequence of this. This development potentially threatens the long-held values of freedom of teaching and research.

CONCLUSIONS

This chapter analyzed the continued interest in the adaptive university and compared recent practical experiences and theoretical findings. There is a continued need to understand university steering as self-reliant, adaptive, entrepreneurial, or innovative. Universities are still in the process of finding the right balance between demand and response. This is further triggered by stark societal developments like digitalization, immigration and integration, and inequality. Higher education institutions have a strong role to play in this area.

For a successful pathway of transformation, it seems necessary

- To use theories and approaches from organization studies

Once institutions of higher education are seen as organization, a whole range of theories and approaches can be applied and can that way help to lead, steer and manage efficiently and effectively. It is this tool-oriented notion that could be beneficial to many colleges and universities.

- To focus on change and new modes of governance and integrate critical aspects

Universities as organizations and organization theory lead to the focus on change and adaption. It is important to keep the environmental vulnerability of universities in mind and develop a culture around that. New governance system would be necessary to scan and understand external trends and developments and to develop adequate responses. Critical aspects like mentioned above need to be integrated like the role of different disciplines, faculties and constituencies.

- To use an entrepreneurial approach as an opportunity

The adoption of an entrepreneurial approach could potentially lead to more diverse models and differentiation in higher education. The concept integrates external expectations, translates them into opportunities and develops new responses. In an ideal world, more differentiation will follow as different types of organizations can offer different services. It could be a counterbalance to the dominant trend of convergence of institutional types. This could in turn help to make higher education more accessible to a wide range of societal stakeholders.

- To continue comparative work of all sorts

The field of higher education research is an important player in this dynamic as well. Through continued case studies, institutional research and theoretical analyses a widened pool of examples and benchmarks can be offered. Practitioners and academics are still in need to understand the different responses and approaches of colleges and universities around the world.

In summary, the role of universities in society is more important than ever. Universities need to view their character and trajectory as fluid and developmental. Only through a process view of change and wise combination of learnt success factors and requirements of the future, will they keep or even enhance their status.

REFERENCES

Aghion, P., Dewatripont, M., Hoxby, C., Mas-Colell, A., & Sapir, A. (2008, July 5). *Higher aspirations: An agenda for reforming European universities* (Bruegel blueprint). Bruegel.

Aghion, P., Dewatripont, M., Hoxby, C., Mas-Colell, A., & Sapir, A. (2010). The governance and performance of universities: Evidence from Europe and the US. *Economic Policy, 25*(61), 7–59.

Bleiklie, I., Enders, J., Lepori, B., & Musselin, C. (2011). New public management, network governance and the university as a changing professional organization. In T. Christensen & P. Laegreid (Eds.), *The Ashgate research companion to new public management* (pp. 161–176). Farnham: Ashgate.

Bok, D. (2009). *Universities in the marketplace: The commercialization of higher education*. Princeton, NJ: Princeton University Press.

Christensen, C. M., & Eyring, H. J. (2011). *The innovative university: Changing the DNA of higher education from the inside out*. Hoboken, NJ: John Wiley & Sons.

Clark, B. R. (1998). *Creating entrepreneurial universities: Organizational pathways of transformation*. Issues in higher education. New York, NY: Elsevier Science Inc.

Clark, B. R. (2004). *Sustaining change in universities. Continuities in case studies and concepts*. London: McGraw-Hill Education.

De Boer, H., Enders, J., & Schimank, U. (2007). On the way towards new public management? The governance of university systems in England, the Netherlands, Austria, and Germany. In D. Jansen (Ed.), *New forms of governance in research organizations* (pp. 137–152). Dordrecht: Springer.

Dill, D. D. (1999). Academic accountability and university adaptation: The architecture of an academic learning organization. *Higher education, 38*(2), 127–154.

Dill, D. D., & Sporn, B. (1995). *Emerging patterns of social demand and university reform: Through a glass darkly* (Issues in higher education). New York, NY: Elsevier Science Inc.

Etzkowitz, H., Webster, A., Gebhardt, C., & Terra, B. R. C. (2000). The future of the university and the university of the future: Evolution of ivory tower to entrepreneurial paradigm. *Research Policy, 29*(2), 313–330.

Ferlie, E., Musselin, C., & Andresani, G. (2008). The steering of higher education systems: A public management perspective. *Higher Education, 56*(3), 325.

Gumport, P. J. (2000). Academic restructuring: Organizational change and institutional imperatives. *Higher Education, 39*(1), 67–91.

Gumport, P. J., & Sporn, B. (1999). Institutional adaptation: Demands for management reform and university administration. In J. C. Smart & M. B. Paulsen (Eds.), *Higher education: Handbook of theory and research* (pp. 103–145). Dordrecht: Springer.

Höllinger, S., & Titscher, S. (Eds.). (2004). *Die österreichische Universitätsreform: Zur implementierung des universitätsgesetzes 2002*. Vienna: WUV Universitätsverlag.

Leih, S., & Teece, D. (2016). Campus leadership and the entrepreneurial university: A dynamic capabilities perspective. *Academy of Management Perspectives, 30*(2), 182–210.

Marginson, S. (2006). Dynamics of national and global competition in higher education. *Higher Education, 52*(1), 1–39.

Mattei, P. (Ed.). (2014). *University adaptation in difficult economic times*. Oxford: Oxford University Press.

Meyer, M., & Sporn, B. (2018). Leaving the ivory tower: Universities' third mission and the search for legitimacy. *zeitschrift für hochschulentwicklung, 13*(2), 41–60

Musselin, C. (2007). *Are universities specific organisations. Towards a multiversity* (pp. 63–84). Bielefeld: Transkript.

Nowotny, H., Scott, P., Gibbons, M., & Scott, P. B. (2001). *Re-thinking science: Knowledge and the public in an age of uncertainty* (p. 12). Cambridge: Polity Press.

Pinheiro, R., & Stensaker, B. (2014). Designing the entrepreneurial university: The interpretation of a global idea. *Public Organization Review, 14*(4), 497–516.

Rhoades, G., & Sporn, B. (2002). Quality assurance in Europe and the US: Professional and political economic framing of higher education policy. *Higher Education, 43*(3), 355–390.

Slaughter, S., & Leslie, L. L. (1997). *Academic capitalism: Politics, policies, and the entrepreneurial university*. Baltimore, MD: The Johns Hopkins University Press.

Sporn, B. (1999). *Adaptive university structures: An analysis of adaptation to socioeconomic environments of US and European universities* (Higher education policy series 54). Philadelphia, PA: Taylor and Francis.

Tierney, W. G. (1998). *The responsive university: Restructuring for high performance*. Baltimore, MD: The Johns Hopkins University Press.

Trow, M. (2000). From mass higher education to universal access: The American advantage. *Minerva, 37*(4), 303–328.

Whitchurch, C. (2008). Shifting identities and blurring boundaries: The emergence of third space professionals in UK higher education. *Higher Education Quarterly, 62*(4), 377–396.

Resources

Database of the IAU and WHED: http://whed.net/home.php

Eurostat Database on Tertiary Education: https://ec.europa.eu/education/resources/european-tertiary-education-register_en

Nonprofit organization for innovative education: www.station1.org

OECD and Commission sponsored platform on the innovative university: https://heinnovate.eu/en

ARWU Academic Ranking of World Universities (Shanghai Ranking): http://www.shanghairanking.com/

S. FEYO DE AZEVEDO

4. GOVERNANCE AND MANAGEMENT – CHALLENGES OF TODAY, ADAPTING TO THE TIMES

INTRODUCTION

I have this feeling and understanding, like a 'Verité de La Palisse', that throughout the history of humankind, in all domains of life, speaking of individuals or institutions, it has not been the 'strongest' (individual or institution) that necessarily survived, but rather the one that proved to be most adaptable to changes ... I am sure that you, reader, have already identified that this speculative and (for some) probably arguable statement is inspired in the studies of Darwin about the evolution of species and has been disseminated (not by Darwin) in relation with the evolution of species. For me, the underlying idea serves as introduction to my short text and to my conference. Indeed, the issue for the talk, that will be limited in scope to Governance and Management of Universities, is structured in these three points/questions – (i) how do we characterize our contemporary days? (ii) what challenges are ahead of us, embedded in our present reality? (iii) How can we, or how should we tackle them, what should we do to adapt to times?

READING THE PAST

We should not put 'memory', the lessons of the past, aside. This means to think about the question – Are these challenges of today so different from those that our ancestors had to face over the past, say, two hundred years? Independently of recognizing the tremendous pace of development that we are going through, as I obviously recognize, it is important to have a 'memory' and keep in mind the type of progress and the shock/clash of progress in society, in institutions and individuals along the times.

The 1st industrial Revolution (~1750–1850) associated to James Watt (1736–1819) and the steam engine,[1] represent the days when, possibly for the first time known, machines replaced hand powered tools. What a shock it has been. And then we identify the 2nd industrial Revolution (~1850–1930), the age of the steel,[2] with locomotives and steam boats allowing for goods to be 'massively exported around the world' as it is commented in some writings about those times, or a period where Europe 'changed dramatically', experiencing 'rapid changes of social and economic patterns'.

Speaking of those days, it has also been written, and rightly so, that the Pasteur's breakthroughs (1822–1895)[3] 'revolutionized the world as it was known', or that discoveries of Thomas Edison (1847–1931)[4] 'changed the world for ever'. And similar sentences for the discovery of penicillin by Alexander Fleming (1881–1955) and how it also 'revolutionized' the health area.

Then, of course, in the area of communications, the first public radio broadcasting in 1910, or the transistor, that revolutionized the field of electronics, first patented by Julius Edgar Lilienfeld in 1926, but really only brought to practice in 1947 by John Bardeen, Walter Brattain, and William Shockley (Nobel prize winners in 1956).[5]

Many other examples could be given about 'times of dramatic changes'. Indeed, many other quotations of the past with the very same words that we use today to characterize contemporary life can be found in the literature.

THE WORLD TODAY

So, with this background in mind, let me 'go back to the present and to the future'. If we look to the trajectories of changes along the past 200 years, yes, we note that the derivative has increased significantly over the past 40 years or so. I take the end of the seventies, and particularly the last decade of the last century as a reference time for very significant changes, for the identification of the 4th Revolution,[6] that is clearly not only industrial.

Main driving forces? For sure social understanding of education, progress in science and technology and the cycles of world politics, the latter having changed much along the last quarter of the 20th century due to the influence of science and religion.

Speaking of Education, there is a clear understanding that the shout 'Education is a Human Right', very much promoted by UNESCO, through the 'Education for All' Movement,[7] initiated in the World Conference on Education for All in 1990, in Thailand, represents a major milestone.[8]

About progress in science, I have identified above some examples of the past, linked to research in the health and the communications areas, with tremendous impact in our lives. For a reason. Recent developments in these very same areas are especially responsible, though of course not exclusively, for this 'revolution of the present'. The developments in the health area experienced by the end of the last century were responsible (together with public policies, of course) for the sharp increase in the expectancy of life and this has clearly put in question the social system in Europe and elsewhere, as it was organized. About ICT (Information and Communications Technology), the known and felt progress in this wide field, as we go wireless with unforeseeable end and consequences, is of course influencing all areas of our life. And politics, with the fall of the Berlin Wall in 1989, has led to all social, political and economic consequences that we are feeling today, not foreseen at the time, having strengthened, accelerated, this reality of the Global World open to the market economy. The social paradigm has changed, with serious consequences of political and social instability, as we all see today, every single day.

It is of course true that we live a 24/7 economy, from East to West, with Europe in the middle, with a sharp increase in global competition. We communicate in real time. Businesses are easily delocalized, because, also, the digital communication is supported by the very significant improvements in physical transportation – we fly East at midday, to work directly early next morning in what was known before, but not anymore, as the 'other side of the world'.

But, let us dedramatize, bringing again statements of La Palisse! We live today times of changes ... as others have lived, before. We simply have to be up to the times ... as others had to be, before.

Universities are, more than any other area or business, in this game, for the simple reason that we have the 'knowledge', we are the main producers of the 'knowledge' that supports all this evolution.

Yes, we are under pressure and have to cope with multiple challenges. Is this new? I do not think so, it is simply different and we are working with the constraints, threats and opportunities of our world, as it is today. And, we shall succeed.

CHALLENGES FOR THE UNIVERSITIES

The next issue is that of the challenges that we face in the universities. To start with, the scope of our mission is of course much wider today than it was not so long ago. And also the dimension – here in Portugal, we have today something like 10 times more students and staff than we had 45 years ago.

Those were the days where Education was centered in the professor and in the classroom, and the main (and almost only) reason to justify the existence of universities (higher education institutions), this picture being naturally different from country to country, depending on the stage of development of each country.

Today, the issue of teaching shifted to student-centered learning, we speak of 'autonomous' classrooms in a model of education progressively without borders, or better saying 'without borders externally and without walls internally'. Significant pedagogical issues are at stake as never before in universities and Faculty must be prepared to give an answer to this new demand – the offer of education, the model of learning, issues that I shall revisit below.

Those were the days where research was essentially driven by curiosity, with predominantly monodisciplinary research groups, with limited external networking.

Today, much of the research is driven by contracts and associated to pre-defined targets. The recognition that knowledge is mainly produced in multidisciplinary environments is (slowly) leading to organizational changes (this important point will be obviously retaken below). In Europe we are pursuing the creation of the ERA (the European Research Area).

Those were also the days where Education and Research were the only two accepted or recognized pillars of the university mission.

With the sharp increase in the demand and with the rising costs of the functioning (namely of the competitive functioning), the pressure of the society and governments for accountability (in several forms) has increased significantly. Of course that this means that we pay a price, possibly a too heavy price in ... bureaucracy, rules and paperwork, an issue that I shall also retake below. They want to feel that universities respond to what they understand to be the needs of the people and want to see those goals embedded in the mission of universities. They rightly want universities to respond for the results of the students. They want to see shorter term results of the investment in research, with impact in the economy.

Independently of some of these issues being very controversial, particularly those related to the discussion of 'what are the educational needs of the society, thinking of future jobs (which jobs?)' or 'what are the driving objectives of research', we have today a well identified and recognized third pillar of the university mission, known as the Third Mission, where major social and economic issues are included, such as the social dimension for the universities and the valorization of knowledge in its several complementary forms of promoting entrepreneurship, protecting intellectual property and launching startups, besides of course the relevant promotion of culture, the basis for the Alma Mater of institutions, and promoting sports.

It is a fact that universities today must be open in very clear terms to society, as never before, and must offer students increasing means for holistic education.

A POLITICAL DIMENSION – MOBILITY, *COOPETITION*, FUNDING

A more political dimension has to be brought into the discussion, with three issues – mobility of students and staff, cooperation & competition of universities (coopetion we say) and the model of funding.

For reasons of the instruments made available by ICT, together with the progress in the long distance transport system and with the borders of the countries more and more open, the World is actually 'shrinking'.

European politicians of the seventies/eighties of the last century anticipated the future, felt this need to promote critical mass in Europe, integration of cultures and the dialogue of civilizations, and they created this model to promote academic mobility, mainly of students, and to promote cooperation, firstly within Europe, but also thinking of the World.

This was (and is) the Bologna Process,[9] today, 20 years after the first agreements, the result of the political will of 48 European countries, that led to the creation of the European Higher Education Area (EHEA) in 2010, that promotes worldwide mobility and cooperation mainly through the different versions of the ERASMUS programme and that is pushing for the development of the ERA.

It is important to stress at this point that this model requires that (and only will survive if) we succeed in developing the most important value in free, open societies: Trust.

Mobility of students within Bologna requires precisely that we build trust among our institutions. How? By agreeing in a qualifications framework (done), in a system to measure objectives of work and work load (done), in a system of quality assurance (done) and in a system to recognize qualifications (partially done), and also by adopting methods of teaching and learning adapted to the reality of the times, to the expectations of the young generations (in slow, but steady progress).

We have also this major political request of the global world – competitiveness, and this brings in, among other aspects, the capacity of institutions of projecting their quality (to promote trust) and of attracting the required funding.

Starting with quality and trust – how? Ideally through transparent models of quality assurance that are understood and accepted by the different stakeholders. Model that should be developed for the meta-level of institutions, for sectoral groups and for field-specific areas. Rankings are in this issue. As we do not live in an ideal world, it so happens that some of these existing rankings lack transparency and are of limited scope. But, the fact is that they exist and have impact, hence we must take them in serious account. It comes to say at this point that at European level an effort has been (is being) made to develop a model that answers and overcomes criticisms raised by many universities about existing rankings, namely that very negative tendency of reducing quality to a single figure, but indeed this effort is far from having been (so far being) convincing and successful.

And a final note about funding, just to stress that gone were the days where funding was guaranteed by the governments. Direct public funding is diminishing, at least in percentage of the required budgets. The University Management and Faculty, together, must find complementary means to support the activity, to support the mission. We can discuss to which extent this has to be done, but it clearly has to be done, be it through competitive funding, or student tuition fees, or mechanisms of fundraising (namely through Alumni) or by selling services other than those of the regular academic education and research activity.

GOVERNANCE AND MANAGEMENT

Some notes, finally, about governance and management of universities in this contemporary environment, reflecting naturally the Portuguese organization.

The distinction between governance (mainly planning the framework for work, setting organizational goals, setting accountability frameworks) and management (mainly organization and allocation of resources, overseeing day-to-day implementation) is often quite blurred, depending on the legislation in place in the countries.

Two keywords concerning the functioning of universities are: autonomy and accountability. It is clear that quality is part of the accountability requirements. These keywords are embedded in the following statement: *'universities should accomplish their contratualized mission in a legal environment of audited autonomy'*. This is my wishful thinking, not what we have.

With this concept in mind, I come back to the opening questions – which issues are at stake, how can we, or how should we tackle them, what should we do to adapt to times?

The answer about issues at stake comes partially from the previous elaboration: (i) new pedagogical environments, with new offer and methods of education; (ii) new multidisciplinary environments, reshaping internal organization for research; (iii) the Third Mission of the universities – knowledge valorization, entrepreneurship;

culture and sports; (iv) the social dimension; (v) internationalization, promoting the institution and cooperation, all over and at all levels; (vi) quality assurance at institutional, sectoral and field specific levels.

University Governance and Management must clearly have these guidelines well present in their political, structural and daily decisions.

What should also be present is that the moment in Europe does not seem to be the best ... at least communicationally, bad *Winds of Discontent* are blowing from all sides: low public financing, austerity, budget cuts, 'research and education budget in shambles', 'universities apparently broke', too much bureaucracy and brain drain, these are buzzwords of concern that we can read all over.

I add: what about the organizational models and the efficiency of the management system that universities adopt, in Europe, or specifically in Portugal?

It seems to me clear that the continuous increase of costs of running universities has led governments to take political decisions of putting pressure in the universities to fight for funding other than public and as consequence to adopt new more forms of organization, more flexible and competitive in attracting such funding. This is simply recognizing a situation or an assessment of a situation. But it should be noted that university organization is a major issue with main consequences other than in the global institutional financing, such as in the quality of academic education and in the managing of human resources and assets (property buildings, common equipment, etc.)

Portuguese universities are of course subfinanced and we have to fight for increasing such public financing. Taking as reference some central European universities and normalizing for the difference of salaries, we end up with a ratio of up to 1:3 in terms of budget for general expenses and capital investment. There are (very) limited resources for strategic investment. This for example hinders action to promote scientific jobs and through that to fight brain drain. The dimension of strategic funding is a measure of the level of development of universities. Yet, most Portuguese Universities are by no means broke, as I read about universities elsewhere. Often money exists, but is not available for rectors and deans to incorporate in their budgets. This means that often problems are related to university organization and to the management model, not so much to the resources available.

We have to understand the new type of multidisciplinary environments required to produce and transfer knowledge and reorganize the institutions accordingly. This should lead to a smaller number of the constitutive entities (Faculties) of the universities, as compared to what larger universities have today. We see this move in many European universities. Also, the new tools available for managing human resources, for monitoring processes and for the university accounting allow for new methods that on the end of the day increase transparency on the overall running of the institution. To adapt to the times, to be competitive in the open world, we have to go through this path of reform.

In this discussion, there are two major underlying values that we should not mix – academic freedom and autonomy. Academic freedom is unnegotiable for all academics. Autonomy is to a large extent also unnegotiable when we speak of academic autonomy (related to, but different from academic freedom), but there are limits when we speak of management. The issue of autonomy in management is of course delicate. We have to decide within the organization what type of autonomy we recognize in each level of activity, otherwise in limit we end up with self-management at cell level, a model that for sure does not lead to good results.

About bureaucracy – it is a burden of modern times embedded in all activities: in daily running with purchases, service contracts and work contracts; in recruitment or promotion competitions; in planning reporting, budget preparation, activity and accounting reporting; in annual exercises of staff appraisal; in periodic exercises of quality assurance. Though these are only (easy) words, for sure management has the obligation of fighting for external and internal review of legislation to minimize such burden. Much easier to write than to do.

TO WRAP UP

Universities represent (or should represent) major instruments for changes in society, in their capacity to anticipate and to model the future; they are very complex environments, among other reasons because they are populated by bright young people, because those that have in their hands the main responsibility to produce and transfer knowledge are, by condition of the job, free, open, dynamic, brilliant minds, and they are supported by very robust staff; it is up to the management, certainly that in close contact with the community, to create the conditions for such high level community to accomplish the so relevant scientific, social, cultural and economic goals of the mission.

NOTES

[1] https://www.britannica.com/biography/James-Watt
[2] http://www.britannia.com/history/euro/1/4_1.html
[3] https://en.wikipedia.org/wiki/Louis_Pasteur
[4] https://www.britannica.com/biography/Thomas-Edison
[5] https://www.aps.org/programs/outreach/history/historicsites/transistor.cfm
[6] https://www.weforum.org/agenda/2016/01/the-fourth-industrial-revolution-what-it-means-and-how-to-respond/
[7] http://en.unesco.org/news/education-all-movement
[8] http://unesdoc.unesco.org/images/0009/000975/097552e.pdf
[9] https://www.ehea.info/

PART 3

CHANGES AND CHALLENGES IN GOVERNANCE AND MANAGEMENT

RENÉ KREMPKOW AND MATHIAS WINDE

5. HUMAN RESOURCE DEVELOPMENT FOR JUNIOR RESEARCHERS IN GERMANY

Stocktaking and Prospects

INTRODUCTION

Personnel development is understood in business administration to be the systematic promotion of an employee's aptitudes and abilities in preparation for future activities. Such a form of personnel development requires defined personnel structures, career paths and appropriate selection criteria for positions and provision for the acquisition of agreed-upon skills.[1] This is still rare for academic personnel at German higher education institutions (HEI). In recent years, structures have been established at HEIs that, as a core element, have adopted measures for professional guidance and skills development. Only relatively recently, however, has another key element of human resource development been placed at the centre of the higher education policy discussion in Germany: predictable career paths. Applicants for the so-called "junior researcher pact" or "tenure-track-programme" must therefore provide evidence of personnel development in their HEI.[2] The aim of the programme is to establish tenure-track professorship via 1,000 new professorships in the next 10 years as an internationally known and accepted career path in Germany.

The Stifterverband, a joint initiative started by companies and foundations focused on consulting, networking and promoting improvements in the fields of education, science and innovation in Germany, has been working on this topic for more than a decade (e.g., Winde, 2006; Briedis et al., 2013). In 2015, a survey on the personnel development of junior researchers[3] was conducted, funded by the German Federal Ministry of Education and Research in cooperation with the German Centre for Higher Education Research Hannover (see Krempkow et al., 2016). Some key results are presented here. The first part of the chapter focuses on which developments in the past ten years have comparable indicators in HEIs. The second part focuses on a small area of personnel development, namely on the extent to which personnel structures and arrangements related to tenure-track and the establishment of permanent positions in HEIs are available and planned for the next three years. The underlying data contain responses from 150 academic institutions in Germany.[4] The results show that human resource development for junior researchers in Germany has generally made significant progress over the past decade, although there is even more potential for development.

OVERVIEW OF CHANGES DURING THE PAST DECADE

Significant Advancement but also Further Potential

The aim of this study was to gain insight into the personnel development of junior researchers in Germany. To show the increase or decrease of activities, we compare the results of our recent survey of HEIs (2015) with the results of two similar previous surveys (2006 and 2012). Considered together, the recent study (Krempkow et al., 2016) and the preceding study in 2012 (Briedis et al., 2013), show a comparison of supplier and user perspectives for the professional development of junior researchers. The surveys discussed in detail the options available at academic institutions based on information provided by human resources managers and the extent to which junior researchers know about or take advantage of these options.

For a comprehensive overview of the results, comparable indicators over the past decade for HEIs that grant funding for Ph.D. degrees should be highlighted (hereafter, simply HEIs) (see Table 5.1). Almost all HEIs believe that it is important to offer junior researchers personnel development as a core activity. In addition, the priority of the topic for HEIs has only become greater since 2006: 93% of HEIs, as opposed to 73% in the past, now believe that the personnel development of junior researchers at their institution is a high priority. The share of HEIs with vocational counselling services increased by 31% to 86% between 2006 and 2012 but has

Table 5.1. Personnel development for junior researchers in Germany over time (values in %)

Indicators	Higher education institutions 2006	Higher education institutions 2012	Higher education institutions 2015	Non-university research institutions 2015
Priority that HEIs place on personnel development for junior researchers	73	86	93	87
Availability of personnel development for junior researchers	56	98	97	86
Availability of non-subject-specific competency training for junior researchers	53	98	98	88
Availability of vocational counselling services for junior researchers	31	86	95	84
Participation rates in personnel development (estimations, median per year)	15	30	33	61
Share of doctoral candidates in graduate colleges or schools	18	31	23	69

Source: Stifterverband/DZHW (2006, 2013, 2016)

again sharply increased to 95%. This is now as strong as the coverage nationwide. Participation rates in the personnel development offered by HEIs have steadily increased since 2006.

The importance of human resource development has not yet been reflected in the management or central administration in all areas of institutions. 60% of HEIs state that for their institution professorships offer little in the way of personnel development support. This percentage has grown since 2012, when it stood at 29% (cf., Krempkow et al., 2016; Briedis et al., 2013). A lack of incentives to do this remains that most HEIs (73%) have no additional financial means for personnel development (e.g., performance-based allocation of funds), even though they have risen in comparison to 2012 (65%). One in three HEIs (34%) also reported the absence of continuous career paths, which is also a greater share compared to 2012 (17%).

A key result for financing is that resources for personnel development have increased in recent years in the vast majority of institutions, especially for basic resources. Higher education institutions now finance the personnel development of junior researchers with as much as 70% coming from basic resources, whereas 30% comes from third-party funds or other resources. However, at 81%, non-university research institutions have an even higher share coming from basic resources compared with third-party resources.

Academic Institutions Are Pursuing Enhanced Institutional Objectives

Higher education institutions are primarily pursuing two institutional goals in their personnel development measures. The first is to increase the quality of their core tasks (in research and – in the case of HEIs – in teaching); the second, as an institution, is to become highly attractive for junior researchers. Objectives that are more geared towards the individual than society, such as comprehensive individual skills development, are considered less important. The prioritisation of targets has also tended to increase since 2012; institutional objectives, particularly those of research, have become ever more important. However, preparation for activities outside academic institutions (2012 was considered the least important) has caught up significantly as an objective (see details in Krempkow et al., 2016, p. 46).

In terms of the conception of personnel development at HEIs, activities outside of the university is an important objective, as they are responsible for training academically qualified personnel for careers outside of the university system (see Schlüter & Winde, 2009, p. 10). In pursuing this objective in academic institutions, the availability of vocational counselling and skills development are central components (in addition to the presence of career paths). For this purpose, it is also important to understand the needs of junior researchers.

In conjunction with the survey carried out as part of this study for the *Stifterverband*, a survey of junior researchers through the DZHW showed that, in line with the 2015 increase in the number of junior researchers who wanted to leave academia, the need for professional orientation and professional competence development has also increased (cf., Krempkow et al., 2016, p. 75f.). In the DZHW survey, junior researchers generally had less clarity about future job requirements, career goals, and paths to achieve their career goals than in 2012. This increased need for guidance, especially for activities outside academia, does not just affect HEIs. The proportion of HEIs that offer professional orientation for activities outside of academic institutions decreased slightly by six percentage points to 80% of HEIs. At the same time, a larger share of academic institutions offers guidance for activities within academia. Their proportion increased slightly by six percentage points to 84%. Thus, for the first time, HEIs offer as many activities inside academic institutions as there are outside. Among the various forms of vocational guidance services offered by academic institutions in 2015, mentoring support and advisory services for start-up entrepreneurs were given particular mention. Increasing the share of providers of mentoring services is encouraging since this had been identified in the 2012 survey as a special area of interest. However, it is only accessible to a small group of people since only 15% of junior researchers, mostly women, can use the mentoring schemes available.[5]

There is availability for interdisciplinary skills development in almost all HEIs nationwide. Particularly widespread are offers for interdisciplinary research and project management skills, organisational and interpersonal skills. The use of these services has significantly increased over the past three years.

Are young Academics Being Discouraged by Academia?

According to the survey, junior researchers are now, for the first time in Germany, seeing their professional future outside rather than inside the academic system. This means that preparation for activities outside academia has additional relevance. Only 45% of these junior researchers cited academia (professor or scientist) as a career goal in ten years' time (2012: 54%, see Figure 5.1).[6] The majority of junior researchers also become aware early on in their academic activity that they did not want to remain in academia permanently (Krempkow et al. 2016, p. 30). Instead, employment in the business sector (including research & development outside academia) is becoming increasingly attractive, with one third of junior researchers (34%) (see Figure 5.1) seeing their professional future in positions in the business sector as part of research and development teams (R&D). Another 22% would also like to work in non-research-and-development teams (no R&D outside academia).

Those respondents who saw themselves most likely to have a position in the business sector in ten years' time, and who wanted to leave academia, cited two reasons. The first is "poorer employment prospects in academia", and the second is the "higher employment security outside academia". These two reasons, which are also indications of a robust labour market for academics outside academia in Germany,[7] have also seen a sharp increase since 2012. Although deciding early, especially after graduation, to seek employment outside academia (despite this only

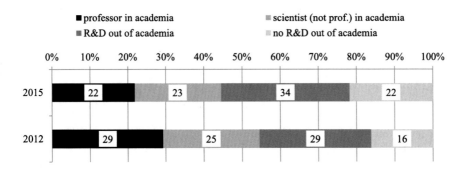

Figure 5.1. Career goals of junior researchers in ten years' time (in %). (Source: Stifterverband/DZHW, 2016)

taking place to a limited extent) rated quite positively, there remains the question of whether academia can still obtain the best junior researchers.[8]

The strategies and measures used by academic institutions to recruit personnel that were discovered in the survey show that these same institutions are beginning to realise the fact that junior researchers are increasingly seeing their future outside the academic system: HEIs are placing increasingly higher priority on the recruitment and retention of (the best) of its junior researchers and, consequently, on their human resources development. Thus, academic institutions are increasingly opening up to a largely untapped potential source for an academic career, such as parents, women and personnel from abroad. One way to increase the attractiveness of some institutions for junior researchers who are in greater demand from many quarters in recent years has been tenure track or similar arrangements and the establishment of permanent positions and professorships. These results of our survey are presented more detailed below.

CAREER PATHS AND THE POSSIBILITY OF POSITIONS BEING MADE PERMANENT

HEIs Are More Capable of Recognising Necessity

For career paths and opportunities for permanent positions, it can generally be determined that compared to the previous survey of the *Stifterverband* in 2012, significantly more HEIs currently have permanent positions or tenure-track positions for young academics. This shows that HEIs have developed a greater recognition of their need. Thus, HEIs are approaching career paths as a central aspect of human resource development, much like companies in the business sector do. They are developing it – from the perspective of university governance research – one step further towards the direction of the "complete organisation" (see Wilkesmann & Schmid, 2012; Grande et al., 2013). This applies to junior professorships in particular:

Tenure-track is now available for junior professorships at all of the responding HEIs (in 2012, it was only present at 64% (see Fig. 5.2)). Junior professorships without tenure track are now only offered at 40% of HEIs, whereas in 2012, more than twice as many (86%) had them. However, junior professorships are not the only possible career path; other paths are also possible in other types of personnel categories. There was also a significant increase for academic personnel with management functions (e.g., junior research group leaders) at 72% (2012: 48%). Employees with focal point academic management roles (e.g., administrative or coordinating positions) were surveyed for the first time in 2015, so a time comparison is not possible in that regard. Despite academic policy demands, they are still relatively rare as a personnel category for young academics. Some HEIs such as RWTH Aachen[9] are already offering corresponding career paths.

The preceding survey of the *Stifterverband* (on the issue of 2012 and beyond) did not ask about "a permanent position or with tenure-track option". Rather, the question was differentiated by the presence of "real tenure-track (or binding position made permanent with trial period)" and "tenure option (or without a binding position

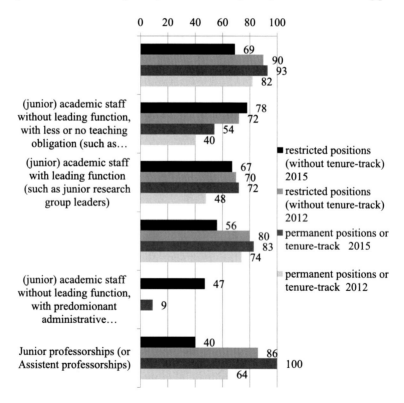

Figure 5.2. Personnel categories for junior researchers and tenure opportunity (in %, multiple responses) (Source: Stifterverband/DZHW 2013, 2016)

made permanent with a trial period)" and "permanent jobs and professorships". The results are presented below. From the responses, it appears that permanent positions are offered only in principle.[10] However, their small number and trial period, which has thus far been largely absent, are often explained by the unpopular perception that a positive tenure evaluation is not necessarily crucial for permanent positions in academia, whereas random vacant permanent jobs are. This is related to situations where not a single permanent position has been conceivable for years in certain areas. In addition, other reasons for incumbents no longer occupying their positions, such as leaving for another institution or random mortality, are considered unpredictable and unimportant by highly qualified young academics. Binding rules on permanent positions could be established here and confidence could be improved by making future employment prospects easier to predict and by allocating jobs according to meritocratic criteria.

Tenure Track/Making Positions Permanent Following a Trial Period, Usually Non-Binding

The possibility of binding positions becoming permanent following a trial period is seldom offered at present (e.g., by means of agreements for personal targets or so-called career points[11]). It is currently associated with tenure track; but it is only available for academic personnel with management functions (e.g., young academic group leaders) in at least 6% of HEIs. For academic personnel without management functions, either with a teaching load (similar to lecturer positions in other countries) or with little or no teaching load (e.g., senior researchers), only 3% of HEIs offer a binding position that becomes permanent following a trial period. For employees with a focus on teaching (e.g., lecturers and senior lecturers) and for employees with a focus on academic management (e.g., administrative positions) the following applies: if a position that becomes permanent following a trial period is provided, this has so far been a non-binding (discretionary) arrangement. At 18%, a non-binding arrangement is three times more likely than a binding arrangement in the case of academic personnel, as opposed to a management position such as young academic group manager. For junior professorships, it is clearly a different picture. Here, a "real tenure track" (with binding positions becoming permanent following a trial period) is, offered by 69% of HEIs. However, there is no indication of how many people benefit from this. The "tenure option" (without binding positions made permanent following a trial period) is offered by 51% of HEIs. This means that both the "real tenure-track" and "tenure option" are offered relatively frequently.[12] However, at 40% of HEIs, temporary junior professorships without agreements concerning the permanency of the position and recruitment agreements are available, and expire after four years (with a positive interim evaluation), default, or are filled again after six years. Thus, many HEIs have basic tenure arrangements, although these are not binding for the most part, even following a trial period.

When interpreting these results, it should be noted that HEIs were surveyed, and thus the results exist on a different aggregate level than, for example, in the surveys of the junior professorships. The results thus differ from those of other surveys. Thus, Schularick et al. (2015), in a study of young academics, who make up 13% of junior professorships with tenure-track contracts, formulate the following as a conclusion to their study: "The German university landscape is far from offering a consistent basis for the introduction of tenure-track professorships that could establish a transparent and nationally and internationally comparable career" (p. 2). Burkhardt et al. (2016, p. 103) reported that 15% of junior professorships were offered a permanent position of W2/W3 (full) professorship at the end of their junior professorship.[13] In particular, they also report a key result, namely that 75% of respondents were dissatisfied with "career planning", and this received the most negative assessment among all the aspects surveyed. There was a greater optimism in a survey by the ERC Starting Grant Research Group Leaders. In a study by Huber et al. (2015, p. 161), 82% said that they either have, or expect to have, a permanent position. Looking at this within the context of our current results on the arrangements for making positions permanent for academics with supervisory responsibilities, it is obvious that in Germany overall, there is a trend towards a particular demand for permanent positions for this specific group. As the literature review on this subject shows, this is a factor that influences the decision to stay in academia, not just for junior professorships and young academic group leaders, but also for Ph.D. holders across Germany (see Krempkow et al., 2014). In a similar vein, the recommendations of the German Science Council (Wissenschaftsrat, 2014) point to the introduction of tenure-track professorships and permanent employment for young academics.

Higher Education Institutions Want the Share of Positions to Be Moderate in Number but to Increase Notably

To obtain an assessment in the current survey of the *Stifterverband* regarding the share of persons who currently possess permanent employment contracts at the HEIs surveyed, these institutions were asked to indicate this proportion for the fields of research, teaching and academic management or administration. In addition, the HEIs were asked to provide the share that were planned and those that were optimally assessed. It turns out that the HEIs have, on average, 26% and 33% of permanent work contracts in the fields of research or teaching, respectively (see Table 5.2). For academic management or administration, there was an average of 48%. In all three areas, a significant increase in making positions permanent is planned in academic management, up to an average of 63%. For academic management and teaching, the planned increase is also considered to be nearly optimal. However, for research, where the planned increase is the lowest, a further increase is estimated to be optimal at 38%. This would then roughly correspond to the proportion of positions made permanent in teaching. Increasing the proportion of permanent jobs is in line with the recommendations of the German Science Council (2014), the German Rectors'

Conference (2015) and professional organisations such as the German Sociological Association (2016). In addition, the values that have been planned and assessed as optimal are also much closer to the proportions of other developed nations in Europe in the areas of teaching and research, such as the Netherlands at 40%, and Norway at 50% (see Höhle, 2015, p. 5). Ateş and Brechelmacher (2013)[14] also cite the UK, Ireland and Poland as countries where at most half of young academics have temporary (short-term) contracts.[15]

Table 5.2. Percentage of people with permanent employment contracts at universities

	At present	Planned	Optimum
Research	26	30	38
Teaching (or further education)	33	41	42
Academic management or administration	48	63	62

Source: Stifterverband/DZHW (2016)

Non-university research institutions were also asked what share of employees currently has permanent employment contracts; more precisely, those planned and those considered to be optimally assessed (no fig.). They indicated an average of 30% of permanent employment contracts for research. For academic management/administration, it is 55%, which is significantly greater than that of the HEIs. However, in contrast to the HEIs, there is no noticeable increase in the permanent positions planned in each area. For academic management, the slight increase planned is also considered optimal. For research in non-university research institutions a moderate increase to 35% is considered optimal.

CONCLUSION

Personnel development for young academics in Germany has, on the whole, advanced considerably over the past decade, but there is still more potential for development. In particular, offers for vocational guidance outside academia are available at fewer institutions than they were three years ago. A large proportion of young academics are searching for a professional future outside academia. In the longer term, an overly strong divergence between supply and demand should be avoided. From the results for personnel structures as a prerequisite for personnel development and, in turn, for career paths and permanent positions addressed in this contribution, the following can be deduced. Academic institutions have a greater awareness of the need to offer more opportunities for permanent positions, especially for young academics who have a Ph.D.. In addition to junior professorships, this most frequently exists for academic personnel with management functions (such as young academic group leaders): one-fifth of HEIs and two-fifths of non-university research institutions offer opportunities for positions that can become permanent in a way that is analogous to tenure-track arrangements for this group. Overall, approximately one quarter to one-third of work contracts for positions in research and teaching become permanent in the institutions surveyed across all personnel categories. According to the institutions' current planning, this proportion is set to increase moderately, but noticeably, over the next three years. In particular, a further increase in positions that will become permanent is also optimally assessed for research at approximately 40%. The HEIs and non-university research institutions obviously want an increase in positions that can be made permanent as a way of achieving a desired increase in their attractiveness as employers in competition with companies and similar institutions overseas and in the area of professorships.

Overall, from the results of the study, the following approaches for action are recommended for personnel development positions at HEIs. As the information broker of strategic coordination and communication of employment opportunities, HEIs should further accelerate acquisition of young academics as well as further advance monitoring through the use of uniform indicators for staffing and resources. Both HEIs and academic policy can create more opportunities for permanent positions, including for professorships, as well as binding arrangements for making positions permanent following a trial period. Furthermore, for recruitment strategies and activities, they should look not only to other HEIs and non-university research institutions, but also to the research and development departments of companies as a way of forming an idea on how to hold onto or "win the best".

ACKNOWLEDGEMENTS

We gratefully acknowledge the cooperation of Thorben Sembritzki and Ramona Schürmann, German Centre for Higher Education Research Hannover. We are also indebted to a lot of colleagues and participants of the 2016 annual conferences of the German-speaking Higher Education Society (GfHf) and the German University Network for Personnel Development (UniNetzPE) for their advice given to this study. Last but not least we would like to thank the track chairs of the track 1 "Governance and Management" at the EAIR 39th Annual Forum in Porto and the editors of this book for their useful comments on former versions of this contribution. This chapter is based on research funded by the German Federal Ministry of Education and Research (FKZ: M517600).

NOTES

[1] For a definition of human resources development in the narrower and broader sense, see Stock-Homburg (2013) and Falk (2007).
[2] See Administrative Agreement of the Joint Science Conference of the Federal and State Governments of Germany of 16 June 2016). However, the final decision on this amendment of the Act on temporary employment in higher education (in German: Wissenschaftszeitvertragsgesetz) was made in 2016 and thus after the surveys for this study, which were carried out in 2015.

HUMAN RESOURCE DEVELOPMENT FOR JUNIOR RESEARCHERS IN GERMANY

[3] The term junior researcher (in German: "Nachwuchsforscher" or "Wissenschaftlicher Nachwuchs") means in Germany all PhD candidates and PhD graduates in a scientific qualification phase below the status of a regular professorship (see BuWiN 2017, p. 65).

[4] The return rate of 42% can be considered very satisfactory for online surveys. Specifically, 46 HEIs granting PhD degrees and 104 non-university research institutions responded; the response rates were similar.

[5] One reason for this can be the capacity of the mentoring programs. Furthermore, in the most cases the mentoring programs in German universities are only offered for women (as part of gender equality programs).

[6] For differences between the subject groups, see Krempkow et al. (2016, p. 32).

[7] For further indications see BuWiN (2017), Krempkow (2017a), Krempkow et al. (2014).

[8] Furthermore we do have a relatively big potential for entrepreneurship in the group of young researchers, notably Postdocs, and at minimum the same as in the group of university graduates at all in Germany (see Krempkow, 2017b).

[9] For a more detailed description and a figure see the Online-Document in URL: http://www.rwth-aachen.de/cms/root/Die-RWTH/Karriere/Karriere-fuer-Wissenschaftlerinnen-und-W/~jgeb/Karrierewege-des-wissenschaftlichen-Nach/?lidx=1

[10] In particular, the following information was provided on the basic availability of permanent jobs (on which nothing is given concerning their number in HEIs). For academic personnel without a management function with teaching load (incl. academic council), 81% of HEIs offered permanent positions, and 53% of those offered with little or no teaching load (e.g., senior researcher). For academic personnel with management functions (such as youth group leaders) it is 64%. For employees with a focus on teaching (e.g., senior lecturers), it is 85%, and for employees with a focus on academic management (e.g., administrative positions) in HEIs, it is 88% (see Krempkow et al., 2016).

[11] For more details to this discussion see the remarks on career positions in Austria, in Kreckel (2016) and Ateş and Brechelmacher (2016).

[12] Junior professorships were offered permanent positions at 3% of HEIs, the trial period of which has probably been confirmed. However, it could, in principle, provide return options in permanent positions. This cannot be determined here from the information provided by the HEIs.

[13] Overall, they report that a quarter of junior professorships stated that a permanent position was promised following the junior professorship. For 15%, this was a W2/W3 professorship – see Burkhardt et al. (2016, p. 103).

[14] Ateş and Brechelmacher (2013) indicate that for Germany, Austria and Switzerland, in the age group 36–45 years, the proportion of temporary employment is extremely high among professorships in comparison with other countries in Europe.

[15] Other publications that intensively cover the topics of job categories and time limitations use data available in the official higher education statistics as a base (although this partly includes PhD positions), but these data are only consistent for academic personnel taken as a whole. They are not specifically targeted at young academics within academic personnel. Thus, Kreckel (2016) arrived at the figure of approximately 35% of academic personnel with permanent contracts for the Netherlands, approximately 60% for the United States (25% tenure-track job not counted), 66% for Britain and approximately 70% for France. Of course, in interpreting these data, the specific features of the national higher education systems must be observed; in the US and the UK, it is possible to have compulsory redundancies in HEIs and research institutes, whereas permanent scientists in France are usually lifetime civil servants (cf. ibid.).

REFERENCES

Ateş, G., & Brechelmacher, A. (2016). Universitäre Beschäftigungsbedingungen in der Doc- und Postdoc-Phase unter Berücksichtigung des österreichischen Laufbahnmodells. *Qualität in der Wissenschaft (QiW), 10*(2), 58–62.

Briedis, K., Jaksztat, S., Schneider, J., Schwarzer, A., & Winde, M. (2013). *Personalentwicklung für den wissenschaftlichen Nachwuchs. Bedarf, Angebote und Perspektiven – eine empirische Bestandsaufnahme*. Essen: Stifterverband (Ed.).

Burkhardt, A., Nickel, S., Berndt, S., Püttmann, V., & Rathmann, A. (2016). Die Juniorprofessur – Vergleichende Analyse neuer und traditioneller Karrierewege im deutschen Wissenschaftssystem. *Beiträge zur Hochschulforschung, 38*(1–2), 86–117.

BuWiN. (2017). *Bundesbericht wissenschaftlicher nachwuchs 2017. Statistische Daten und Forschungsbefunde zu Promovierenden und Promovierten in Deutschland*. Bielefeld: Konsortium bundesbericht wissenschaftlicher nachwuchs (Ed.).

Falk, S. (2007). *Personalentwicklung, Wissensmanagement und Lernende Organisation in der Praxis: Zusammenhänge – Synergien – Gestaltungsempfehlungen* München und mering: rainer hampp.

Frank, A., Krempkow, R., & Mostovova, E. (2017). *Gründungsradar 2016. Wie Hochschulen Unter nehmensgründungen fördern*. Essen: Stifterverband (Hg.).

Grande, E., Jansen, D., Jarren, O., Rip, A., Schimank, U., & Weingart, P. (Eds.). (2013). *Neue Governance der Wissenschaft: Reorganisation, Externe Anforderungen Medialisierung*. Bielefeld: Transkript.

GWK. (2016). Eine Milliarde Euro für den wissenschaftlichen Nachwuchs – GWK stellt Weichen für neues Bund-Länder-Programm. Pressemitteilung der Gemeinsamen Wissenschaftskonferenz vom 20.05.2016, Berlin/ Bonn.

Höhle, E. (2015). From apprentice to agenda-setter: comparative analysis of the influence of contract conditions on roles in the scientific community. *Studies in Higher Education, 40*(8), 1423–1437.

Huber, N., Wegner, A., & Neufeld, J. (2015). *MERCI (Monitoring European research council's implementation of excellence). Evaluation report on the impact of the erc starting grant programme* (iFQ Working Paper 16). Berlin.

Kreckel, R. (2016). Zur Lage des wissenschaftlichen Nachwuchses an Universitäten: Deutschland im Vergleich mit Frankreich, England, den USA und Österreich. *Beiträge zur Hochschulforschung, 38*(1–2), 12–41.

Krempkow, R. (2017a). Können wir die Besten für die Wissenschaft gewinnen? Zur Rekrutierung von Nachwuchsforschenden in Wissenschaft und Wirtschaft. *Personal- und Organisationsentwicklung (P-OE), 12*(2+3), 59–64.

Krempkow, R. (2017b). *Der Beitrag von Absolventenstudien zur Analyse des Gründungspotentials. Jahrestagung des Kooperationsprojektes Absolventenstudien (KOAB) der Hochschulen Deutschlands*. Kassel: Universität Kassel.

Krempkow, R., Huber, N., & Winkelhage, J. (2014). Warum verlassen Promovierte die Wissenschaft oder bleiben? Ein Überblick zum (gewünschten) beruflichen Verbleib nach der Promotion. *Qualität in der Wissenschaft, 8*(4), 96–106.

Krempkow, R., Sembritzki, T., Schürmann, R., & Winde, M. (2016). *Personalentwicklung für den wissenschaftlichen Nachwuchs 2016. Bedarf, Angebote und Perspektiven – eine empirische Bestandsaufnahme im Zeitvergleich*. Berlin: Stifterverband (Ed.).

Schlüter, A., & Winde, M. (2009). *Akademische Personalentwicklung. Eine strategische Perspektive*. Essen: Stifterverband (Ed.).

Schularick, M., Specht, J., & Baumbach, S. (2015). *Berufungspraxis bei Juniorprofessuren in Deutschland 2005-2013. Studie der AG Wissenschaftspolitik der Jungen Akademie*. Berlin.

Stock-Homburg, R. (2013). *Personalmanagement: Theorien – konzepte – instrumente*. Wiesbaden: Springer-Gabler.

Wilkesmann, U., & Schmid, C. J. (Eds.). (2012). *Hochschule als Organisation*. Wiesbaden: Springer-VS.

Winde, M. (2006). Stiefkind Personalmanagement – Ergebnisse einer Stifterverbands-Umfrage. In *Akademisches Personal management* (pp. 5–9). Essen: Stifterverband für die Deutsche Wissenschaft (Ed.).

Wissenschaftsrat. (2014). *Empfehlungen zu Karrierezielen und -wegen an Universitäten*. (Drs. 4009-14).

TON KALLENBERG

6. SHADOWS OF HIERARCHY

Managerial-Administrative Relationships within Universities under Pressure

It happens at the edges.

INTRODUCTION

Universities can be described as hybrid organizations (In 't Veld, 1995), in which two types of employees work: academics and administrators. They each have their own values, stakes and interests, work in more or less segregated domains, and are independently trying to accomplish different goals. Academics are the executives of the organization's primary process: providing education and conducting research. Administrators are focused on organizing and supporting that primary process. The relationship between these domains has long been described as conflicting, competitive, negative or tense (Birnbaum, 1988; Conway, 1998, Hanson, 2001, Anderson, 2008). Some simply see this tension as an organizational feature of universities and not necessarily as something negative (Warner & Palfreyman, 1996; Lauwerys, 2002; Bacon, 2009). Others suggest it is a dysfunctional separation, negatively affecting the outcome of processes, projects or innovations (Dearlove, 1998; Tourish, 2000; Wohlmuther, 2008).

In the last decade, under the influence of the so-called 'New Public Management' (NPM), the focus has been on issues such as cost cutting, transparency in resource distribution and increasing performance management (Pollitt & Bouckaert, 2011). As a result, academics and administrators have been more closely linked and it is harder for them to isolate themselves within their own domain (Deem & Brehony, 2005; Winter, 2009). This has led to more conflict between the logic of both domains, to more resistance and to a lack of understanding (Anderson, 2008).

A third domain has developed between these two domains, particularly at the faculty and thus decentralized level within the university organization; a domain in which employees operate who represent the interests of both domains and do pursue common goals. This new group of employees, also known as 'blended professionals' or 'third space professionals' (Klumpp & Teichler, 2008; Whitchurch, 2006, 2008), consists mainly of faculty managers and senior administrators. The faculty managers are mostly members of the academic staff who perform a governing role for a certain period, such as: Dean, Vice-dean, Academic Director, Director of Studies, and are also called academic middle managers (Kallenberg, 2013; Floyd, 2016). The senior administrators are employees of the non-academic staff who fill positions such as: Head of Educational and Student Affairs; Head Quality Control; Director of Operational Management, Director of Academic Affairs, and are also called educational administrators (Kallenberg, 2016).

The manner in and the extent to which the faculty managers and senior administrators cooperate with each other is not only important for the functioning of the separate domains of academics and administrators, but also for the faculty organization as a whole. Faculty managers and their senior administrators are dependent on each other when it comes to the realization of initiatives and policy intentions. Of course, each has its own frame of reference and different backgrounds, but simultaneously, there are many striking similarities between them. They face the challenges of NPM, resulting in increased bureaucratization, administrative overload, resource constraints and governing (academics and/or administrators) by influence. They have an expanding scope of their job, with new demands linked to the 'management side' such as setting performance targets, quality assurance and risk management – areas that did not previously fall within the traditional ambit of academic middle managers and educational administrators.

They are constrained by the effects of managerialism, which has resulted into a tyranny of bureaucracy with red-tape and minute-detail reporting (Fitzgerald, 2009). This tyranny of bureaucracy translates them into disempowered academic middle managers and educational administrators, because it results into command-and-control attitudes, authorial leadership and adherence to rules within a culture of conformance. To cope with the identified negative effects of managerialism, the academic middle managers and their educational administrators create their own systems outside the bureaucracy and provide more support to peers and subordinates (Davis et al., 2016).

For managers and senior administrators the challenge is how to deal with this external control based on hierarchical interventions using legislative or executive decisions. Externally, both the managers and the administrators must fulfil all kinds of requirements, but at the same time they want to keep their relationship with their employees, based on academe's notions of collegiality and consideration, grounded in the revered values of academic freedom and autonomy. So the question is: do they contribute to the efficacy of policymaking or do they require the shadow of hierarchy, i.e. legislative and executive decisions, in order to deal effectively with the problems they are supposed to solve?

Because these groups of actors have not been researched much, little is known about how they do that. We have a far better understanding of the work of college Presidents than we do of academic Deans or Vice-Presidents, and their administrative and academic managers (Bastedo, 2012). Therefore, this study seeks to gain more insight into the managerial-administrative relationships within the faculties. How do they cooperate? How do they experience this cooperation? How do they relate to each other? And, are there certain factors that influence this cooperation? In order to obtain a better understanding of these relationships and factors, interviews were conducted with faculty managers and senior administrators within several faculties and universities in the Netherlands. The interviews centred on their mutual relationships, the way in which they cooperate and their views about managing faculty developments.

RESEARCH METHOD

The research was conducted to gain more insight into the managerial-administrative relations and what factors may influence those relationships. The focus of this research was on understanding, comprehending and sensing rather than on refuting or falsifying theories. It is about empathizing with the (experienced) reality of managers and senior administrators while realizing that these experiences cannot represent the factual or entire truth. It is not about objective truth finding in the physical, natural and measurable reality, but about objectified interpretations of a unique, social and created reality. The subjective story of the managers and senior administrators was the starting point and the objectivity principle was mainly to do this subjective story justice (Latour, 2005; Vickzo, 2015).

The objective was therefore to identify key points for a possible underlying, measurable pattern in managerial-administrative relationships. After all, managers and their senior administrators act on the basis of ambiguity and continuing uncertainty (Randall & Proctor, 2008). Therein, complete objectivity is impossible. In addition, it often concerns morally charged issues in the contact with others. Encounters are rather interactions than transactions. It is about core values that affect, appeal and matter in human contact.

The focus thereby was on the managerial-administrative relationship itself rather than its effects on the processes in the organization. It is self-evident that the managerial-administrative relationship does not exist in isolation and that the relationship is influenced by, for instance, the *governance culture* and *organizational culture* (the collective mind-set or programming) and the structure of the organization (Vickzo, 2015). However, these elements were not included in this study.

With the aforementioned in mind, a total of 21 interviews were conducted with managers and senior administrators from different faculties and different universities in the Netherlands. The interviews were semi-structured, in which a number of themes were used to respond to specific cases brought forth by the interviewees during the conversations. There were 9 interviews where both the manager and the administrator were present at the same time (resulting in a so-called 'trilogue') and 12 interviews with either the manager or the administrator (6 each). The interviews were then transcribed and encoded, which gave insight into recurring themes and topics. A content analysis and a division has been done on these recurring themes and topics, which leaded to two main themes, namely social and substantive relationships; professional and political rationality.

RESULTS

Relationship (Social and Substantive)

Both the literature (Kuo, 2009; Wohlmutter, 2008; Whitchurch, 2006; McMaster, 2005; Conway, 1998; Kallenberg, 2016) and the interviews quickly reflect on the 'soft' side of the relationship between the manager and the administrator. Therein, a distinction can be made between a social component and a substantive component.

Regarding the social relationship the following morally charged elements are regularly mentioned regarding the relationship between faculty managers and senior administrators: trust, security, transparency, respect and integrity.

Almost all respondents identified 'trust' as one of the first values as a basis for cooperation. Trust is not self-evident between managers and administrators and should grow and develop during the period of their cooperation. During the interviews it was found that there are still quite a lot of administrators that said they did not always feel backed by their managers. The following statements illustrate this.

> When push comes to shove, managers will let you down …. [Administrator 02-10]

> In practice we coordinate things a lot via the informal route. But when problems arise, she always reverts to the formal route. That's just not right. [Administrator [06-01]

> With us, mutual trust is not a given. At least not on my part. I have not, for instance, forgotten that last year she failed to support me when there was a conflict about the year plan and I had to back down before the programme chairs. [Administrator 13-12]

> Bilaterally we do manage to establish a relationship of trust, but it's difficult in larger groups because my manager sometimes steers his own course. [Administrator 08-03]

In line with trust, the value 'security' is very regularly mentioned. Security is used in the sense that managers and administrators support each other when it is necessary.

> As long as the manager supports me. [Administrator 07-09]

> You can never be sure that you will be supported. [Manager 04-13]

In some interviews respondents indicated that they missed security. Several arguments were given such as that the organization is not transparent, or that decisions seem to be made on the basis of personal preferences, and governance occurs on the basis of power. In those cases, it seems that managers return to their authority to make decisions rather than make use of valid arguments.

In conversations in which respondents indicated that they experienced (mutual) trust and security, the cooperation was in all cases experienced as pleasant and stimulating.

Other commonly mentioned values, in the relationship between manager and administrator, were mutual transparency and respect. Mutual transparency and informing each other in a timely manner contributes to the core values trust and security. An advantage is that when managers make their wishes and ideas known immediately administrators can develop the necessary political sensitivity. Administrators should have room to contradict a manager. It is striking that managers regularly indicate that they appreciate critical advice about their ideas from their senior administrators, while contrarily administrators say that managers want to hear very few opposing thoughts. Some emblematic examples:

> You shouldn't surprise each other, so I really like it that [name] is as clear as possible. I'd rather hear it directly during our own bilateral, than suddenly hearing it in a meeting. [Manager 07-15]

> When he gets something in his head, it's difficult to talk him out of it and he's not receptive to substantive arguments. In those cases, his word is law and I can do nothing but settle. [Administrator 19-03]

Some respondents linked transparency to respect, in the sense that when you know what the manager is doing and with what he or she is dealing, that you, as an administrator, automatically gain respect for what the manager carries out. Thus, respect has to do with acknowledging each other's roles. Some examples:

> You have to allow other people to fulfill their role. [Manager 02-13]

Mutual loyalty can cause a barrier when interests conflict with each other. On the one hand, an administrator is loyal to the manager, on the other hand, the administrator manages a department, in which he or she must be deemed trustworthy. If the management does a one-eighty on a political decision, the senior administrator can end up in a difficult position in the eyes of employees from their own department.

At the beginning of this paragraph it was mentioned that the relationship between manager and administrator has a social and a substantive component. Both managers and administrators independently from each other identified the importance of the conversation about 'content and process'. In almost all cases, both actors indicated that they want to know from each other what they think about topics both substantively and process wise. The substance mainly concerns the content of the topic, while the procedural thinking is of a strategic-political and organizational nature. Administrators, for example, indicate that they want to know how a manager thinks and how he or she views the content and process and also that they want to protect their manager from 'slip-ups'. Managers indicate that they would like to have an idea of the strengths and weaknesses of their 'own' senior administrators and also what competencies they can expect. Necessary therein is of course a good social relationship between senior administrator and manager, though the substantive component is also very important. Several administrators are very critical of this point:

> I don't have the impression that my manager sees what skills I have. It's not uncommon that a topic comes up that I really know a lot about and I just don't even get the chance to say anything substantive about it. Either because he starts to lecture us or because he says we should just ask for advice from [name] or [name]. I don't get it, but I just can't seem to get rid of his blind spot. [Administrator 01-16]

> We too often have too many topics on the agenda to discuss. This results in us rarely being able to really delve deep into a topic. And because my office is too far from hers, there's no opportunities in between meetings either. The result is that we really just get superficial business done and rarely or never achieve any substantive depth. [Administrator 13-08]

Professional Versus Political Rationality

Another striking discussion topic was related to the content and the perspective from which topics are dealt with. The interviews showed that managers and administrators operate from different perspectives, which creates a different rationality for each of them: administrators mostly think from professional rationality, while a manager primarily thinks from a political rationality.

Striking was, for instance, that a lot of managers used their own field or experiences from a former employer as a frame of reference in their examples, while administrators are inclined to think from organizational – or theoretic – knowledge.

> He [name] has to understand that I can't only be led by diagrams and checklists. They might offer him guidance or a sense of control, but I think he is way too focused on it. I deal with the meaning behind those diagrams. [Manager 06-12]

> My manager is a chemist and it seems as though he relates this to everything. Including the reactions. But I studied Organizational Sciences, so I look at a problem from a completely different angle. [Administrator 11-12]

There were also examples in which an administrator operated much more from the political rationality, while her manager had the tendency to micro-manage within the educational logistics of the faculty, and thus worked from the professional rationality.

Related to this are the short term and long term perspectives. A manager is usually appointed for a specified period of time (e.g. four years). During that period managers want to create something new and important. Administrators work on the periphery; their popularity is not linked to realizing a certain prestigious project but to professionalism. This leads to managers having a short term perspective and being inclined to finish business faster and sooner, while administrators consider both the short term and the long term.

My manager is difficult to persuade once he has adopted a standpoint. He ignores the valid arguments in the discussion, just because he wants to get the deal done. He listens to the people who are like-minded and agree with him, ... but what's the use in that? ... [Administrator 05-11]

The fact that the manager quickly makes way has to do with the period for which he or she is appointed and the management knowledge he or she has. Vice-Deans are generally former academics, emerging from a traditional collegial space and catapulted into the relatively unknown domain of executive management, with its related problems (Gmelch, 2002). There is a body of literature on (Vice-) Deanship that points to its evolving nature in a contemporary setting, in the academe characterized by complexity and change (Gmelch, 2002; Meek et al., 2010). What emerges from these dialogues is that (Vice-)Deans nowadays are required to be more than collegial, intellectual leaders. They are also meant to be fiscal and human resource experts, fund-raisers, politicians and diplomats. Seale & Cross (2016) concludes that (Vice-)Deans – although credible scholars – do not have the necessary management know-how or experience, neither are they prepared to deal with role ambiguity and, in some cases, additional capacity and support, especially with relation to the management dimensions of their role.

From the given examples about the differences in perspective, it was also found that there is a kind of continuing tension between the political-managerial rationality of the manager and the administrative-professional rationality of the administrator.

We have quite an informal organizational culture. Which is nice, but it does mean that I can't always act according to the regulations or procedures. And it can also mean that I might not be able justify my actions afterwards. I think that's quite risky. [Administrator 04-05]

Our management strongly disagrees with each other on all kinds of matters. It's truly a power culture, where only achievements and results count. This results in me having to arrange things under immense pressure. Sometimes outside the regulations. [Administrator 07-03]

Finally, the changing (external) environment was also regularly referred to as a source for differences in views. Examples were given such as the ever-increasing (external) pressure of accountability and performance. Especially administrators regularly indicated that they experience being increasingly addressed by managers on the performance of the organization and that this performance is also associated with their individual performance.

INTERPRETATION

This study has attempted to discover key points for a possible underlying, measurable pattern in managerial-administrative relationships. In the interviews the focus was mainly on the managerial-administrative relationship in itself rather than its effects on the organization. It was about gaining insight into factors that might affect those relationships. From this perspective, there are a few notable elements that can contribute to the objective.

The managerial-administrative relationship within the faculty is mostly characterized by the *social and substantive relationship* between both. This relationship can be strong, when they cooperate well with each other and also acknowledge and stimulate each other's competencies. The relationship can also be weak, when their characters do not match and/or when they do not acknowledge each other's competencies and as a result start working parallel to each other instead of together. Or, as one administrator put it:

> Best case scenario is riding a twin bike together, that way you reach your destination much faster. But more often than not I feel like we are both on our own bikes … one person on a racing bike and the other on a box bike … and everyone is going their own way, and sometimes everyone has a different destination. [Administrator 5-12]

The managerial-administrative relationship also seems to be characterized by the *political-managerial rationality and the administrative-professional rationality*. The more managers and administrators have a sense of both these rationalities the better their relationship is.

As this study progressed, a useful perspective emerged for the organization of the impressions and insights from the meetings with the managers and senior administrators. The core of this perspective is formed by the political-managerial and the administrative-professional rationalities. By placing these rationalities on two axes, four types of managerial-administrative relationships arise (see Figure 6.1).

The *portfolio type* is characterized by both the manager and the administrator's low activity on, respectively, political-managerial and administrative-professional rationality. Coupled with the fact that their relationship is not strong, this leads to a situation in which both actors work separately from each other and are mainly focused on their own portfolio. They protect themselves against – too much – influence of the other. An advantage of this type could be the individual administrative profiling and sway of the manager. Disadvantage is the compartmentalized management.

The *manager type* is characterized by the administrator's low level of administrative-professional rationality and the manager's high level of political-managerial rationality. The manager takes responsibility for the policy formulation and policy implementation. The role of the administrator is limited in this type. Advantage of this type is the stronger administrative integrative capacity. Disadvantage and risk of this type is an overworked management, because they do the educational management 'on the side'.

The *secretary type* is characterized by the administrator's high level of administrative-professional rationality and the manager's low level of political-managerial rationality. This type is characterized by strongly governing administrative top and a remotely governing management. The focus in the governance of policy

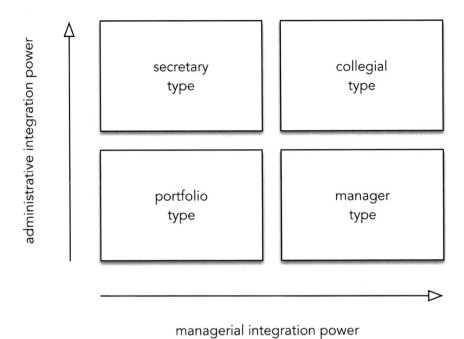

Figure 6.1. Four types in the managerial-administrative relationships

and the educational management lies with the administrator. Advantage is the continuous attention for the 'issues of the day'-processes; disadvantage is the limited attention to political-managerial control.

Due to the politicization of the faculty board, managers claim their role in the faculties more explicitly and the expectation is that this type will disappear as a result. This type fits well with a-political organizations, in which the management has a primarily monitoring role.

The *collegial type* is characterized by both the manager and the administrator's high activity on respectively political-managerial and administrative-professional rationality. The responsibility for the education management lies explicitly with the administrative top. The administrator is, in this type, a sparring partner for the manager. Advantage of this type is the high degree of integrative capacity of the model and the opportunities it offers the management to more distinctly orient itself externally. This is possible because the administrative top is relieved of policy implementation, operational management, and coordination.

It seems logical to assume that the collegial type of managerial-administrative relationship is the most desirable, because it can contribute to a more socially-oriented style of governance and coherence in policy.

Despite the intention of many interviewees for well-functioning managerial-administrative relationships (everyone acts in good faith) the reality is different. The history, the skills of managers and administrators, their mutual chemistry, and the governmental wish to delegate responsibility to the administrators are determining factors in the extent to which an organization is actually governed according to the collegial type. A first attempt to organize the respondents according to the types resulted in a diffuse image, where, within each type, multiple respondents could be positioned.

FACTORS FOR SUCCESSFUL COOPERATION

This study only considered the managerial-administrative relationships itself. Both managers and administrators have to find their way through a sometimes impenetrable forest of paradoxes, dilemmas and 'wicked problems' (Ramalay, 2014). Situations are unique, complex, uncertain and the problem is often finding the problem itself. They must deal with time constraints, incomplete information and often conflicting interests and diverging interests. Logic, emotions, difference in perspective, views and interests are often intertwined in unique ways. Both managers and administrators are also dealing with the increasing (external) pressure. From this common context, I see based on these interviews the following relevant factors for a collegial cooperation between the administrative top and the management:

1. Be explicit about the (desired) role fulfillment and focus
   Despite the fact that the manager is formally responsible for the entire organization, it is impossible to take on and the policy formulation and policy implementations and the operational management and the organizational development and the coordination. It is important to choose and bring focus to what the manager considers his or her primary task. This view on key tasks, of course, also depends on the situation of the faculty. One explanation for differences in role fulfillment by administrators is that one institution. For example, can have its education coordination completely streamlined, while the other institution still has to make significant progress in this respect.
   Furthermore, it is important to be clear about the choices on which the manager will be primarily governing and to make explicit agreements about this. By making explicit agreements, governing on the basis of these agreements, and evaluating them, it also becomes clear where the focus should not be and possible unrealistic expectations are avoided.
2. Invest in the relationships of the arena.
   No matter how well the top structure is set out, the quality of the mutual relationships and affiliations remains of pivotal importance. The administrator and manager have to allow each other to fulfill their roles and trust in each other. This does not only apply to the relationship between managers and administrators, but to all relations at the top. For managers and administrators it means that they must invest in each other. It sounds simple, but seeking each other out informally, chatting, informing each other about wishes and goals remains crucial. In some

universities we saw that managers did not want to invest time in discussions with their administrators because they thought it was ineffective and 'a waste of time': "the administrator should just carry out the decisions". This is either a sign that the manager has no confidence in the administrator or that there is a denial of the administrative professionalism.
3. Focus your energy: first things first, then the 'sexy' topics
   Even though it is not set in stone, there is still a certain logic in the development of the role of the administrator. First things first (coordination of the operational management of the educational organization, organization development), before the administrator can successfully focus on the (strategic) policy formulation and implementation. On the one hand this has to do with the efforts of managers who feel that the educational management should have everything in order before it orients itself externally, on the other hand this development is logical, because the management's trust in the administrative top needs to grow.
4. Make consistent choices in role distribution
   A management structure and the managerial-administrative relationships must be consistent. Good management structures are characterized by consistency. The position of the managers and the administrators, the portfolio holder's meeting, the sector management and department management, the concern staff, the controller and other control positions are all interrelated and cover the entirety of the responsibilities and tasks.
5. Grow alongside societal developments.
   In the past years, there have been quite a few managers at universities and faculties that were forced to leave. In many cases the skills of the managers no longer fit the required competencies. For instance, managers were asked to play a much larger role in the implementation of the policies, while they themselves had a much more limited role in mind. It is important for a manager to be able to adapt to new ideas from managers and new developments in or for the organization.

CONCLUSION

It is striking that managers and administrators are rarely in dialogue about the functioning of the organization and the managerial-administrative relationships. It very much seems like an administrative practice is growing in which questions can be asked about the effectiveness of the role distribution. We also see often that the expectations of managers and administrators about the desired role distribution vary. And because of the fact that they don't discuss the desired role fulfillment and don't discuss about the aspects which are (dis)satisfying, this results to a basis for conflict. When a conflict has arisen it is almost impossible to mend the mutual relations and than – more often than not – it ultimately results in the dismissal or retreat of members of the administrative top. In our view, administrators and managers should periodically discuss policy and operational issues they face and see which structure and mutual relationships are most appropriate. That way the mutual role distribution remains open for discussion, the effectiveness of the managerial-administrative relationships is periodically evaluated and a basis is formed for better governance and with that a better performing university organization.

REFERENCES

Anderson, G. (2008). Mapping academic resistance in the managerial university. *Organization*, 15(2), 251–270.
Bacon, E. (2009). Do professional managers have a profession: The specialist/generic distinction amongst higher education professional services staff. *Perspectives: Policy and Practice in Higher Education*, 13(1), 11–17.
Bastedo, M. N. (2012). Organizing higher education. In M. N. Bastedo (Ed.), *The organization of higher education. Managing colleges for a new era*. Baltimore, MD: John Hopkins University Press.
Birnbaum, R. (1988). *How colleges work. The cybernetics of academic organization and leadership*. San Francisco, CA: Jossey-Bass.
Conway, M. (1998). Academics and administrators: Competitive collaborators? *Journal of Institutional Research in Australia*, 7(2), 26–35.
Davis, A., Jansen van Rensburg, M., & Venter, P. (2016). The impact of managerialism on the strategy work of university middle managers. *Studies in Higher Education*, 41, 1480–1494. Retrieved from http://dx.doi.org/10.1080/03075079.2014.981518
Dearlove, J. (1998). The deadly dull issue of university 'administration'? good governance, managerialism and organising academic work. Higher Education Policy, 1(1), 59–79.
Deem, R., & Brehony, K. J. (2005). Management as ideology: The case of 'new managerialism' in higher education. Oxford Review of Education, 31(2), 217–235.
Fitzgerald, T. (2009). The tyranny of bureaucracy: Continuing challenges of leading and managing from the middle. Educational Management Administration & Leadership, 37(1), 51–65.
Floyd, A. (2016). Supporting academic middle managers in higher education: Do we care? Higher Education Policy, 29(2), 167–183.
Gmelch, W. H. (2002). Deans' balancing acts: Education leaders and the challenges they face. Washington, DC: AACTE. Retrieved from http://files.eric.ed.gov/fulltext/ED481388.pdf
Hanson, E. M. (2001). Educational administration and organizational behaviour (4th Eed.). Boston, MA: Allyn and Bacon.
In 't Veld, R. J. (1995). *Spelen met vuur. Over hybride organisaties* [Playing with fire. About hybrid organizations]. 's-Gravenhage: Vuga.
Kallenberg, T. (2013). Prisma van de verandering? De rollen van academische middenmanagers bij strategische innovaties in het onderwijs. Den Haag: Boom/Lemma. Dissertation Tilburg University [English: Prism of Change? The roles of academic middle managers within strategic innovations in Higher Education].
Kallenberg, T. (2016). Interacting spheres revisited. Academics and administrators between dualism and cooperation. In R. Pritchard, A. Pausits, & J. Williams (Eds.), From here to there: *Positioning higher education institutions*. (pp. 177–198). Rotterdam, The Netherlands: Sense Publishers.
Klumpp, M., & Teichler, U. (2008). Experten für das Hochschulsystem: Hochschulprofessionen zwischen Wissenschaft und Administration. In B. M. Lehm, E. Mayer, & U. Tiegel (Eds.), *Hochschulen in neuer Verantwortung. Strategisch, überlastet, divers?* . (pp. 169–171). Bonn: Klemens.
Kuo, H. M. (2009). Understanding relationships between academic staff and administrators: An organizational culture perspective. *Journal of Higher Education Policy and Management*, 31(1), 43–54. Retrieved from https://doi.org/10.1080/13600800802559278
Latour, B. (2005). *Reassembling the social: An introduction to actor-network theory*. Oxford: University of Oxford Press.
Lauwerys, J. (2002). The future of the profession of university administration and management. Perspectives, 6(4), 93–97.

Marini, G., & Reale, E. (2015). How does collegiality survive managerially led universities? Evidence from a European survey. *European Journal of Higher Education, 6*(2), 111–127. Retrieved from http://dx.doi.org/10.1080/21568235.2015.1070676

McMaster, A. (Maddy). (2005). *A theory of the university organisation as diarchy: Understanding how deans and faculty managers in Australian universities work together across academic and administrative domains* (Doctorate thesis). Centre for the Study of Higher Education, The University of Melbourne, Melbourne.

Meek, L., Goedegebuure, L., Santiago, R., & Carvalho, T. (Eds.). (2010). The changing dynamics of higher education middle management. Dordrecht: Springer.

Pollitt, C., & Bouckaert, G. (2011). *Public management reform: A comparative analysis: New public management, governance, and the neo-Weberian state*. Oxford: Oxford University Press.

Ramalay, J. A. (2014). The changing role of higher education: Learning to deal with wicked problems. Journal of Higher Education Outreach and Engagement, 18(3), 7–22.

Randall, J., & Proctor, S. (2008). Ambiguity and ambivalence: Senior managers' accounts of organizational change in a restructured government department. *Journal of Organizational Change Management, 21*(6), 686–700. doi:10.1108/09534810810915727

Seale, O., & Cross, M. (2016). Leading and managing in complexity: The case of South African Deans. *Studies in Higher Education, 41*(8), 1514–1532. Retrieved from http://dx.doi.org/10/1080/03075079.2014.988705

Tourish, D. (2000). Management and managerialism: Mis/managing Australian Universities? New Horizons in Education, 103, 20–42.

Viczko, M. (2015). Beginning in the middle. Networks, processes, and socio-material relations in educational administration. In D. Burgess & P. Newton (Eds.), *Educational administration and leadership. Theoretical foundations*. New York, NY: Routledge.

Warner, D., & Palfreyman, D. (1996). Higher education management. The key elements. Buckinghamshire: Society for Research into Higher Education/Open University Press.

Whitchurch, C. (2006). Who do they think they are? The changing identities of professional administrators and managers in UK higher education. Journal of Higher Education Policy and Management, *28*(2), 159–171.

Whitchurch, C. (2008). Shifting identities and blurring boundaries: the emergence of third space professionals in UK Higher Education. Higher Education Quarterly, *62*(4), 377–396.

Winter, R. (2009). Academic manager or managed academic? Academic identify schisms in higher education. Journal of Higher Education Policy and Management, *3*(2), 121–131.

Wohlmuther, S. (2008). 'Sleeping with the enemy': How far are you prepared to go to make a difference? A look at the divide between academic and allied staff. Journal of Higher Education Policy and Management, *30*(4), 325–337.

MELINDY BROWN, JAMES WILLIAMS AND DAVID KANE

7. HIGHER EDUCATION INSTITUTIONS RESPONDING TO ISSUES

Gender-Based Violence on Campus

INTRODUCTION

Gender-based violence (GBV) against students has been highlighted as one of the crises currently confronting universities and an issue that requires concerted action (Universities UK, 2016; Batty et al., 2017; Livingston, 2017). The scale of the problem is still unclear although some surveys have indicated that as many as 25% of women students have 'been on the receiving end of unwanted sexual behaviour' (Phipps & Smith, 2012, p. 360). However, media attention and subsequent research has tended to focus on traditional universities, students and higher education culture. Concomitantly, there is a particular focus on 'laddish' behaviour, that is, the boisterous activities of young men, often in the context of sports clubs. Whilst this may reflect the experience of some institutions and their cultures, it cannot be applied to all institutions. Modern higher education is characterised by diversity, especially in the demographics of the student body. It is therefore important to explore the extent to which the common depiction of GBV applies to a broad range of students. Although there is evidence that university senior management teams are beginning to take GBV seriously, to date, there has been little work with university students and staff that examines their perceptions of GBV in the university context.

GBV is a broad term that covers a range of activity. It is best described as 'violence that occurs as a result of the normative role expectations associated with each gender, along with the unequal power relationships between the two genders, within the context of a specific society' (Bloom 2008, p. 14). It is widely acknowledged that the majority of people affected by GBV are women and girls, as a result of the unequal distribution of power in society between women and men. GBV is also often understood as a way of describing any violent act against women (United Nations, 1993). Forms of GBV often fit within the following four categories: physical violence, sexual violence, emotional and psychological violence and threats of violence (Murthy et al., 2010).

Recent research has indicated that GBV is an issue in higher education. Indeed, some reports in the UK describe the incidence of sexual harassment and GBV at university as an 'epidemic' (Batty et al., 2017; Livingston, 2017). A cross-campus study involving a number of universities in England found that all participants who had been victims of sexual violence had been affected psychologically, physically or emotionally (Stenning et al., 2012). This is a clear indicator of the negative impact GBV is having on students' experience of higher education, particularly within the United Kingdom. This research coincided with work investigating the rise of 'lad culture', which was perceived as becoming problematic for female students and which led to the UK National Union of Students (NUS) commissioning a report into the phenomenon (Phipps & Young, 2013). The resulting report found that there is an awareness of 'lad culture' affecting women, however less of an understanding in respect of the lesbian, gay, bisexual and transsexual communities.

Phipps and Young's study (ibid.) with 40 female undergraduate students concluded that 'lad culture', is a dominant part of university life. 'Lad culture' was characterised as having a pack mentality and linked predominantly with sporting activities and the consumption of alcohol. A further feature was the idea of 'banter' that quite regularly encompassed misogynistic, sexist or homophobic behaviour (Phipps & Young, 2013). This is a direct link to GBV, as suggesting that such actions are 'just banter' minimises its effect and leads to a societal acceptance of such behaviour.

The study also linked 'lad culture' to the sexual objectification of women, with on the extreme scale, the promotion of rape:

> Seen by some as just a bit of fun, 'lad culture' has been criticised by others as at best being dismissive and objectifying towards women and at worst glamorising the sex industry and normalising sexual assault. It has been linked to a broader 'sex object' culture which has been identified in student communities. (Phipps & Young, 2013, p. 7)

> It should be recognised that ideas of behaviours linked to 'lad culture' are not necessarily solely male-oriented, with a survey by the National Union of Students noting that both males and females were victims of unwanted sexual harassment. (Stanton, 2014)

Evidently, there is a clear link between 'lad culture' and the student population. Silver and Silver refer to the traditional image of students being described as 'alcoholic layabouts' (1997, p. 14). Concern at what they considered to be high levels of alcohol consumption amongst (male) students led the National Union of Students (2009) to enforce minimum tariff levels within their Student Union premises at universities across the country. Consuming alcohol in large amounts has been normalised within the student population (Piacentini & Banister, 2009). Furthermore, research indicates that if the culture of excessive drinking is not addressed, then eliminating lad culture will be particularly hard (Sanghani, 2014).

'Lad culture' is closely linked with the well-researched area of masculinity, in particular hegemonic masculinity. A study in South Africa suggested that a reason for gendered violence against women could be due to a male backlash against the rise of female empowerment (Andersson et al., 2000). This implies that resisting a perceived loss of power is one of the reasons behind GBV. Hegemonic masculinity is referred to as the dominant form that the majority of men aim to reach, causing women, and men who do not fit the criteria, to be subordinate to them (Connell & Messerschmidt, 2005). This mimics laddish behaviour in the form of subordinating women and men who present as homosexual, bisexual or transsexual.

Key factors such as reporting and tackling certain behaviours in relation to GBV have been identified as needing attention. Despite the severity of GBV, it has been recognised that the number of women who have reported being victims is unrepresentative due to this culture of 'normality', which acts to reduce the willingness to report (Mirsky, 2003). Burton et al. (1998) explain this 'normality' in a UK study that found half of men and a third of women were tolerant of women being hit or raped in certain circumstances.

Issues with reporting are present amongst both staff and students, often due to doubts about the institution's appetite to actively accept that a problem exists and/or to try and tackle the issue (Mirsky, 2003). Goldhill and Bingham (2015) in a recent study found that over half of female students and 60% of male students had not reported instances of sexual abuse experienced at university. Cases are not reported for two main reasons: a) it is part of accepted norm; b) victims are too afraid to do so because of potential stigmatisation, being blamed or simply not being believed (NHS Health Scotland, 2015).

This anxiety about reporting an incident can be increased when the perpetrator is someone who is known to the victim (The Good Lad Workshop, 2013). Furthermore, a key finding of the Drinkaware (2016) study was that around half of students were unaware of the protocol for reporting drunken sexual harassment. Additionally, around a third of participants were not confident that their report would be taken seriously. This lack of awareness and/or confidence in university procedures and attitudes demonstrates that more work is required by institutional management to ensure their position on GBV and accompanying reporting procedures are both clear and well publicised.

In the United Kingdom, various initiatives have been developed to raise awareness and tackle GBV within universities. The 'Good Lad Initiative' for example, is one project that has been developed to help men handle difficult situations where GBV might occur and help encourage positive masculine behaviour. This initiative has involved running workshops at 15 universities within the UK to generate a cultural change in views towards GBV (Good Lad Initiative, 2016). The National Union of Students (NUS) Women's Campaign and Sexpression UK developed the 'I Heart Consent' initiative designed to 'facilitate positive, informed and inclusive conversations and campaigns about consent in universities and colleges'. Twenty Students' Unions within the UK were involved in piloting workshops that aimed to promote consent and decrease sexual abuse on university campuses (NUS Connect, 2016).

These campaigns, along with Phipps and Young's (2013) 'That's What She Said' and the NUS (2010) 'Hidden Marks' report demonstrate an awareness that GBV exists in the higher education environment and work is needed to tackle the issue.

Despite this, management in UK institutions has been criticised for the manner in which they handle instances of GBV. This was highlighted by the Office of the Independent Adjudicator (OIA) (2014) who argued that universities needed to address issues of sexual harassment and lad culture. Their 2015 report noted that the OIA 'continue to receive a small but steady number of complaints about sexual harassment and welcomed the establishment of the Universities UK task force' (p. 21).

The Universities UK task force report, 'Changing the Culture', was published in 2016 and made a series of recommendations to assist institutions through effective prevention and response. Universities were encouraged to embed a zero-tolerance approach to sexual violence, harassment and hate crime; take an institution-wide approach to tackle the issues and develop clear and accessible response procedures and centralised reporting systems for dealing with such incidents, working with relevant external agencies where appropriate (Universities UK, 2016).

Much of the literature mentioned above considers the issue on a national level, particularly in the UK, although it should be noted that sexual harassment at universities was first identified as an issue in the USA (see Zimmerman, 2016 for a timeline of work in the USA). While the existing literature might reflect the general experience of institutions, we were keen to explore student and staff perceptions of GBV in a modern inner-city university with a diverse student body. Our reading of the issue in the UK was that it tended to foreground a traditional notion of both institution and student i.e. pre-1992 universities comprising students drawn largely from white, middle-class backgrounds. We wanted to test if the sexual harassment epidemic, or crisis, was prevalent in an institution that does not correspond to these norms.

METHODOLOGY

A case study approach was adopted using a post-92 university located in the West Midlands, UK. The institution is characterised by a diverse student body, numbering over 20,000, many of whom are recruited from the immediate area. Statistics from the 2011 census indicates that the West Midlands is second only to London in the numbers of Black, Asian and Minority Ethnic groups (BAME) (Medland, 2011).

This study used a mixed methods strategy, comprising quantitative and qualitative elements, as this was considered the most pragmatic method of gathering information relating to the phenomenon under investigation (Brannen, 2005). Given the subject matter, it was particularly important to consider the ethical concerns of the work ensuring that all participants were fully informed about the nature of the project and gave informed consent prior to taking part. Participants were also made aware that all reporting of comments made by participants would be anonymised. The project comprised three stages: an initial survey with students, a series of focus groups with student participants and interviews with university staff.

The initial survey was designed to capture baseline data on the perceptions of students of GBV at university. The survey was implemented by the Birmingham City University Students Union 'Student Voice Assistants' who routinely conduct on-campus surveys of student experience and opinion. The survey was designed to capture baseline date relating to students' perceptions of GBV and instances of GBV behaviours they were aware of both on and off campus.

The survey was based on themes drawn from the literature and included questions on topics such as awareness of invasion of personal space, offensive comments, 'laddish' and homophobic behaviour. The institution's Student Union was invited to implement the survey as the Union had been visible in previous initiatives that engaged students with issues around sexual harassment and GBV. A total of 600 students were approached at random, with 173 agreeing to complete the survey. To ensure safety and sensitivity, students were only approached when clearly alone. Participants across the university's dispersed campuses were approached to ensure that students from different disciplines were provided with an opportunity to take part.

The majority of participants who agreed to take part in the survey were female and from the traditional student age of between 18 and 21 years old. However, there was still representation from students who would fit within the other gender and age categories that participated. One of the key rationales of the research was to highlight how GBV can potentially differ in a culturally and ethnically diverse university. The majority of participants were white British, however over 50% of the total number of participants were either from ethnic minority backgrounds or international students. In addition, just over 30% of students lived in student accommodation, however nearly half were living in the family home. The respondents' demographic make-up reflects the case study university's diverse student body.

The second phase of the project comprised a series of focus groups with students. The focus groups followed a standardised schedule of questions structured round a core set of concerns drawn from the existing literature and responses to the initial survey. Questions covered areas that probed students' understanding of GBV, awareness of it both on and off-campus and awareness of initiatives undertaken to tackle GBV. Again, to ensure diversity, students from across the various university campuses were invited to take part.

The third phase of the project comprised a number of in-depth semi-structured interviews with a range of staff at the university. The aim of this phase was to provide an overview of university policy and practice as well as to gather an understanding of awareness of issues relating to GBV on and off- campus from the perspective of those with responsibility for students. The sample of interviewees included eight staff members with varied job roles, from student liaison officers to a member of the University Executive Group. A standardised interview schedule was devised with questions adapted to suit participant's roles. Questions were structured around a particular series of concerns including understanding and awareness of GBV both on and off campus and awareness of any campaigns and/or initiatives aimed at tackling GBV.

OVERVIEW OF SURVEY RESULTS

As noted above, the initial survey was designed to capture baseline data on the perceptions of students of GBV at university. The survey was implemented by the Birmingham City University Students Union 'Student Voice Assistants' who routinely conduct on-campus surveys of student experience and opinion.

The majority of students demonstrated a higher level of awareness of GBV issues occurring off-campus, rather than on campus. Laddish behaviour and offensive jokes were the two behaviours that students were most aware of, with some highlighting the issue of verbal altercations. A third of respondents agreed that GBV behaviours had a negative effect and affected their sense of safety both on and off campus.

To ascertain the level of GBV at the institution, respondents were invited to look at a list of GBV behaviours and asked to indicate if they had been directly affected by any. The highest single response was 'none of the above' (25%). However, the remaining 75% of participants responded a total of 240 times to various types of GBV that they had personally been affected by. Similar to awareness, laddish behaviour was highlighted as the issue that participants were more likely to face.

The survey indicated that the majority of students were not aware of support systems available should they experience GBV and 80% of students had no knowledge of any activities that the Student Union were involved in to address issues of GBV. Of those students who took part in the survey and were personally affected by GBV, 80% did not discuss the issue with anyone. Participants justified this decision with varied responses.

I wasn't that bothered by it.

I didn't know who to talk to.

This raised the question as to whether GBV is seen as a real issue to students and also whether reporting and support services need to be made clearer to students.

Overall, findings from the initial survey suggested that students have a general awareness of GBV and a high number of students have experienced it. However, there is an underlying sense that the behaviour has been normalised. It is implied that GBV is more apparent off-campus and more likely to appear in a verbal context. There is an overall lack of awareness of reporting procedures, support systems and Student Union activity.

These findings informed the subsequent phases of the research, staff interviews and student focus groups, that were undertaken to develop a greater understanding of issues initially explored in the survey. Findings from these phases of the research are discussed in the following sections.

KEY THEMES EMERGING FROM FOCUS GROUPS AND INTERVIEWS

The survey findings highlighted a range of issues that were explored in greater depth in the second and third phases of the research: focus groups with students and interviews with staff respectively, as discussed in the methodology above. From the set of data derived from these phases of the research, we were able to discern, a range of perceptions about GBV within the higher education context. A number of key themes emerged from the focus groups and interviews. The themes gathered are similar and as such will be discussed together in the following paragraphs.

Awareness and Perceptions of Gender-Based Violence

Student perceptions coalesced around a few specific issues. One participant highlighted power and control within relationships: 'in relationships, it's often about who is the dominant character and who's in control' (Focus Group 4). Two other participants argued that difference could lead to incidents of GBV, noting that 'the element of difference can play a part' (Focus Group 4) and 'difference plays a part, so for example not having the latest clothes' (Focus Group 4). Other participants highlighted, as in the work of Phipps and Young (2013), the role of alcohol in encouraging inappropriate behaviour. One observed that 'Alcohol makes a real difference on behaviour, it can lead to verbal abuse' (Focus Group 4) and another that 'the alcohol element, potentially causes the inappropriate behaviour' (Focus Group 6). Another participant argued that 'there's a media portrayal, for example taking a drink is seen as the first stage in a bigger story' (Focus Group 3).

Students were also aware that GBV affects both women and men, albeit in varied forms. There was an overall perception that GBV has been normalised within society and that people, as a result, handle situations differently depending on their own personal tolerance levels. The idea that certain behaviours relating to GBV are accepted as a normal part of modern society is demonstrated in the survey results. When participants who did not seek support or help for GBV were asked to clarify why, the most popular answer was 'I wasn't that bothered by it'.

Gender-Based Violence and the Media

Students are aware of the media portrayal of GBV with some noting that the media reinforce stereotypical views of student life that present sexist interpretations of women as vulnerable and men in control:

> [There is a] general idea of what you see in the media of what a typical university student should be. I think a lot of people come to university thinking they can live the typical student lifestyle opposed to actually getting the degree itself. Like going out on the pull is definitely part of the typical University lifestyle.

Gender Based Violence and Social Media

Both male and female students reported that GBV is more prevalent on the internet due to it being a platform that, in some instances, encourages irresponsibility. Staff noted that increased access to the internet has allowed GBV to be displayed more regularly, to the point where one interviewee referred to it as 'the normal diet'. One group agreed that social media was a challenge:

> It's about social media responsibility and accountability. People don't realise the damage they do to themselves. We all have views and see one of those examples and think it's funny and share it. (Focus Group 7)

There have been incidences involving internet-based GBV at the university. However, the use of social media as a means of abusing others has made it possible for authorities to prove allegations of abuse. For example, a member of the senior executive team described how:

> We've had issues of social media being used to bully people and using gender as a way of doing that. I think the ways in which students talk to one another is more likely to be documented if through social media whereas in the past it would have been a lot harder to prove. (Executive Management Team 2)

Types of GBV at the University

Staff members agreed that GBV is an issue, with women considered to be the main target. In addition, GBV is also recognised as a societal issue that has been normalised. Staff also identified other groups as vulnerable including young Asian women, members of the LGBT+ community and men who are less likely to come forward due to stigma. Staff also thought that the university should take the lead on promoting diversity awareness, education, support and guidance and enlist Student Union involvement to address the issues.

The most common form of GBV observed by students was verbal abuse such as comments made by men directed at women. The majority of cases that were reported were of builders making comments. For example, a woman student said that 'I got shouted at by the builders at the [building site by the entrance to the new buildings]' (Focus Group 4). Participants also referred to another group of young men who can be found in the public space in front of the City Centre Campus, who do not appear to be students and make students, especially women, uneasy. One participant (Focus Group 5) noted that 'the group of guys at the front of the City Centre Campus is a big issue. The number of them scares students, particularly female students'.

However, in limited cases, groups of male students were reported to have made comments directly to women. One participant observed that 'inside [the Main Building], on the 1st floor, there are groups of guys who sit in the social space seemingly all day and they watch women going up and down the stairs and make comments like "Ooh, I know about you"' (Focus Group 5). Some cases of physical assault by students have been mentioned. For example, one student said:

I have a friend who was groped by a fellow student. She wanted to report him but decided not to and to try and give him a chance. She's changed courses to avoid him now. (Focus Group 7)

There is little awareness of how GBV incidents are managed at the university. Some participants felt that it was not the university's responsibility but rather the students' obligation to educate themselves. However, students who have experienced GBV have not been impressed by the response of the university:

Unsure what the university could do to tackle it. (Focus Group 1)

It's a societal issue so it's our responsibility to educate ourselves and not the responsibility of organisations such as universities or indeed religions. (Focus Group 3)

I've not really had experience of it. (Focus Group 6)

You get a brief mention of consent during Fresher's. I haven't heard anything since, I think this should be made clearer to students, what actually happens? (Focus Group 7)

For some participants, the issue of GBV was felt to be one that young people address at school and college. It was something they should have grown out of by the time they come to university. However, if they were to experience it, it was felt that they should be prepared to tackle it due to their previous experience during growing up.

It is really no longer an issue at this age, we are past the 'name calling' stage. (Focus Group 6)

We have more of an idea of how to stop it if it was to happen at this age. (Focus Group 6)

Laddish Behaviour

Laddish behaviour was a term recognised by the majority of participants. It was noted that universities can often provide a platform that encourages a culture of laddish behaviour with sports teams, 'pack mentality' and student nightlife identified as principle areas of concern. It was acknowledged that women take part in this behaviour, but this was not seen as problematic. Challenging instances of laddish behaviour was seen as the most effective way of tackling the behaviour.

Participants reflected on the meaning of 'laddish behaviour' in practice and on contemporary attitudes amongst students. It was recognised that laddish behaviour was evident at the university and had been experienced by undergraduates. This led to a discussion of questions of inclusivity and how what is acceptable and what is not is defined. It was felt that a group dynamic feeds into this. This was referred to by one participant as a 'pack mentality':

May be different behaviours depending on what course, different [group] focuses. (Focus Group 4)

Comments and whistles are often referred to as 'being lads'. (Focus Group 5)

Lads will encourage each other, try and wing man each other, but it gets pushed too far. (Focus Group 7)

They say its banter, being just a lad. It's their excuse, as if saying that makes it okay. (Focus Group 7)

If a girl sleeps with a guy, she's a slut. If a guy sleeps with a girl, it's 'ooh well done mate, that's 10 lad points for you'. (Focus Group 5)

One participant felt that 'laddish behaviour is making [gender-based violence okay] by not confronting it and it's quite concerning as the problem will continue to grow'. This reinforced the views of other participants who considered 'laddish behaviour' to be a social norm. 'Laddish behaviour' was referred to as an 'everyday' activity and one that some people within society see as amusing:

A cultural thing rather than university abused. (Focus Group 4)

We live in a culture that tries to make laddish behaviour funny, look at all the viral videos. (Focus Group 7)

Outside of university 'lads' culture is definitely problematic. (Focus Group 5)

To be honest, my perceptions as a mature student, were always aware that there would be this kind of culture and stuff but seeing it first hand, as well, it's kind of like, I try and distance myself. (Focus Group 7)

Some participants aware of the phenomenon of 'laddish' behaviour associated it with university sports societies:

You would expect the Rugby team to do GBV, of laddish behaviour. Even football, but not as much as Rugby. You get the stereotypical people in the rugby group, afterwards they go on a night out. That's the stereotype. I saw something on TV, Rugby players were asked what they do in their free time and they were all shouting on camera. (Focus Group 1)

Laddish behaviour, like men's football vs women's football. Men in the football team consider themselves the alpha males. It's more a verbal behaviour than physical. (Focus Group 4)

Additionally, laddish behaviour was associated with student nightlife. It was thought to be a particular problem during students' nights out and more likely to occur in clubs off-campus than on campus:

Groups of men on a lads' night out who will be walking and shouting. If you're on your own it can be intimidating, but if you're with your friends it's fine. (Focus Group 1)

Laddish behaviour was a problem during Freshers' week, through touching women without consent. (Focus Group 4)

In clubs, in the evening. Not a problem within the university. (Interview, Media Student)

Women expect to experience laddish behaviour on a night out. (Focus Group 4)

Indeed, some participants felt that it was wrong to condemn a whole culture although it was felt that 'we do appear to be living in a culture of aggression, demonstrated by both men and women'. It was acknowledged that women take part in this behaviour but this was not seen as problematic. It was felt by some participants that women have played a role in promoting 'lad culture':

I see it across both genders. Although laddish behaviour is automatically associated with men, there may be women who act in the same way. (Focus Group 7)

Girls contribute to lad culture, they agree and react in the same way as guys do in relation to some topics, for example the girl sleeping with a guy topic. (Focus Group 5)

If women act in a laddish way, for example touching a man's bum, the behaviour is considered acceptable but not if men do it to women. Men feel that they should be flattered by this behaviour, if they complain then they look weak. (Focus Group 7)

Participants were asked to reflect on how cases of laddish behaviour should be handled and responded in a variety of ways. Some of the students felt that incidents should be dealt with immediately and challenged. However, some participants highlighted that incidents of laddish behaviour may not be as threatening as they are initially perceived to be:

In some groups of women, it may be easier to call someone out for unacceptable behaviour which could therefore discourage the behaviour from occurring again. (Focus Group 7)

I will not attack the individual if they say something unacceptable but rather talk to them about it so that they listen. (Focus Group 7)

More guys need to feel comfortable with challenging people's views if they are unacceptable. It's often labelled lad culture so they are expected to agree [with the behaviour]. (Focus Group 7)

I will say that's wrong and use my history as a reason for why. I may take some backlash to start off with but its best to make your opinion known. It takes only one person to say they believe it's wrong to change things. (Focus Group 7)

… large groups can lead to an element of intimidation, more than what is potentially perceived. (Focus Group 7)

However, participants in Focus Group 3 felt that laddish behaviour is a part of exploration. One participant reflected that 'some [lads] grow out of it some don't'. The group agreed that actions such as wolf-whistling might be part of a 'phase that is probably best ignored'. One participant mentioned a feeling of being 'more protective towards friends' than for themselves.

Some participants highlighted the existence of a university sub-culture. In common with many other institutions, there appears to be a 'university chant' that is recognised by some students. The university, like other institutions, is home to a wide range of student societies but the presence of groups of students from different societies in venues such as the university pub can lead to tensions. Interestingly, a participant highlighted the role of the Women's football club in challenging behavioural stereotypes:

Uni chants are often sexual. You often hear it at the end of a night out. I, as a female, even have to admit that I go along with it, but I know it is something that shouldn't be continued. I think it's a cultural issue, but I'm unsure where it came from though. (Focus Group 7)

I am not originally from England, so when I heard the Uni chants I was surprised by it. It must be a cultural thing as no one else seemed to see it as a problem. (Focus Group 7)

It's more of a university culture rather than something that would be accepted in normal society. (Focus Group 7)

It can be intimidating having different types of societies together in the SU pub. For example, I am in the theatre society and if the Rugby team were in there it would be like "what if they are going to say something, what if they comment; they say anything?". (Focus Group 6)

Women's football, there are sexist issues in relation to status and stereotypes. (Focus Group 6)

The only way I know about the chants is due to me knowing people from the sports societies. (Focus Group 7)

Gender-Based Violence Off-Campus

All participants had a clear awareness of GBV issues off-campus with women considered as the main target. Public transport and 'nights-out', were seen as particularly problematic. Alcohol was often seen as an influencing factor in such behaviour. Students perceived university-owned student accommodation to be less likely to have incidences of GBV than privately-owned student accommodation. Staff described the university's responsibility for students off-campus as 'blurry', particularly in relation to student accommodation and the outskirts of the university campus. Overall there is a perception that the university has a responsibility to offer support and guidance to students.

Anti-Gender-Based Violence Campaigns

Awareness of university events and campaigns amongst students was varied. A number of students were unaware of university events aimed at raising awareness of GBV issues. However, some students had received information in lectures or through the Student Union and a number of students mentioned the 'Tea consent' video. The most well-known campaign was the 'It's Not Banter' campaign. There was an understanding that promotion needs to be more university-wide. Staff were more aware of campaigns and outlined their desire for a clear, all-encompassing campaign around all aspects of GBV.

University Jurisdiction and Responsibility

Although the university has responsibility for the safety of students and staff within its own buildings and on its land, it has no jurisdiction over areas close to it, such as local streets and parkland. This is a challenge because it is difficult for direct action to be taken. This distinction was highlighted by a member of the senior executive management team:

> The other incidents we have had are in the park [outskirts of campus] – the park is a challenge. That's where the potential for homophobic incidents can happen. This is why our security people patrol the park as well, but our security staff have no jurisdiction. (Executive Management Team 1)

One member of staff felt that the university could not be held responsible for student behaviour off campus but there was a responsibility to support them:

> Students do a lot of things outside the university that the university cannot be held responsible for but could do in terms of supporting students. (Research Fellow 2)

A member of the senior executive management team and a student liaison officer both suggested that support could be provided in the form of warning and educating students of the dangers of living in the city:

> What we can do as the Student Union does is to warn them to be careful on their level. Warn them to be sensible. (Executive Management Team 1)

Yes, it can affect students outside the university we cannot physically do anything about this. However, we can educate and arm students with knowledge on how to prevent and deal with this if it happens. I think the SU need to play an active role in this. (Student Liaison Officer 2)

Student Accommodation

The discussion about university jurisdiction and responsibility is reflected in the students' discussions about safety on and off campus. Most students felt safer in university-owned halls of residence but less safe in privately owned halls. For example, one interviewee, a woman who was an international student, explained that she had felt 'safer at [university-owned accommodation] as there is more security' (Interview, Media Student). By the time of the interview, she had moved to a City Centre based private student accommodation and her feelings of safety had changed. She described her experiences of GBV there:

Around the area there is a lot of homeless people who are holding alcoholic drinks – they always look and sometimes shout comments as I walk past. They shout this because I am a woman. One day it was very distressing because there was a girl who screamed 'please don't hurt me' in the middle of the day and I could hear men laughing but I couldn't see what was happening from my room. Next minute there was guys running away and the girl stopped screaming. (Interview, Media Student)

However, despite the anxiety of living in such accommodation, some students feel that they have little real choice because of the cost of accommodation:

I don't like the situation of [my] accommodation (City Centre based private student accommodation) but I won't move though due to it being cheap. (Interview, Media Student)

Whilst accommodation itself might generally be viewed as safe, discussions highlighted a lack of security in the immediate vicinity of the accommodation. For example, one participant observed 'the accommodation itself is safe, it is the walk there that is intimidating' (Focus Group 4). Furthermore, getting to and from accommodation to the main university buildings were felt to be insecure:

The walkway of [a local hall of residence] is unsafe. (Focus Group 4)

I would not like to walk from campus to [a local hall of residence] by myself after 8pm if I lived there, I would not feel safe. (Focus Group 4)

However, there was also evidence that contradicted this perception that accommodation was safe. A lecturer mentioned an incident that she had been told about:

One of my students told me how in her halls recently a fellow student had been raped by a fellow student and I think that the fact that is happening irrespective if it is on campus or not but is still associated with the university is a really big problem. (Lecturer 1)

However, where incidents are reported in university owned halls of residence, the university is in a position to act. The member of the executive team commented that:

I've also had issues of women reporting feeling threatened in her student accommodation of other students who were male, so we dealt with that as a complaint. (Executive Management Team 2)

Varying Tolerance Levels

Student participants in the focus groups generally agreed that there were levels of tolerance of GBV. One participant felt that 'behaviour such as wolf-whistling can be tolerated, it's when it escalates past that point that it can be problematic' (Focus Group 3). A commonly expressed distinction was between verbal comments and physical contact. One participant felt that 'when it's verbal comments, I have a 'move on, get on with it' mentality' (Focus Group 4). Another observed that 'physical violence I take very seriously' (Focus Group 6). In general, however, participants agreed that 'outside of university [gender-based violence] is considered "a real-life situation"' (Focus Group 7). More depressing is the resigned response to incidents of GBV: 'I think it's a behaviour that people just put up with' (Focus Group 6).

There was recognition, however, that tolerance levels also vary between individuals. One student argued that 'reaction to gender-based violence largely depends on an individual's views' and therefore the 'level of tolerance' to the violence varies. Another participant noted that 'if it does not have an emotional effect then it's not normally followed up, it depends on the level' (Focus Group 7). Another participant observed that 'it comes down to your perception of what you are classing violence as, not necessarily your background but your own experiences' (Focus Group 2). Only a few participants indicated they had a 'zero tolerance' approach to GBV: one participant responded: 'It's definitely not acceptable behaviour' (Focus Group 5). One focus group highlighted the development of an 'invisible line' that each individual has that helps them to determine the difference between tolerable behaviour and that which is unacceptable.

Reporting Gender-Based Violence

The apparent existence of an 'invisible line' of tolerance makes it difficult to ensure that incidents are reported. It was clear from student participants in the research that they were unclear about how to report incidents of GBV at the university. In the focus groups, one participant reflected: 'reporting occurrences of gender-based violence? No idea who to go to' (Focus Group 4). Another said, 'I don't know who I would go to in the university if anything happened' (Focus Group 5). Yet another participant reported on an actual incident that occurred during 'Freshers' Week': 'it was reported to the Student Buddies [helpers], but nothing formal was done. I was not made aware of where to go now and I still do not know' (Focus Group 6).

The survey highlighted that victims of incidents of GBV would tend to seek support from a range of different groups, including campus security officers for more serious issues, student services, parents and friends. This was reflected in the focus group discussions. Students said that they reported issues to a wide range of services and individuals. One participant said that 'It's Security's job to deal with it – they have cameras' and another suggested 'security guards perhaps?'. A few comments indicate that some students would report incidents to their tutors, but others would not, depending how comfortable the student felt. Some participants indicated that students might ask their fellow students for advice and help. A participant in Focus Group 4 suggested that a victim 'might speak to peers, expect them to point you in the right direction'. Another said that in some cases, 'sometimes you have to get your male friend to stand up to the guy for you' (Focus Group 7).

Students felt that more needs to be done to make such procedures clearer. One participant felt that 'there should be somewhere to report GBV that is [made aware to students by being] included in induction programme perhaps' (Focus Group 4). Participants referred to how location and complexity of the incident can also affect where it should be reported and how it should be handled. This was particularly the case with male experiences of GBV. Participants were wary of the potential repercussions of reporting GBV. Students and staff noted issues regarding truth due to the sensitivity of the topic and potential repercussions. This can be heightened by cultural challenges. An interviewee who was an international student observed that:

> I've not made a complaint about my own experience as it is hard to explain it to others ... It's more of a general attitude towards women from people of this culture. I understand that culture is a delicate topic and I need to understand that people act in different ways so wouldn't report it. (Interview, Media Student)

What more can Be Done?

Discussions such as the above developed into participants highlighting what more they felt needed to be implemented by the university to help with incidences of GBV. The issue of cultural differences and education was reiterated:

> An idea for next year is that there should be a clearer guide for people, especially for people coming in from abroad. Just useful information. You know, I had to be with her to help her and support her. It is terrifying, especially if you are on your own. Thing is it is also; the guy is trying to be friendly but ends up making you uncomfortable then something is wrong. (Focus Group 6)

Students and staff felt that education was key to raising awareness about GBV issues, specifically how to report incidents and the consequences that can occur. The use of media and technology was seen as the most effective way to raise awareness and engage with as many students as possible. The majority of students were in agreement that the topic should be discussed in intervals, consistently throughout the year.

CONCLUSIONS

Exploring the perceptions of GBV amongst staff and students at a diverse inner-city university has indicated that there is a general awareness of the issue and that dealing with personal experiences of it can be challenging. However, this study indicates that the national depiction of GBV on campus as a crisis or an 'epidemic' is more complex than at first it may appear. Whilst many of the issues that commentators such as Phipps and Smith (2013) have highlighted have been referred to by staff and students within the context of this case study university, students generally have not felt that GBV has had an impact on their lives at university. Rather, it is a societal challenge that everyone faces. Students in this case study have to negotiate life in the wider community as well as on campus and the issue for many of the participants is that they are more likely to be faced with GBV in off campus settings.

Notably, discussions with students have highlighted a recurring notion of an 'invisible line' of tolerance of GBV. According to this argument, individuals develop their own tolerance levels, particularly towards verbal forms of abuse but recognise that any physical abuse is unacceptable. For some students, the levels of tolerance are high, and they tend to accept and ignore incidents. For others, tolerance levels are much lower and lead to a greater concern to report such incidents.

When that 'invisible line' of tolerance is crossed, however, reporting procedures are not always clear to students. They respond in a range of different ways, from not reporting incidents to sharing it with friends or family and possibly taking it further to university security or even the police. The situation is complicated by cultural differences: in particular, reporting of incidents may not be possible for women from particular cultural, ethnic and religious backgrounds.

The issue is further complicated by the question of university jurisdiction and this is one that deserves greater attention. The answer probably lies in educating students about what is acceptable behaviour and what is not and how to report incidents whether within university grounds or in public. The clear confusion relating to this issue between managerial and non-managerial staff should be clarified by providing all staff with the necessary training. Policy on university jurisdiction should also be made clear to staff and students along with training on how to report incidents when outside university jurisdiction.

REFERENCES

Anderson, K. (2005). Theorizing gender in intimate partner violence research. *Sex Roles, 52*, 853–865.
Batty, D., Weale, S., & Bannock, C. (2017). Sexual harassment 'at epidemic levels' in UK universities. *The Guardian* (Online). Retrieved November 21, 2017, from https://www.theguardian.com/education/2017/mar/05/students-staff-uk-universities-sexual-harassment-epidemic

Bloom, S. S. (2008). *Violence against women and girls. A compendium of monitoring and evaluation indicators* (Online). Retrieved November 21, 2017, from https://www.measureevaluation.org/resources/publications/ms-08-30

Bourne, L. Jr., & Russo, N. (1998). *Psychology: Behavior in context.* New York, NY: W. W. Norton.

Brannen, J. (2005). Mixed methods research: A discussion paper. *ESRC National centre for research methods. NCRM methods review papers* (NCRM/005, ESRC, national centre for research methods) (Online). Retrieved from November 28, 2017, http://eprints.ncrm.ac.uk/89/1/MethodsReviewPaperNCRM-005.pdf

Braskamp, L. A., & Ory, J. C. (1994). *Assessing faculty work: Enhancing individual and institutional performance.* San Francisco, CA: Jossey-Bass.

Burton, S., Kitzinger, J., Kelly, L., & Regan, L. (1998). *Young people's attitudes towards violence, sex and relationships.* Edinburgh: Zero Tolerance Charitable Trust.

Creswell, J. (1998). *Qualitative inquiry and research design.* London: Sage Publications.

Denscombe, M. (2003). *The good research guide.* New York, NY: McGraw-Hill Education.

Drinkaware. (2016). *Students call for universities to take action against drunken sexual harassment* (Online). Retrieved November 28, 2017, from https://www.drinkaware.co.uk/press/students-call-for-universities-to-take-action-against-drunken-sexual-harassment/

European Institute for Gender Equality. (2014). *Estimating the costs of gender-based violence in the European Union* (Online). Retrieved November 29, 2017, from http://eige.europa.eu/rdc/eige-publications/estimating-costs-gender-based-violence-european-union-report

Global Protection Cluster. (2017). *Gender-based violence* (Online). Retrieved November 28, 2017, from http://www.globalprotectioncluster.org/en/areas-of-responsibility/gender-based-violence.html

Goldhill, O., & Bingham, J. (2015). One in three UK female students sexually assaulted or abused on campus. *The Telegraph* (Online). Retrieved November 28, 2017, from http://www.telegraph.co.uk/women/womens-life/11343380/Sexually-assault-1-in-3-UK-female-students-victim-on-campus.html

Good Lad. (2016). *Good lad initiative: promoting positive masculinity* (Online). Retrieved November 28, 2017, from http://www.goodladworkshop.com/about/

Hamilton, P., & Russo, N. (2006). Women and depression: Research, theory and social policy. In C. Keyes & S. Goodman (Eds.), *Women and depression: A handbook for the social, behavioral, and biomedical sciences* (pp. 479–522). New York, NY: Cambridge University Press.

Kangas, A., Haider, H., Fraser, E., & Browne, E. (2015, July). *Gender-based violence. GSDRC applied knowledge services* (Online). Retrieved November 28, 2017, from http://www.gsdrc.org/topic-guides/gender/gender-based-violence/#costs

Livingston, E. (2017). When will universities wake up to this epidemic of sexual harassment? *The Guardian* (Online). Retrieved November 21, 2017, from https://www.theguardian.com/commentisfree/2017/mar/07/when-will-universities-wake-up-to-sexual-harassment

Medland, A. (2011). *Regional trends. Portrait of the West Midlands. Office for national statistics* (Online). Retrieved March 22, 2018, from http://www.sustainabilitywestmidlands.org.uk/wp-content/uploads/portraitw_tcm77-2260021.pdf

Merton, R. K., & Kendall, P. L. (1946). The focused interview. *American Journal of Sociology, 51*, 541–557.

Mirsky, J. (2003). *Beyond victims and villains: Addressing sexual violence in the education sector.* London: The Panos Institute.

Murthy, P., Upadhyay, U., & Nwadinobi, E. (2010). Violence against women and girls: A silent global pandemic. In P. Murthy & C. L. Smith (Eds.), *Women's global health and human rights* (pp. 11–24). Sudbury, MA: Jones and Bartlett Publishers.

NHS Health Scotland. (2015, July). *Who is affected?* (Online). Retrieved November 28, 2017, from http://www.healthscotland.com/equalities/gender-based-violence/demographics.aspx

NUS. (2010). *Hidden marks: A study of women student's experiences of harassment, stalking, violence and sexual assault* (Online). Retrieved November 28, 2017, from https://www.nus.org.uk/global/nus_hidden_marks_report_2nd_edition_web.pdf

NUS Connect. (2016). *I heart consent* (Online). Retrieved November 28, 2017, from http://www.nusconnect.org.uk/winning-for-students/women/lad-culture/i-heart-consent

Office of the Independent Adjudicator. (2014). *Annual report 2014* (Online). Retrieved November 28, 2017, from http://www.oiahe.org.uk/media/99897/oia-annual-report-2014.pdf

Office of the Independent Adjudicator. (2015). *Annual report 2015* (Online). Retrieved November 28, 2017, from http://www.oiahe.org.uk/media/109675/oia-annual-report-2015.pdf

Phipps, A., & Young, I. (2013). *'That's what she said': Women student's experiences of 'lad culture' in higher education*. London: National Union of Students.

Reinharz, S. (1992). *Feminist methods in social research*. Oxford: Oxford University Press.

Schwartz, M. D., & Leggett, M. S. (1999). Bad dates or emotional trauma? The aftermath of campus sexual assault. *Violence Against Women, 5*, 251–71.

Stenning, P., Mitra-Kahn, T., & Gunby, C. (2012). *Gender-based violence, stalking and fear of crime: Country report United Kingdom*. Bochum: Ruhr-university Bochum; Keele: Keele University.

The Good Lad Workshop. (2013). Men and gender based violence: part of the problem, but also the solution? *Oxford Human Rights Hub* (Online). Retrieved November 28, 2017, from http://ohrh.law.ox.ac.uk/men-and-gender-based-violence-part-of-the-problem-but-also-the-solution/

United Nations. (1993). *Declaration on the elimination of violence against women*. New York, NY: Oxford University Press.

United Nations Department of Public Information. (2011, November). *Violence against women* (Online). Retrieved November 28, 2017, from http://endviolence.un.org/pdf/pressmaterials/unite_the_situation_en.pdf

Universities UK. (2016). *Changing the culture: Report of the Universities UK Taskforce examining violence against women, harassment and hate crime affecting university students* (Online). Retrieved November 29, 2017, from http://www.universitiesuk.ac.uk/policy-and-analysis/reports/Documents/2016/changing-the-culture.pdf

Zimmerman, E. (2016). Campus sexual assault: A timeline of major events. *The New York Times* (Online). Retrieved November 21, 2017, from https://www.nytimes.com/2016/06/23/education/campus-sexual-assault-a-timeline-of-major-events.html?_r=0

PART 4

QUALITY MANAGEMENT AND THE RELEVANCE OF STRATEGY

TINA KLUG

8. STRATEGIC QUALITY MANAGEMENT – A CONTRIBUTION TO AUTONOMY

The Example of TU Darmstadt, Germany

INTRODUCTION

Against the backdrop of the visible changes in Higher Education Institutions (HEI) in Europe, this chapter analyses how quality management can contribute to configuring autonomy. One important premise is the connection between quality management and strategy making. In addition, it is shown how an integrated approach to quality management promotes autonomy. The instruments that support the connection between quality management and strategy making are introduced and discussed with reference to TU Darmstadt as the first autonomous university in Germany. Based on these practice examples, it is shown how the instruments presented contribute to appropriate governance to underpin TU Darmstadt's autonomy.

The higher education system in Europe has undergone tremendous changes within the last decades. Amongst other aspects, the autonomy of HEI has grown and quality assurance and quality management activities have increased (e.g. Dobbins & Knill, 2017). With this in mind, the chapter addresses the question as to the connection between two phenomena: increasing autonomy and increasing quality assurance activities. The assumption underlying this chapter is that autonomy can benefit from quality management that both integrates the institutions' core activities and is closely linked with strategic management.

In the second section, the chapter therefore discusses the developments in autonomy and quality management in HEI in Europe. Based on practice examples at Technische Universitaet Darmstadt (TU Darmstadt), indicators are derived to support the argument demonstrating how strategic quality management can contribute to using the growing autonomy of institutions in a most effective and beneficial way. The third section therefore introduces TU Darmstadt, its autonomous status and its quality management system before presenting and discussing the instruments applied in the fourth section. Complementary, international viewpoints on strategic quality management that were collected during a recent international staff week at TU Darmstadt are introduced in the fifth section. The chapter closes with a summary highlighting strategic quality management as an important strategic tool in HEI.

DEVELOPMENT OF AUTONOMY AND QUALITY MANAGEMENT IN HEI IN EUROPE

With increasing autonomy from governmental institutions, the autonomy of HEI has also been growing for several decades. In Germany, the idea of autonomy and deregulation was accepted in the 1990s (Huether et al., 2011a, 2011b). Increasing autonomy saw a rise in the need for more and different leadership as well as responsibility for strategy making (Pausch, 2009; Kuepper, 2009; Lange, 2009). Also, due to the increasing complexity of society and HEI, the need to manage this complexity grew (Kruecken, 2008). Furthermore, the Bologna Process initiated a broad reform of the entire programme of studies at European universities and colleges (see Bayerisches Staatsinstitut fuer Hochschulforschung und Hochschulplanung, 2012a). Closely connected to this development was the emergence of quality assurance and quality management activities within HEI in Europe and worldwide (see Bayerisches Staatsinstitut für Hochschulforschung und Hochschulplanung, 2012b; Nickel, 2014; Berg, 1993). The European Commission recently identified a need to further improve sector specific quality assurance in HEI in Europe (European Commission, 2014).

Considering various approaches to quality management in German HEI, key success factors emerge (Nickel, 2014): amongst others, a close connection between quality management and strategy making, persuasive leadership and acceptance by stakeholders.

One of the most important challenges of New Public Management in HEI is defining goals. Agreements on objectives are therefore an important management tool. One concrete outcome of increasing autonomy has been the introduction of this tool in the higher education sector. Agreements on objectives are also increasingly used as strategic instruments in German HEI. They are a qualitative addition to quantitative instruments like the performance-based allocation of resources and strategic controlling, which are also tools that emerged as the autonomy of institutions grew. There are agreements on objectives at different organisational levels: between university leadership and professor, between unit and university leadership and between university and state. All three forms of agreement on objectives should ideally fit into the format known as the cascade model. The most important function of agreements on objectives is the systematic development of the organisation because it addresses aspects not covered by strategic controlling. Other important functions include transparency and supporting communication about best practices (Berthold & De Ridder, 2008; HRK, 2005; Jaeger, 2006; Klug, 2011; Nickel, 2007; Ziegele, 2006).

Originally, it was important to discuss and define the challenges, opportunities and limitations of this instrument (Zechlin, 2005). Nowadays, agreements on objectives are common practice at many German and European universities. At some European universities, they are closely connected to institutional evaluations. In these informed peer review processes, agreements on objectives are based on the results of feedback from external experts. The combination of agreements on objectives with peer review evaluation enhances the outcomes and acceptance of both instruments. It also contributes to transparency because objectives are discussed and explained much more widely when external feedback is taken into consideration.

In addition to the autonomy of the institutions, the autonomy of the units and individuals within the institutions has to be taken into account. There are voices and studies that argue that only the leadership benefits from autonomy and quality management and that, by contrast, the members of the institution have less autonomy and are subject to more control and formalisation. The benefits of autonomy are questioned and the loss of autonomy in the decentral units and for individuals is emphasised (Kuehl, 2011). However, it seems to depend on how autonomy and quality management are applied. If, for example, the principles of accountability, transparency and fairness are employed, more members of the institutions benefit from autonomy and quality management (Hoecht, 2006).

Another instrument emerging that improves quality in HEI are advisory boards. Advisory boards can be composed of internal experts, external experts or both. Depending on the composition of the board, the function and roles differ and the contribution to quality enhancement also differs. In internal combined advisory boards, the members can operate as multipliers within the organisation, informing their peer groups about strategic discussions and decisions at the institution. They can also represent the voices of their status groups. Their expertise with reference to the institution and quality management can be used to further develop and improve quality management approaches and instruments. With internally composed advisory boards, the above-mentioned criticism about less autonomy for the units and individuals and more control and formalisation can be addressed to some extent. Members of the institution have a voice and can therefore influence the impact on the autonomy of both their units and themselves. Boards of external experts have a different role, also providing helpful feedback for quality enhancement, but not being able to take the voices of the institution into account as well. Many institutions have therefore instituted more than one advisory board, adopting the different roles as appropriate (e.g. Boentert, 2014 for external advisory boards). In addition, the introduction of advisory boards is an example of how standard, well-received approaches in science are also accepted in the context of quality management and therefore produce valuable results for enhancing quality.

All in all, with the backing of these instruments, autonomy can be seen as an opportunity rather than a duty. The implementation of appropriate management tools means greater strategic self-determination and thus results in enhanced performance.

TU DARMSTADT AND ITS AUTONOMOUS STATUS

TU Darmstadt is a medium-sized German university of technology. It was established as a higher vocational school and polytechnic institute in 1836, becoming an institute of technology in 1877. Currently, there are about 26,360 students (29% women,

18% foreign students), 306 professors (52 female, 254 male) and 4,310 academic and non-academic employees (1,380 women, 2,930 men). Of the total budget of approx. 452 million euro, about 245 million derive from state funding, 164 million from third party funding, 35 million from the Higher Education Pact and 7.9 million from other sources (https://www.tu-darmstadt.de/universitaet/selbstverstaendnis/zahlenundfakten/index.en.jsp).

In 2005, TU Darmstadt was designated a model university under the "Autonomy Law" by the state parliament of Hesse, a status which conferred a degree of autonomy and self-determination that was unprecedented nationwide. With the introduction of the law known as the "TUD-Gesetz" (TUD Law), TU Darmstadt became autonomous in the fields of personnel, finance and organisation. Technically speaking, TU Darmstadt changed from being an exclusively state financed public institution into an independent institution governed by public law. This change in status and the concomitant gain in freedom brought with it a huge growth in responsibility for strategic governance and strategic management. Besides new responsibilities for university management and new controlling and strategy instruments, like performance-oriented allocation of resources, the meaning of quality management acquired greater importance as well (Pautsch, 2011; Huether, 2011; Proemel, 2010).

In Darmstadt, quality assurance activities relating to studying, teaching and research were already in place before the university received its autonomous status. As the scope of autonomy grew, these mainly unconnected quality assurance initiatives were further developed into an integrated quality management system with a close connection to strategy making. Quality management at TU Darmstadt today addresses strategy, structure, research, studying and teaching, promotion of early career researchers and administration. Its integrated quality management system incorporates a mixture of top down and bottom up elements, including and addressing all internal stakeholders such as students, professors, teachers and administrative staff. Quality management also embraces external stakeholders like state politicians, representatives of industry and society as well as local citizens.

In 2017, TU Darmstadt was awarded the so-called "system accreditation" certificate for its quality management system. This certificate strengthens its autonomy and responsibility for quality management and quality development even further. Especially in the field of study programmes, TU Darmstadt is now much more autonomous as the former obligatory accreditation of study programmes by external agencies is no longer necessary: the quality management system itself has been accredited. This means that TU Darmstadt is certified to assure the quality of its study programmes itself, which opens the door to strategic developments: The (further) development of study programmes can be linked even more closely with developments in profile building and research. Moreover, external experts can be chosen by the university. Experience shows that this leads to high-quality expertise and matching amongst the experts involved. For the results of TU Darmstadt's system accreditation, visit http://aaq.ch/verfahrensberichte/.

STRATEGIC QUALITY MANAGEMENT – A CONTRIBUTION TO AUTONOMY

TU DARMSTADT'S QUALITY MANAGEMENT INSTRUMENTS TO SUPPORT AUTONOMY

Considering the general conditions described above and the instruments that support the autonomy of HEI, the following section illustrates how these instruments are employed at TU Darmstadt. The relevant critical success factors are analysed and discussed.

Institutional Evaluations

Analysis shows that it is important to implement quality management as leanly as possible with methods that are accepted, especially in the scientific community. In this regard, peer review based institutional evaluations or advisory boards are convenient in at least two ways. Firstly, peer review is a firmly established and widely-used process in the scientific community and is therefore more acceptable in the context of strategic quality management than other methods which have their origin, for example, in industry. Furthermore, it is perceived as less bureaucratic than other quality assurance instruments. It must, however, be remembered that the peer review of institutions is public and often driven externally whereas the peer review of publications or scientific projects tends to be internal and is initiated by the person evaluated (Torka, 2011). It emerges that by integrating several quality assurance activities, such as peer review, survey results and statistical information, important insights can be gained into the quality of units and strategies.

At TU Darmstadt, evaluation of all faculties and central institutions was introduced in 2009. The evaluations are conducted by the quality management unit of the university on behalf of the university President. The method used is the informed peer review approach, which generates recommendations by external experts on the future development of the unit under evaluation. The external experts are recruited from other institutions, mostly from universities or research institutions. Sometimes, external experts from industry supplement the peer groups which also include one external student respectively. TU Darmstadt has defined selection criteria for the external experts that are based on criteria developed by the German Research Foundation (DFG) and the Leibniz Association. The most important criterion for recruiting external experts is scientific excellence. In a nutshell, the institutional evaluations at TU Darmstadt involve highly-respected researchers from external institutions but are organised internally. On the basis of the external experts' recommendations, the university leadership negotiates agreements on objectives with the respective faculty or institution.

TU Darmstadt also strives to achieve the four goals of evaluations proposed in the relevant literature: acquiring knowledge, executing control, creating transparency to enable dialogue and document success and thus legitimating the activities and decisions of the units evaluated (Stockmann, 2002). Evaluations at TU Darmstadt emphasise the knowledge and dialogue functions, but the control function is also used, stressing the aspect of strategic decision making. The control function is therefore understood in the context of "controlling" rather than "control". Consequently, the results of the evaluation process are used by the university leadership to negotiate the agreements on objectives with the units evaluated. They are thus both knowledge based and strongly strategy oriented. The legitimation function is employed as well. The results of the evaluation are communicated transparently to the important boards at TU Darmstadt, e.g. the University Council and the Senate, and can be used for communication with the ministry and other public stakeholders.

Agreement on Objectives at TU Darmstadt

The practice example of TU Darmstadt shows, furthermore, how agreement on objectives between organisational units and the head of the institution are especially valuable when they are embedded in a strategic quality management process that includes the perspective of an external review. Agreements on objectives with units encourage profile building and, as a result, support the systematic and strategic development of the higher education institution.

Since 2009, the agreements on objectives negotiated between the units of TU Darmstadt and the President of the university have been closely linked to the results of the institutional evaluations, which had been introduced previously. With the exception of one faculty, several other units and the central administration were evaluated institutionally. In total, between 2009 and 2016, 300 goals were negotiated between the faculties and the university President. Even though the process of implementing the goals is still ongoing and some of the agreements on objectives have only recently been negotiated, approx. 25 per cent of the goals have already been reached. About the same percentage has not yet been launched and about 50 per cent are ongoing (see Figure 8.2). Only after the first cycle of agreements has been completed in 2022, will it finally be possible to determine the full extent to which goals have been reached. It is, however, already evident that important goals pertaining to structural and organisational aspects as well as to the appointment of professors are being achieved to a greater extent. Interestingly, but also obviously, stakeholders are less driven and engaged in pursuing objectives that have less strategic significance.

Advisory Board on Quality Management

The Advisory Board on Quality Management at TU Darmstadt is composed of internal members of the university. The chair of the board is the President of the university; the members are all stakeholders: students, professors, scientific and administrative staff. As a group, they represent all the academic fields at the university: engineering, natural sciences and humanities. The board meets approx. twice a year and allows guests to attend if it is helpful in discussing specific topics. The minutes of the meeting are published on the university intranet.

STRATEGIC QUALITY MANAGEMENT – A CONTRIBUTION TO AUTONOMY

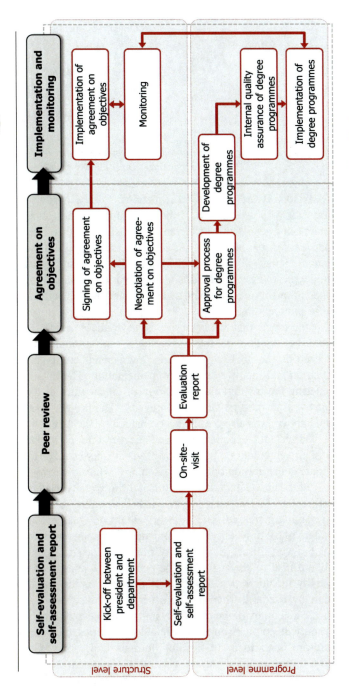

Figure 8.1. *Institutional evaluation procedure at TU Darmstadt 2017 (© Quality Management Unit, TU Darmstadt)*

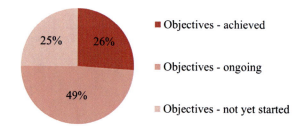

*Figure 8.2. Current state of objectives implemented at TU Darmstadt
(© Quality Management Unit, TU Darmstadt)*

The Advisory Board has several functions. Firstly, it advises the President of TU Darmstadt who uses it as a sounding board to reflect on the goals of quality management and to discuss forthcoming decisions in this area. The board offers opportunities for participation and actively designing the university's quality management. It is a forum that facilitates the exchange and communication of different perspectives. The board is also tasked with establishing transparency and acceptance of quality management at TU Darmstadt. It is neither a control body nor an alibi for participation.

One of the topics that has been discussed by the Advisory Board to date is the institutional evaluation of the university's central administration. Discussions have centred on the goals of the process, agreement on objectives resulting from the evaluation and monitoring goal implementation. The board was also involved in considering the institutional evaluation of all faculties at the university, which was adjusted after the first "evaluation cycle". The project "system accreditation", mentioned above, was also closely accompanied by the Advisory Board.

In TU Darmstadt's experience, there are several important factors governing the successful implementation and outcome of an advisory board on quality management. Such a board concretely embodies the autonomy of the university. With the increasing autonomy of the university itself, the role of the university leadership and the official legal entities at TU Darmstadt changed; in particular, responsibility for strategic decision making increased. The Advisory Board on Quality Management supports the President of the university concerning quality management aspects in a relatively informal but very direct way. Quality management strategies that are discussed by the board tend to accommodate the perspectives and needs of a broader group of university members than instruments that are implemented top down without discussion by a board. Therefore, the perspectives on how quality management supports the autonomy of the university and its units can be disseminated throughout the university. In comparison with official legal entities, the board is less formalised and therefore open to more meeting formats and topics. Generally, the board provides a forum for involving members of the university in strategic decisions on quality management at an early stage. It contributes to the development of an overall understanding of quality at the university. The exchange of the various stakeholders' sometimes differing points of view on quality management approaches is facilitated by the Advisory Board whose discussions help to pinpoint strategic key aspects of quality management. An important premise for the success of the Advisory Board is a sound communication strategy. At TU Darmstadt there are several channels that are considered important. For example, the President regularly reports back to the university Senate on topics discussed and results achieved. Also, important topics are published in the university newspaper and the results are communicated on the university intranet. In addition, the members of the board transfer topics and results to their groups and prepare the board meetings within their different status boards. This ensures that the board's recommendations are supported by other members of the university. Bendermacher et al. (2017) also advocate, amongst others, commitment, shared ownership and the importance of communication as important organisational elements that contribute to quality culture.

There are several challenges that need to be addressed before an Aadvisory board on quality management can function successfully. The relationship to the other working groups and boards already in existence and their different responsibilities needs to be clearly defined and transparent. Moreover, the results of the meetings must be acted upon and conscientiously followed up, as appropriate. The members of the board need to act as multipliers within the university, which involves effort and commitment. It is also important that the board itself sets the right topics, which means those that are not only of interest to board members but also drive the university forward, especially its quality management. Not getting too caught up in micromanagement but, rather, concentrating on strategic questions of quality management is another important aspect.

Taking the example of TU Darmstadt, the three instruments described show how quality management that is closely connected with strategy making promotes the university's autonomy. Institutional evaluations help the units evaluated to develop their profile further and to discuss their strategic approaches in their core areas in a systematic way. The increasing responsibility for profile building and strategic development of the university as an institution as well as the units of the university resulting from increased autonomy can be developed in a much more targeted fashion by involving informed external peers. The agreements on objectives that are based on the results of the institutional evaluation lead to knowledge-based negotiation about these plans with the leadership of the university. Agreements on objectives are per se an instrument to configure the autonomy of an institution. Embedding them in the institutional evaluation instrument of external peer review and basing them on the results of this process leads to systematic, strategic and comprehensive agreements on objectives which support the autonomy of the units and the university leadership. With the agreements on objectives the units acquire a coherent development programme for the next five to seven years whilst the university leadership has a defined programme for its units which can be used for communicating with government and the public as well. An emphasis on the dialogue function of quality management is set by instituting an advisory board chaired by the university President. At an early stage of drawing up concepts and strategies, university members are involved in the decision making on the university's quality management system. This instrument illustrates the development function for autonomy. The scope in the field of quality management that exists due to the university's autonomous status can be boldly and systematically developed.

INTERNATIONAL PERSPECTIVE ON STRATEGIC QUALITY MANAGEMENT AND AUTONOMY

Following on from a workshop on strategic quality management that took place recently during an international staff week at TU Darmstadt, interesting perspectives from other European countries can be added to the above analysis. Overall, the input from about twenty participants from twelve European countries confirms the strategic significance of quality management. However, its status and strategic significance in the various countries' respective HEIs are quite diverse.

Interestingly, there seems to be a pattern amongst European HEI with regard to the status of the quality management systems already in place, and especially the narrower or broader approaches to quality management, with the less integrated approaches displaying a looser connection to strategy making and the more integrated approaches a closer connection to strategic decision making. The instruments in Europe range from process-oriented to evaluation-oriented approaches. The former are usually accompanied by a stronger focus on quantitative data and indicators, the latter take greater account of more qualitative information. All quality management systems are based on national and European standards and include objectives and goals specific to their own institution. In general, the northern and western European countries seem to place a greater emphasis on integrational and strategic perspectives than the eastern and southern European countries.

Despite the very different approaches and quality management instruments used in European HEI, the consensus amongst workshop participants on the challenges of and critical success factors for strategic quality management was very clear. Challenges that were mentioned by participants during the event ranged from a lack of understanding of quality management goals to a stubborn resistance to change. The need for clear objectives and the challenges posed by constant changes of policy were also mentioned. The group agreed on the following critical success factors: first and foremost, communicating appropriately, closing the quality cycle by actually using the outcomes of quality assurance for strategy making and demystifying the quality jargon. Furthermore, it became clear that in all the European countries present, it helps if quality management is based on scientific approaches and if scientists are addressed by and integrated in the quality management activities. Finally, the leadership of the institution must emphasise the significance of quality management for its own institutions.

These observations are not representative or statistically proven. But taking note of these random, subjective conclusions may be an interesting starting point for further Europe-wide research on quality management practices and their effects on quality, autonomy and governance. They also support the approach formulated by the European Commission which has identified the need for better cooperation on quality assurance in Europe (European Commission, 2014).

CONCLUSION

Strategic quality management has great potential to promote the development of HEI. Studying is one core area of higher education institutions to which it is important to apply quality management. The analysis presented here, however, shows that it is even more valuable to adopt an integrated approach to quality management that includes not only studying but also other core areas of HEI such as research, promotion of early careers, structure and administration, and that is closely linked with strategy making. Whilst this integrated perspective is already being practised in auditing in various European countries, quality management in Germany still mainly addresses the field of studying (Nickel & Ziegele, 2012).

Against the backdrop of these findings, one goal of quality management in higher education should be to rescue it from its wallflower existence as a necessary evil and to enhance its status as an important strategic tool in HEI. To achieve this goal, quality assurance instruments should be as scientifically oriented as possible and should address all stakeholders' perspectives in an appropriate way. Quality assurance must, moreover, be closely connected with strategy making because this is the way to make results visible.

REFERENCES

Bayerisches Staatsinstitut für Hochschulforschung und Hochschulplanung (2012a). *Beiträge zur Hochschulforschung. Thema: Umsetzung des Bologna-Prozesses 1*. München.

Bayerisches Staatsinstitut für Hochschulforschung und Hochschulplanung (2012b). *Beiträge zur Hochschulforschung. Thema: Qualitätssicherung in Lehre und Forschung 3*. München.

Beise, A. S. et al. (2014). *Qualitätssicherung von Studiengängen jenseits der Programmakkreditierung. Neue Herausforderungen für Hochschulsteuerung und Organisationsentwicklung, Forum Hochschule 1*. Hannover.

Bendermacher, G. W. G., Oude Egbrink, M. G. A., Wolfhagen, I. H. A. P., & Dolmans, D. H. J. M. (2017). Unravelling quality culture in higher education: A Realist review, *Higher Education, 73*(1), 39–60.

Berg, C. (1993). University Autonomy and Quality Assurance. *Higher Education in Europe, 18*(3), 18–26.

Berthold, C., & de Ridder, D. (2008). Interne Zielvereinbarungen als hochschulisches Steuerungsinstrument. In C. Berthold, B. Tag, H. H. Seidler, & G. Scholz (Eds.), *Handbuch Praxis Wissenschaftsfinanzierung* (A 1.8). Berlin: Raabe.

Boentert, A. (2014). Externe Evaluation durch Beiräte: Das Modell der Fachhochschule Münster. In A. S. Beise, I. Jungermann, & K. Wannemacher (Eds.), *Qualitätssicherung von Studiengängen jenseits der Programmakkreditierung. Neue Herausforderung für Hochschulsteuerung und Organisation* (pp. 57–66). Hannover: Deutsches Zentrum für Hochschul- und Wissenschaftsforschung GmbH (DZHW).

Dobbins, M., & Knill, C. (2017). Higher education governance in France, Germany, and Italy: Change and variation in the impact of transnational soft governance, *Policy and Society, 36*(1), 67–88.

European Commission. (2014). *Report from the commission to the European parliament, the council, the European economic and social committee and the committee of the regions. Report on progress in quality assurance in higher education.* Retrieved February 17, 2017, from http://ec.europa.eu/dgs/education_culture/repository/education/policy/higher-education/doc/quality_en.pdf

Hoecht, A. (2006). Quality assurance in UK higher education: Issues of trust, control, professional autonomy and accountability, *Higher Education, 51,* 541–563.

HRK. (2005). Entschließung des Plenums der HRK vom 14.06.2005. Grundsätze zu Gestaltung und Verhandlung von Zielvereinbarungen. Bonn: HRK.

Hüther, O., Jacob, A., Seidler, H., & Wilke, K. (2011a). *Hochschulautonomie in Gesetz und Praxis. Eine Analyse von Rahmenbedingungen und Modellprojekten.* Essen: Stifterverband für die Deutsche Wissenschaft.

Hüther, O., Jacob, A., Seidler, H., & Wilke, K. (2011b). Hochschulautonomie in Gesetz und Praxis. *Forschung & Lehre.* Retrieved from http://www.forschung-und-lehre.de/wordpress/?p=8852

Jaeger, M. (2006). Steuerung an Hochschulen durch interne Zielvereinbarungen. *Aktueller Stand der Entwicklungen, die Hochschule, 2,* 55–66.

Klug, T. (2014). Profilbildung und Qualitätsentwicklung – Monitoring von Zielvereinbarungen an der TU Darmstadt. In S. Nickel (Ed.), *Implementierung von Qualitätsmanagementsystemen: Erfahrungen aus der Hochschulpraxis* (pp. 37–47). CHE Arbeitspapier 163.

Klug, T. (2015). Institutionelle Evaluationen und ihre strukturverändernden Effekte auf Wissenschaftsorganisationen. Am Beispiel der Technischen Universität Darmstadt. In O. Vettori, G. Salmhofer, L. Mitterauer, & K. Ledermüller (Eds.), *Eine Frage der Wirksamkeit? Qualitätsmanagement als Impulsgeber für Veränderungen an Hochschulen.* (pp. 191–206). Bielefeld: UniversitätsVerlagWebler.

Krücken, G. (2008). Lässt sich Wissenschaft managen? *Wissenschaftsrecht, 41*(4), 345–358.

Kühl, S. (2011). *Was heißt hier Autonomie? Wider den Mythos von der „deregulierten Hochschule".* Working Paper 11.

Küpper, H.-U. (2009). Effizienzreform der deutschen Hochschulen nach 1990 – Hintergründe, Ziele, Komponenten. *Beiträge zur Hochschulforschung, 4,* 50–75.

Lange, J. (2009). Wie viel Management braucht und verträgt die Wissenschaft? *Beiträge zur Hochschulforschung, 4,* 76–88.

Nickel, S., & Ziegele, F. (2012). *Audit statt Akkreditierung. Ein richtiger Schritt zu mehr Hochschulautonomie und weniger Bürokratie.* CHE Positionspapier.

Nickel, S. (2007). *Partizipatives Management von Universitäten. Zielvereinbarungen, Leitungsstrukturen, staatliche Steuerung.* München: Rainer Hampp Verlag.

Nickel, S. (2014). *Implementierung von Qualitätsmanagementsystemen: Erfahrungen aus der Hochschulpraxis.* CHE Arbeitspapier 163.

Pautsch, A. (2009). Neue Organisationsmodelle für Hochschulen – Ein Ländervergleich. *Beiträge zur Hochschulforschung, 4,* 36–49.

Prömel, H. J. (2010). Noch selbständiger. Das neue, fortschrittliche TU Darmstadt-Gesetz. hoch3. *Die Zeitung der TU Darmstadt, 6,* 18.

Stockmann, R. (2002). *Qualitätsmanagement und Evaluation – Konkurrierende oder sich ergänzende Konzepte?* CEVAL Arbeitspapiere 3.

Torka, M. (2011). Institutioneller gleich handlungspraktischer Wandel? Das Beispiel von Begutachtungspraktiken bei der Evaluation wissenschaftlicher Einrichtungen. In S. Hornbostel & A. Schelling (Eds.), *Evaluation: New balance of power?* (pp. 69–81). Berlin: iFQ-Working Paper 9.

Zechlin, L. (2005). *Entwicklungspläne und Zielvereinbarungen. Die strategische Steuerung von Universitäten zwischen staatlichen Vorgaben, Wettbewerbsdruck und autonomer Profilierung. Was kann und soll ein universitärer Entwicklungsplan leisten.* Wien: Workshop der Österreichischen Forschungsgemeinschaft.

Ziegele, F. (2006). Zielvereinbarungen als Kern des „Neuen Steuerungsmodells". In HRK (Ed.), *Von der Qualitätssicherung der Lehre zur Qualitätsentwicklung als Prinzip der Hochschulsteuerung* (pp. 77–105). Bonn: Beiträge zur Hochschulpolitik 1/2006.

CINDY KONEN

9. INNOVATIVENESS OF HIGHER EDUCATION INSTITUTIONS

Preconditions for the Development of Co-Operative Innovations

RESEARCH QUESTION AND RELEVANCE

The classical understanding of the role of higher education institutions (HEIs) in Germany (universities and universities of applied sciences) is subjected to profound change under the current conditions. The HEIs are becoming more and more of an actor in the economic competition and are thus expected to contribute their resources, knowledge and competencies to create co-operative innovations with enterprises. (e.g. Krücken, Blümel, & Kloke, 2012; Nickel, 2011; Schneidewind, 2016; Vega & Krücken, 2014).

The changed expectations from politics and society are, for example, expressed by the increasing importance of the third mission (e.g. Henke, Pasternack, & Schmid, 2015; Roessler, Duong, & Hachmeister, 2015; Vega & Krücken, 2014), a financing structure which is increasingly changing in the direction of higher third-party interests (e.g. Aljets & Lettkemann, 2012; Stifterverband, 2014), or, more recently, the federal and state government initiative "Innovative higher education system (Innovative Hochschule)" (Bundesministerium für Bildung und Forschung, 2016). However, it is increasingly driven by the higher education system itself. In 2014, 93% of the presidents of HEIs wanted more co-operation with enterprises. In addition to financing their research activities, they want to gain access to relevant research questions, technologies and know-how as well as contribute to the transfer of knowledge (Stifterverband, 2014).

This changed expectation does not replace the classic tasks of German HEIs of basic research and teaching. Instead, it needs to be understood as an additional task which superimposes the original pillars (Krücken et al., 2012). Thus HEIs are faced with the challenge of organising the traditional and complementary tasks into a hierarchy in a suitable target system by using the available human and material resources tactically with the goal of a best possible target achievement (Konen, 2017a).

A prerequisite for the emergence of co-operative innovations between companies and HEIs is sufficient innovativeness among all partners of the co-operation. Therefore, this chapter defines innovativeness of HEIs as the capability to support the demand-driven development of innovations in co-operating enterprises utilising resources, knowledge and competencies from the HEIs (Konen, 2017a, based on the understanding of Faix, 2017).

An innovation co-operation is therefore understood as the complete process from the initiation to the conclusion of a co-operation between at least one HEI with at least one company and possibly other partners, such as non-university research institutes, with the aim of producing innovation (Konen, 2017a).

When looking at the innovative success of German HEIs, there are considerable differences despite similar legal and social conditions. Therefore, it can be assumed that the orientation of the internal institutional factors has a significant influence on the innovativeness. While the influence factors of the innovativeness of economic orientated organisations have already been widely explored by empirical studies (e.g. Lawson & Samson, 2001; Smith, Busi, Ball, & Van der Meer, 2008; Stern & Jaberg, 2010; Wagner, Slama, Rogowski, & Bannert, 2007), only few detailed studies have been conducted for the field of German HEIs to date and most of them only examine a subarea of innovativeness (e.g. Aljets & Lettkemann, 2012; Hüther & Krücken, 2013; Kloke & Krücken, 2010; Krücken et al., 2012; Ringelhahn, Wollersheim, & Welpe, 2015 or for the international context e.g. Paradeise & Thoenig, 2013; Thoenig & Paradeise, 2016). The research presented here tries to contribute to closing this research gap. It intends to show how HEIs could organise their internal institutional factors to increase their innovativeness and thereby (successfully) generate co-operative innovations.

DESCRIPTION OF THE GERMAN HIGHER EDUCATION SYSTEM

The German higher education system consists of 428 HEIs, of which 106 belong to the universities, 217 are universities of applied sciences and 105 are art, administrative, educational and theological universities (Statista, 2017). Thereby a distinction is made between state and privately funded, but state-approved HEIs (Hochschulrahmengesetz § 1). In the further course, due to the research objective of the work presented here, only the universities and universities of applied sciences are analysed in detail. In these, about 96.5% of the students in Germany are enrolled (Statistisches Bundesamt, 2017b).

The tasks of the HEIs are differentiated according to their type (university and university of applied sciences) in the State Higher Education Act. The research focus at universities of applied sciences is usually less pronounced, and research that occurs is usually more application-oriented. With a few exceptions, the right to award doctorates in Germany lies with the universities (Keller, 2016). The following quotation from the Law on the HEIs of the Federal State of North Rhine-Westphalia shows the different roles of the HEI types (Gesetz über die Hochschulen des Landes Nordrhein-Westfalen § 3):

(1) The universities serve the gaining of scientific knowledge as well as the care and development of the sciences through research, teaching, study, promotion

of young scientists and knowledge transfer (in particular scientific further education, technology transfer). They prepare for occupational activities at home and abroad that require the application of scientific knowledge and methods. [.......]

(2) The universities of applied sciences prepare by application-based teaching and study for professional activities in Germany and abroad, which require the application of scientific knowledge and methods or the ability to artistic design. They perform research and development tasks, artistic-creative tasks as well as tasks of knowledge transfer (in particular scientific training, technology transfer). [.......][1]

The universities of applied sciences have a much younger tradition in Germany than the universities. While many universities were founded centuries ago, the first universities of applied sciences were founded in the 1960s. Since the beginning of the research and teaching in universities of applied sciences, they were first and foremost practice-oriented (Nickel, 2011).

Table 9.1 gives an overview of some statistical key figures of HEIs differentiated between universities and universities of applied sciences. The effects of the key figures will be discussed at the end of this section.

Table 9.1. Statistical key figures of HEIs

	University	University of applied sciences
Professors (2016)[2]	24,256	19,306
Teaching input professors in semester periods per week[3,4]	8–9	16–19
Scientific and artistic assistants (2016)[5]	168,070	11,856
Lecturers and assistants (2016)[6]	2,125	603
Students (winter semester 16/17)[7]	1,747,515	956,717

In 2015, German HEIs had revenues of €26.23 billion. These consisted of the basic as well as third-party funding. The share of third-party funding amounted to €7.44 billion, of which approximately 93.5% was awarded to the universities and about 6.5% to the universities of applied sciences. Thus, the share of third-party funding in relation to the total funding of the HEIs makes up about 28% (Statistisches Bundesamt, 2017a). There was a slight increase compared to 2005 when the share of third-party funding was 24.5% (Statistisches Bundesamt, 2007). Around 20% of the third-party funding of the HEIs are from co-operations with enterprises (Stifterverband, 2014).

Regarding funding, the state approved HEIs face the particular challenge of not receiving any state funding. They are primarily financed by tuition fees and income from business activities and assets. Usually, they, therefore, have a particularly high percentage of third-party funding from the business sector, and their internal institutional frameworks actively focus on the possibility of entering into such co-operations (Buschle & Haider, 2016).

The above-indicated conditions clearly show that the framework conditions set at the universities of applied sciences (high teaching input, few scientific assistants, doctoral degrees only in exceptional cases, little third-party funding) are initially much less suitable for generating innovations. Due to the high orientation towards the creation of practice-oriented knowledge, they can in other cases, however, prevail over the strongly basic research-oriented universities.

THEORETICAL FRAMEWORK

The above-presented understanding of the tasks of HEIs is particularly found in the literature discussed in Germany. Here two definitions of HEIs have come out on top where an HEI is understood either as an organisational actor (Krücken & Meier, 2006; Meier, 2009) or by the concept of the "entrepreneurial university". According to Etzkowitz (2008), a university can be regarded as entrepreneurial if it implements the goal of economic exploitation in addition to research and teaching in its target system. The approach of the HEI as an organisational actor, on the other hand, focuses on the organisational building-up processes that make the HEI an autonomous, increasingly centrally-controlled, efficient and profiled organisation without emphasising a specifically economic orientation (Kosmützky & Borggräfe, 2012). This contribution is situated between the two approaches by turning away from a predominantly economic orientation of HEIs, but interpreting the new tasks in a way that (potential) research results are proactively applied to the exploitation of enterprises and society (Konen, 2017a).

With regard to innovations, HEIs find themselves in a dynamic context characterised by uncertain expectations. This is justified by the fact that different internal and external units are involved in the development of innovations. These are located on different hierarchical levels (researcher, leadership positions, administration) and are characterised by different cultures (administration vs department) (Konen, 2017a). The ability to innovate differs from unit to unit. They differ in their willingness to innovate, their feasibility to innovate, their ability to innovate and their responsibility to innovate (according to Auernhammer & Hall, 2014). Due to the specific socialisation and competencies, the units differ in their perceptions and situation assessments.

This dynamic context requires an understanding of innovation as a dynamic capability in accordance with Teece, Pisano and Shuen (1997). Therefore an institution is not permanently endowed with a competitive advantage but must continuously redesign it through a reconfiguration of the resource and competence base through processes of coordination, learning, reconfiguration and transformation. Thereby the basis of knowledge and resources (position) determines the possible paths an HEI can use for the learning, coordination reconfiguration and transformation processes.

In 2007 Teece presented an evolution of the concept of Teece et al. (1997) by defining dynamic capabilities more detailed via microfoundations. In this context he defines dynamic capabilities as follows:

> Dynamic capabilities can be disaggregated into the capacity (a) to sense and shape opportunities and threats, (b) to seize opportunities, and (c) to maintain competitiveness through enhancing, combining, protecting, and, when necessary, reconfiguring the business enterprise's intangible and tangible asset. (p. 1319)

On this basis he defines the capacity to sense and shape opportunities and threats in the following way:

> Sensing (and shaping) new opportunities is very much a scanning, creation, learning, and interpretive activity. Investment in research and related activities is usually a necessary complement to this activity. (p. 1322)

To be able to seize and shape opportunities, institutions must therefore regularly search the market for opportunities. This includes not only a permanent research activity and the consistent observation of the technological possibilities and customer needs, but also an assessment of the future demand, development of the markets as well as an estimation of the future behaviour of the competitors. On the one hand, this has to happen through the cognitive processes of the individual members of the institution but also through institutionally controlled research and development processes. Thereby the ability to identify relevant developments must be present at both individual and institutional levels. This also implies that appropriate access to information must be made possible by the governance of the HEI.

On this basis, an institution must be able to seize opportunities by initiating development and commercialisation measures. In this context, the institution needs to develop an integrated investment and marketing strategy. It is necessary for the institution to be open enough for the emergence of new ideas and to not exclusively stick to established programs. They need to know the mechanisms (decision rules, powerful actors, etc.) for decisions for or against potential innovations. At the heart of the capability to seize opportunities is the design of institutional structures, procedures, designs and incentives to exploit opportunities.

The capacity to maintain competitiveness through enhancing, combining, protecting, and, when necessary, reconfiguring the business enterprise's intangible and tangible assets is about reconfiguring an institution to adapt to changing market and competitive conditions. As well as trying to avoid path dependencies and the repetitive reiteration of existing inertia leading to past successes but present dysfunctional processes.

Thoenig and Paradeise (2016) adapted the dynamic understanding to the context of HEIs by analysing how universities can act as strategic institutions in the context of a dynamic environment and environmental situations by using strategic capacity. Thus they can react proactively to changing circumstances and thereby achieve a high (international) reputation and excellence.

Strategic capacity itself is formed by the appropriate combination of internal resources and the mastery of social processes. This succeeds if the subunits work together on the same strategic goal. The prerequisite for this is the inclusion of the subunits in the strategic development and decision-making processes, as well as the achievement of a balance between integration and differentiation, as the researchers are both members of the HEI as well as of their respective peer group each with specific requirements.

If the conceptions of Thoenig and Paradeise (2016), Teece et al. (1997) and Teece (2007) are summarized regarding their gain for the conception of innovativeness, it can be seen that the innovativeness has to be differentiated with regard to several levels. First, the endowment of specific resources pictures the level of the causes of innovativeness. This is to distinguish from the level of manifestation of innovativeness. In this research the conceptions of Teece et al. (1997) and Teece (2007) are combined, by achieving manifestation through coordination, reconfiguration, transformation and learning processes, while each of them is found within the capacities to sense and shape opportunities and threats, to seize opportunities, and to maintain competitiveness through enhancing, combining, protecting, and, when necessary, reconfiguring the business enterprise's intangible and tangible assets. Furthermore, a level of innovation results has to be distinguished.

In this context, the results of the work on the innovative capacity of non-university research institutions of Faix (2017) are also of great benefit because Faix also follows a dynamic approach and distinguishes innovative capacity by the three levels of causes, manifestation and effects. Thereby the model can generally be used by its basic structure but needs a comprehensive specification for HEIs as they differ in many contexts from non-university research institutions (e.g. economic orientation, internal and external communication behaviour, leadership models). This specification is achieved by using the results of Teece et al. (1997), Teece (2007) and Thoenig and Paradeise (2016) as well as the results of appropriate studies of higher education research. In the following paragraphs, the resulting model of innovativeness will be described in greater detail.

Level of Causes

The level of causes focuses on the internal factors that influence the abilities, the motivational and other cognitive orientations of the actors as well as the courses of action in the context of research and innovation relevant behaviours. Based on studies about the success factors of the innovativeness of enterprises (e.g. Stern & Jaberg, 2010; Smith et al., 2008; Wagner et al., 2007; Ernst, 2002; Lawson & Samson, 2001; Johne & Snelson, 1988), Thoenig and Paradeises (2016) study on HEIs and Faix (2017) study on non-university research facilities, the following general cause factors were determined and brought into the context of HEIs (see detailed Konen, 2017a):

- *Personnel management and leadership* (esp. innovation-oriented leadership, agreement on objectives, incentive system, hr development and recruitment)
- *Structures and processes* (esp. innovative organisational structures like collaborative research centres, possibilities for restructuring the administrative innovation support units like transfer agencies)
- *Culture* (esp. willingness to learn and change including an error learning culture, co-operative communication and information behaviour, possibilities for autonomous action, innovation as value)
- *Financial and material resources* (esp. impact of the financial and material infrastructure)
- *Methods for innovation appearance* (esp. use of planning, analysis, decision making and control methods)

Their expression defines the possibilities offered to the HEI to manifest their innovativeness (current position).

Level of Manifestation

By using microfoundations, Teece (2007) pictures the manifestation of innovativeness as mentioned above via three part capabilities. This basic idea is also found in Faix (2017), although he developed a manifestation concept for the specific context of non-university research institutions. For these specific requirements, a more detailed subdivision of the ability to sense and shape opportunities and threats is needed. Thus Faix covers these issues through two part capabilities and thereby distinguishes four different part capabilities in total. The following figure shows how the conceptions of Teece (2007) and Faix (2017) cohere with regard to the goal of the here presented contribution. This is because although the concept of manifestation of innovativeness of HEIs uses the four part capabilities of Faix, these do require a specification for the HEI context. For this specification, a recourse to Teece findings is needed.

As a result, the part capabilities of manifestation of innovativeness of HEIs can be defined as follows:

The ability to attract new scientific and technological knowledge is based on the exploitation of knowledge with a direct or an indirect applied approach. These can be generated by the researchers themselves, or they can investigate existing research results and apply them (in a modified way) to their problems. In this context, it is also of high importance that the governance of the HEI provides structures that make it possible for a researcher to gain the needed knowledge. Additionally, the HEI governance has the task to allow and to encourage researchers to gain knowledge outside of the mainstream sector even if it is sometimes politically inopportune (see also cause factor culture).

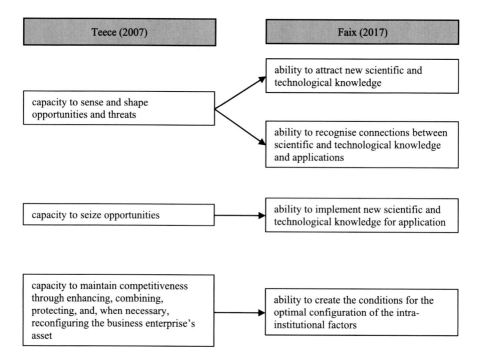

Figure 9.1. Part capabilities of manifestation from Teece (2007) and Faix (2017)

The ability to recognise connections between scientific and technological knowledge and their applications analyses how well the researchers can identify references between existing or planned research and current or planned applications. On the one hand, the initiative may come from the HEI, which is actively looking for companies to co-operate with to implement planned or already realised research results. This activity can start via the initiative of the researchers themselves or through the researchers but supported by the HEI governance or administration. On the other hand, an enterprise facing an innovation problem may hope to find a solution by using existing or not yet realised research output of an HEI. A massive problem in this context is the lack of professional marketing departments at most HEIs.

The object of the ability to implement new scientific and technological knowledge for application is to generate, develop and introduce innovations into the market co-operatively. For this, it is necessary to master all the processes for the initiation, implementation and termination of the innovation co-operation. In this context, there is a high need for the HEI to know the mechanisms (decision rules, powerful actors, etc.) for decisions for or against potential innovations.

The ability to create the conditions for the optimal configuration of the intra-institutional factors is characterised by the fact that an HEI must be able to create the internal prerequisites for the other abovementioned partial capacities of the innovativeness by providing an appropriate institutional configuration of the internal institutional factors. Therefore the HEI must permanently enhance, combine, protect and reconfigure the basis of knowledge and resources to meet current challenges. This is, for example, achieved through the implementation of project structures, the reorganisation of the administration or the implementation of innovation support methods.

Furthermore, the part capability concept is based on the assumption that nearly every HEI is able to produce knowledge exceedingly. However, this knowledge is often not checked for its practical applicability or for the possibilities of transferring it into applications. Only if an HEI is equipped with all part capabilities, a realised innovativeness can be adjudicated. Otherwise, it is only equipped with potential innovativeness.

Level of Effects

The innovativeness of an HEI can be reflected through various impact categories. It can be distinguished into the individual level (e.g. increasing experience of involved professors), the level of individual innovation projects (e.g. patents, licenses) and the level of institution (faculty/department, HEI). It is common in the German HEI system to measure the research and innovative power of an HEI by (exclusively) using the third-party funding as an indicator. Though, the measurement of third-party funding seems to be insufficient for this research. There is a need for a set of more widely spread indicators, like, for example, (contributions to) spin-offs because only through these the build-up of technology parks like Silicon Valley was possible. However, although patents, resulting publications, as well as additional experiences and insights of the researchers originating from the co-operations, are not considered to be "perfect", yet they still are the best possible indicators.

Figure 9.2 gives a holistic overview of the model of the innovativeness of HEIs.

METHODOLOGY AND DATA BASE

The above-described model of innovativeness is twice empirically examined in a two-step process following the case study approach of Yin (2009). First, an exploratory expert interview series was held. According to Yin, the exploratory interviews act as pilot studies which provide a deeper understanding of the context of the research objects as well as a sharpening of the theoretical concepts which must be elaborated upon. The pilot studies may be conducted in an orientation-oriented manner, but they must have thematic and constructive relevance to the later developed cases.

In the interviews professors of state universities and universities of applied sciences in the fields of engineering, natural sciences and economics were interviewed utilising semi-structured interview guides. In addition, interviews were conducted with employees of innovation support units and with a senior lecturer

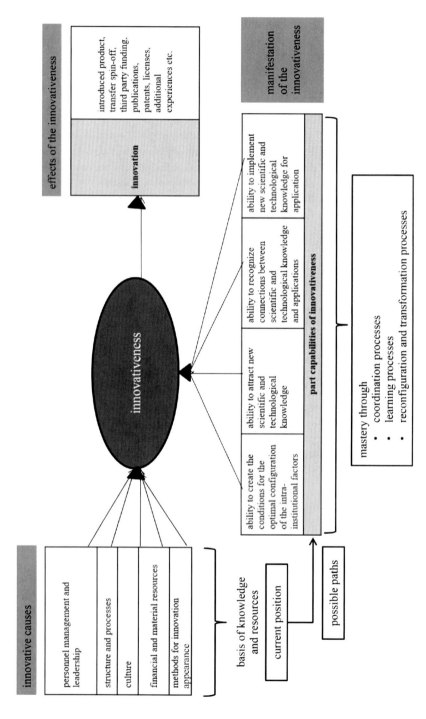

Figure 9.2. Model of the innovativeness of HEIs

at a non-European university, this senior lecturer previously worked as a post-doctoral researcher at a German university for several years. The interview with the Senior Lecturer focused on the discussion of the evaluation of research impact. The interviews usually had a duration of 60–90 minutes. The pilot studies worked with an n of 7. Due to the exploratory character, the resulting findings have limited representativeness.

The evaluation was carried out with the qualitative content analysis according to Mayring (2008) using MaxQDA 10.

In the following second step, the theory elaboration will take place using cross cases. In this context, professors from the fields mentioned above will be asked about the causes, the manifestation and the effects of the innovativeness at their respective HEIs. The selection of suitable cases has to be purpose directed so that each case has a contribution to the elaboration of the theory. The inclusion of supplementary documents (e.g. strategy and development plans) ensures the required data triangulation.

By using cross cases, better conclusions can be drawn to declare why innovation-friendly conditions, considering the individual willingness to innovate, do not lead to an increase in innovativeness.

RESULTS

In the following sections, selected interview results are presented subdivided according to the levels of causes, manifestation and effects.

Causes of Innovativeness

The expert interviews showed that all of the revised causes of innovation affect the innovativeness. This effect is expressed by various drives of innovation. Other cause factors could not be identified.

Personnel management and leadership. In German HEIs leadership cannot be established via the specification of expectations, coercion or control (also Hüther & Krücken, 2013). The interviews showed that, in accordance to French and Raven's, 1959 concept of the bases of social power, leadership has to be based on three kinds of power: identification (referent power), legitimation and reward.

In the interviews, the desire of identification was, for example, expressed by the fact that four interviewees wanted the executives (president/dean) to show the relevance of innovations within their daily actions. For example by taking part in important meetings for the initiation of innovations. Furthermore, four interviewees wished for an improvement of the frame conditions with the goal of linking innovation strategy, objective agreement and incentive system.

During the design of the (innovation) strategy, legitimate power must be utilised. The results of the interview showed evidence for the Thoenig and Paradeise (2016) hypothesis which states that the acceptance of a strategy depends on the extent of involvement of the affected units.

Reward power is needed during the design stage of the objective agreement and the incentive system. In this way, desired results, here the successful conclusion of a co-operative innovation (action result), should occur. An explanation is possible by using the expectancy theory by Vroom (1964). If a researcher should be motivated to strive for the action result "conclusion of a co-operative innovation", they must first be animated to the desired action" initiation of co-operative innovations". Whether this will be successful depends on several factors. First and foremost, it is essential for the researcher that they achieve desirable effects, such as the satisfaction of intrinsic motivation, an increase in reputation, material or immaterial rewards for their research or themselves (sequence of action), or a combination of the preceding. In this context, the valence must be taken into account, which expresses the subjective perception of the sequence of action. For example, a reward system considered inappropriate would only have a low valence.

Furthermore, it is essential to consider the instrumentality that expresses the subjective assessment of the probability that the action sequence is based on the action result. A co-operative innovation may not be undertaken because it does not help to satisfy the intrinsic motivation, the increase of reputation or the right rewards are not expected by the researcher.

Also, the expectation which expresses subjective assessment of the probability of reaching the action result based on the desired action must be considered. In this context, the action-result expectation, which is expressed by personal characteristics (e.g. the ability to initiate co-operative innovations) and the result-consequence-expectation (internal institutional framework) must be distinguished.

The expectancy theory, therefore, states that the motivation for the initiation of co-operative innovations (desired action) only arises when the sequence of actions has a high value, and it is assumed that the action result leads to the desired sequence of action and the desired action leads to the sequence of action. Figure 9.3 illustrates the use of the expectancy theory adjusted to HEIs.

For the interviewees, the intangible component of the incentive system is of prime importance. The effect of appreciation and public recognition is enormous. The (partial) exemption from other tasks or the granting of additional human resources also has a particular effect. Direct material incentives were considered least efficient in the interviews. These findings correspond to the results of other studies (e.g. Ringelhan et al., 2015).

All interviewees agreed that an incentive system could only have an effect if the researchers are already intrinsically motivated.

Furthermore, four interviewees mentioned problems in the context of the personnel development system (see also Krempkow, Sembritzki, Schürmann, & Winde, 2016; Briedis, Jaksztat, Schneider, Schwarzer, & Winde, 2013; Pellert & Widmann, 2008). An interviewee described the HEIs personnel development system

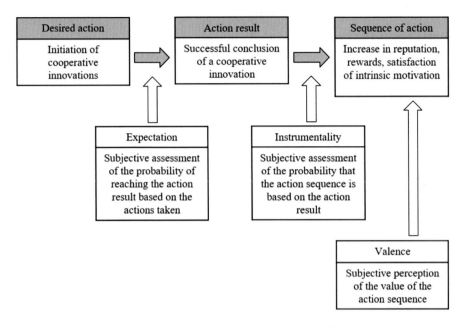

Figure 9.3. Expectancy theory adjusted for HEIs

as being in its infancy. Another explained that although there was an extensive personnel development system at the HEI, it was hardly known to anyone.

Structure and processes. While the influence of transversal (time-limited) organisational forms which superimpose the primary structure like collaborative research centres, industry on campus co-operations or individually aligned innovation co-operations (Reichert, Winde, & Meyer-Guckel, 2012) was considered significant the interviewees focused on the optimisation potentials in the context of implementation and coordination of the innovation supporting units like transfer agencies (critically Kloke & Krücken, 2012; Meier & Krücken, 2011).

As a success factor for the emergence of innovations, all interviewees emphasized the presence of flexible, unbureaucratic administration and support processes. Two interviewees said it would be useful if the state HEI would follow the example of private HEIs in this context. Concrete wishes were fast contract negotiations, extensive service times, clear representation rules, area-specific support and the one-face-to-the-customer principal.

Culture. All except one of the respondents felt that there was no distinctive culture of innovation in their HEI. Five interviewees, however, observed that there currently is a more or less significant change towards an innovation culture. They justified this observation in particular with the advent of young colleagues.

The interviewees, for example, missed the sustainable anchoring of innovations in the value system, e.g. through the implementation of an innovation strategy or the presence of pronounced economic ways of thinking and action (e.g. orientation to (innovation) outcomes and key financial figures).

Furthermore, based on the success factors of an innovation culture according to Auernhammer and Hall (2014) the interviewees also saw deficits in the following areas:

The opportunity to learn from innovation co-operations is, for example, limited through a scarcely present or non-existent error learning culture. An interviewee defined error learning culture in the way that in the case of a quality-conscious work execution, researchers should not have to fear a formal sanction by the leadership or committees (e.g. by not granting funds) for mistakes committed and it should also include the liberty to take moderate risks.

Co-operative working and communication behaviour is also often limited. Four interviewees criticised the limited exchange of researchers within the HEI, in particular across faculty boundaries, and saw little action taken by the rectors and deans as well as the administration to counter this. In this context, also the low exchange with external units was criticised. Kloke and Krücken (2012) found in this context that transfer agency employees often do not have sufficient economic contacts due to their professionally stringent positioning in the science system and therefore are only partially able to provide support.

Furthermore, the possibility of self-responsible action is sometimes limited if the research aims are defined in a too restrictive way. Two interviewees explicitly pointed out that they often pursue long-term research on the emergence of innovation, for which there is as yet no demand for entrepreneurial co-operation partners, since these often formulate their needs ad hoc and without a long-term strategic perspective. In HEIs, on the other hand, there is often a vision of the possible potential for innovation.

Financial and material resources. Thoenig and Paradeise (2016) already pointed out the need for sufficient resources for research projects. Two interviewees reported that inadequate equipment hinders their innovativeness. This may relate to inadequate research laboratory equipment or, for example, a lack of adequate premises or budget to receive the co-operation partners.

Furthermore, three interviewees argued that the amount of overhead costs make sure that they lose their competitiveness compared to other HEIs, research institutes or consulting companies.

Methods for innovation appearance. The interviews showed that a systematic application of methods that can support an innovation (e.g. roadmaps, innovation scorecards) rarely take place or only unconsciously. Right now mostly methods for planning, the analysis and monitoring of innovations, e.g. in the form of project management plans and process flows, have been implemented. Methods of controlling, documenting or assuring learning processes, e.g. lessons learned or other knowledge management systems, are only used to a limited extent.

Manifestation of Innovativeness

Furthermore, the need for a part capability concept of manifestation was examined. This too was temporarily confirmed by the preliminary results. The interview results showed a relevance of all part capabilities as well as numerous circumstances, which could lead to disruptions.[8]

The *ability to attract new scientific and technological knowledge* is first and foremost characterised by the fact that knowledge at HEIs, especially at universities, is often not gained with the focus on economic exploitation (also Nickel, 2011). Two interviewees indicated that disruptions could occur if an innovation co-operation ends without (scientifically) exploitable research results for the HEI. An interviewee from a university of applied sciences reported that they could not be part of the top-level international research because there was not enough money at their HEI to attend high-calibre conferences.

The interviews also showed a variety of disturbances concerning the *ability to recognise connections between scientific and technological knowledge and applications*. Four interviewees stated that they were actively seeking application potential for their (future) theoretical knowledge. However, they also stated that limits had to be taken into account. For example, an interviewee from the business informatics department at a university explained that in their research area there were independent theoretical and application-oriented research strands that would not typically be linked.

Furthermore, two interviewees pointed out that they do not have sufficient time to deal with application potentials and did not receive enough support from the executives, the administration or through other innovation-friendly structure elements.

Concerning the *ability to implement new scientific and technological knowledge for application* five interviewees initially perceived it as problematic that the expectations placed on co-operative innovations differ between HEIs and enterprises. While HEIs focus on expanding the scientific knowledge base and their reputation, enterprises want a fast market maturity and profits (also Jostmeier, 2013). An interviewee from a transfer unit pointed out that it sometimes requires extensive negotiation processes until the HEI is adequately involved (see also the remarks by Meier & Krücken, 2011). They also reported on cases in which a co-operation could not end successfully due to a disagreement over exploitation rights.

Furthermore, three interviewees expressed that the primary responsibility for the innovation co-operation process often lies with the HEI or that responsibilities were not adequately regulated or perceived.

The explanations of the causes of the innovativeness have already shown, how disturbances of the *ability to create the conditions for the optimal configuration of the intra-institutional factors* arise. This applies, for example, to bureaucratically oriented innovation support units or poorly configured incentive systems.

Effects of Innovativeness

Ultimately, it should be examined whether the effectiveness of innovation should be measured using a multidimensional concept. While the possibilities for the measurement of (socially relevant) innovation or research performance is currently given significant attention in the literature (e.g. Bell, Shaw, & Boaz, 2010; Bormann, 2014; Donovan, 2011; Göransson, Maharajh, & Schmoch, 2009; Mardis, Hoffmann, & McMartin, 2012; Toole, 2012) the interview results showed a lack of differentiated and evaluated concepts in the interviewees' HEIs. The interviewees particularly criticised the measuring indicators. Two interviewees complained that third-party funds are the only used indicator. Three interviewees mentioned a need for more indicators specific to the area of expertise.

In the development of appropriate indicators, German HEIs could make use of internationally proven models such as the Performance Based Research Fund (PBRF) utilised by New Zealand's universities and specify this for the innovation context. The PBRF has the advantage that the individual, project and institution levels are taken into account. In addition, a planned innovation-relevant performance can be rewarded even if it does not come to a successful conclusion. If unsuccessful innovation efforts are not rewarded by the incentive structures of the HEI, much of the efforts of the researchers remain unrewarded. In relation to the Expectancy theory of Vroom, this would often lead to no striving for co-operative innovations to occur. Furthermore, learning effects can also arise from unsuccessful innovations as long as the processes are subsequently analysed reflexively. Thus, there is a knowledge gain that can be valuable for the success of follow-up operations. Also, the networks that result from innovation efforts can lead to future innovations (see also Konen & Faix, 2017).

In this case, indicators of the research output (e.g. publications, applications, conference contributions, grey literature) and the research contribution (e.g. network activities, development of new disciplinary methods, assumption of management positions, development of new disciplinary methods, supervision of young scientists, commercialisation of research outputs) are differentiated. Thus, the willingness to generate innovations and the positive effects arising therefrom may be utilised to reward the researchers (Tertiary Education Commission, 2015).

If HEIs link the measurement level with the incentive system, they can achieve a motivational effect.

CONCLUSION

This contribution has shown that, due to the changed expectations from politics and society, German HEIs are becoming (e.g. third mission, changing finance structure, federal and state government initiatives) more and more of an actor in the economic competition and are thus expected to contribute their resources, knowledge and competencies to create co-operative innovations with enterprises. Thereby the HEIs are faced with the challenge to fulfil this additional task without neglecting their traditional tasks of basic research and teaching.

For that reason, this contribution's goal was to examine the innovativeness of HEIs about the co-operative development of innovations in co-operation with enterprises. For that purpose a model has been developed that analyses the innovativeness at the level of causes, manifestation and effects and thus offers a possibility for assessing and, if intended, improving the innovativeness.

The model must respond to the fact that HEIs are traditionally autonomous decentralised expert institutions. As a result, its members pursue multiple individualised goals, belong to different subcultures and have a shared affiliation between the HEI and the peers. Traditional top-down leadership is not possible because the autonomous members on the one hand often do not recognise the executives as authority to give directives and on the other hand, there is little reciprocal knowledge about strategies, objectives and the appropriate ways to achieve the objectives available. A model must both consider these specialities as well as set the framework conditions in such a way that the resulting potentials are used, and barriers are minimised.

On this basis, conclusions can be drawn which are subdivided into "Overarching Conclusions" and "Conclusions directly derived from the model".

Overarching Conclusions

1. The innovativeness of an HEI largely depends on the motivation of its members. Central management by the executives is only possible to a limited extent.
2. The executives can set framework conditions with a positive influence on the innovativeness if they are suitable to satisfy the professor's motivation. The framework conditions that have the most significant impact on the innovativeness vary from person to person. Right now not all HEIs are systematically guided by their executives. The emergence of innovations is often almost exclusively driven by the professors' intrinsic motivation and willingness to perform.
3. There is a difference between the framework conditions provided by the executives and the framework conditions perceived by the professors.

Conclusions Directly Derived from the Model

1. To manage the innovativeness of an HEI the three levels causes, manifestation and effects must be analysed and shaped by the executives.
2. The cause factors of innovativeness can be found in the areas personnel management and leadership, structure and processes, culture, financial and material resources and methods for innovation appearance. The professors mostly wish for the following aspects:

- Personnel management and leadership: The executives should lead by example and implement an incentive system, which on the one hand corresponds to the individuals' motivation and on the other hand, is linked to the innovation strategy, the objective agreement and personnel development system.
- Structure and processes: Although transverse units can support innovation, the primary focus of innovative structure and processes seems to lie within the quality of administrative support.
- Culture: Initially an innovation culture must have visibly anchored to the value of innovation and include factors like an error learning culture and an internal and external openness. A sufficient autonomy of the professors is of high importance for long-term innovativeness.
- Financial and material resources: While an adequate endowment with resources is prerequisite for the appearance of innovations the occurrence is determined by the overhead costs.
- Methods of innovation appearance: Some HEIs are right now hardly aware of the importance of methods.

3. The manifestation of innovativeness is realised through several part capabilities. Only the expression of all part capabilities leads to the emergence of innovations. Furthermore, the professors must not only be willing and able to generate future relevant knowledge and go into co-operations, but the HEI must also grant them free spaces and qualitative support services.
4. The measuring and rewarding of the impact can have a motivating effect on the professors if it is related to the incentive system and recognises as many achievements as possible in connection with the development of innovation.

NOTES

[1] Translated from German.
[2] Statistisches Bundesamt (2017c).
[3] One semester period is 45 minutes.
[4] Franz and Dümpler (2010).
[5] Statistisches Bundesamt (2017c).
[6] Statistisches Bundesamt (2017c).
[7] Statistisches Bundesamt (2017b).
[8] For a more detailed overview of the part capabilities of innovativeness see Konen (2017b).

REFERENCES

Aljets, E., & Lettkemann, E. (2012). Hochschulleitung und Forscher: Von wechselseitiger Nichtbeachtung zu wechselseitiger Abhängigkeit. In U. Wilkesmann & C. Schmid (Eds.), *Hochschule als Organisation* (pp. 131–153). Wiesbaden: Springer.

Auernhammer, J., & Hall, H. (2014). Organizational culture in knowledge creation, creativity and innovation: Towards the freiraum model. *Journal of Information Science, 40*(2), 154–166.

Bell, S., Shaw, B., & Boaz, A. (2011). Real-world approaches to assessing the impact of environmental research on policy. *Research Evaluation, 20*(3), 227–237.

Bornmann, L. (2013). What is societal impact of research and how can it be assessed? A literature survey. *Journal of the American Society for Information Science and Technology, 64*(2), 217–233.
Briedis, K., Jaksztat, S., Schneider, J., Schwarzer, A., & Winde, M. (2013). *Personalentwicklung für den wissenschaftlichen Nachwuchs. Bedarf, Angebote und Perspektiven – eine empirische Bestandsaufnahme.* Retrieved from http://www.dzhw.eu/pdf/22/projektbericht_personalentwicklung.pdf
Bundesministerium für Bildung und Forschung. (Ed.). (2016). *Innovative Hochschule: Eine Förderinitiative von Bund und Ländern.* Retrieved from https://www.bmbf.de/pub/Innovative_Hochschule.pdf
Buschle, N., & Haider, C. (2016). Private Hochschulen in Deutschland. *WISTA* 1/2016. Retrieved from https://www.destatis.de/DE/Publikationen/WirtschaftStatistik/2016/01/PrivateHochschulenDeutschland_012016.pdf?__blob=publicationFile
Donovan, C. (2011). State of the art in assessing research impact: Introduction to a special issue. *Research Evaluation, 20*(3), 175–179.
Ernst, H. (2002). Success factors of a new product development: A review of the empirical literature. *International Journal of Management Reviews, 4*(1), 1–40.
Etzkowitz, H. (2008). *The triple helix: University-Industry-government innovation in action.* New York, NY: Routledge.
Faix, A. (2017). *Befähigung zur Innovation: Grundlagen und Ergebnisse des Projekts „Enabling Innovation" als Ansatz zur Stärkung der Innovationsfähigkeit außeruniversitärer Forschungseinrichtungen.* Frankfurt am Main: Peter Lang.
Franz, A., & Dümpler, D. (2010). *Übersicht der Lehrverpflichtungsverordnungen der Bundesländer – Lehrverpflichtung der Professoren und Juniorprofessoren.* Institut für hochschulforschung an der martin-luther-universität Halle-Wittenberg (HoF). Retrieved from http://www.hof.uni-halle.de/daten/lvv_gesetze_2/lvv_profs.pdf
French, J. R. P. Jr., & Raven, B. (1959). The bases of social power. In D. Cartwright (Ed.), *Studies in social power* (pp. 259–269). Michigan: Research Center for Group Dynamics, Institute for Social Research, University of Michigan.
Gesetz über die Hochschulen des Landes Nordrhein-Westfalen (edition 01.11.2017). Retrieved from https://recht.nrw.de/lmi/owa/br_bes_detail?sg=0&menu=1&bes_id=28364&anw_nr=2&aufgehoben=N&det_id=385551
Göransson, B., Maharajh, R., & Schmoch, U. (2009). New activities of universities in transfer and extension: Multiple requirements and manifold solutions. *Science and Public Policy, 36*(2), 157–164.
Henke, J., Pasternack, P. & Schmid, S. (2015). Viele Stimmen, kein Kanon. Konzept und Kommunikation der Third Mission von Hochschulen. Institut für Hochschulforschung (HoF) (Ed.). *HoF-Arbeitsberichte* (no. 2/15). Retrieved from http://www.hof.uni-halle.de/web/dateien/pdf/01_AB_Third-Mission-Berichterstattung.pdf
Hochschulrahmengesetz. (Ed.). (23.05.2017). Retrieved from https://www.gesetze-im-internet.de/hrg/HRG.pdf
Hüther, O., & Krücken, G. (2013). Hierarchy and power: a conceptual analysis with particular reference to new public management reforms in German universities. *European Journal of Higher Education, 3*(4), 307–323.
Johne, A. F., & Snelson, P. A. (1988). Success factors in product innovation: A selective review of the literature. *Journal of Product Innovation Management, 5*(2), 114–128.
Jostmeier, M. (2013). Transdisziplinäre Forschung als Kooperation heterogener Akteure – Divergierende Handlungslogiken und Integrationsansätze. In S. Jeschke, F. Hees, & A. Richert (Eds.), *Innovationsfähigkeit und neue Wege des Wissenstransfers: Expertisen aus dem IMO-Aktionsfeld Transfer"* (pp. 11–42). Aachen: RWTH aachen university – department of information management in mech. engineering. Retrieved from http://www.internationalmonitoring.de/fileadmin/Downloads/Trendstudien/Trends_V2/imo_innovationsfaehigkeit_expertisen_transfer_jeschke_hees_richert_2013.pdf
Keller, A. (2016). *Promotionsrecht für Fachhochschulen und Promotionszugang von Fachhochschulabsolventen und Fachhochschulabsolventinnen in der Bundesrepublik Deutschland.* Hochschule für Technik und Wirtschaft Berlin (Ed.). Retrieved from https://www.htwberlin.de/fileadmin/HTW/Zentral/HSL_Promotion/Synopse_Promotionsrecht_Fachhochschulen.pdf

Kloke, K., & Krücken, G. (2010). Grenzstellenmanager zwischen Wissenschaft und Wirtschaft? Eine Studie zu Mitarbeiterinnen und Mitarbeitern in Einrichtungen des Technologietransfers und der wissenschaftlichen Weiterbildung. *Beiträge zur Hochschulforschung, 32*(3), 32–52.

Konen, C., & Faix, A. (2017). Innovationsfähigkeit von hochschulen: Einflüsse auf die entwiclung von innovationen in kooperationen mit unternehmen. *Hochschulmanagement, 12*(2+3), 69–78.

Konen, C. (2017a). Innovationsfähigkeit von Hochschulen: Voraussetzungen für das Entstehen von Innovationen in Innovationskooperationen mit Unternehmen – Ergebnisse einer explorativen Experteninterviewreihe. *Beiträge zur Hochschulforschung, 39*(3+4), 134–153.

Konen, C. (2017b). Innovationsfähigkeit von Hochschulen: Ansatzpunkte zur Bewältigung einer neuen Herausforderung für die Institution Hochschule. In J. —P. Büchler & A. Faix (Eds.), *Markt- und Innovationsmanagement: Innovationsstrategien – Grundlagen, Gestaltungsansätze und Handlungsbedingungen* (In print).

Kosmützky, A., & Borggräfe, M. (2012). Zeitgenössische Hochschulreform und unternehmerischer Aktivitätsmodus. In U. Wilkesmann & C. J. Schmid (Eds.), *Hochschule als organisation* (pp. 69–85). Wiesbaden: Springer.

Krempkow, R., Sembritzki, T., Schürmann, R., & Winde, M. (2016). *Personalentwicklung für den wissenschaftlichen Nachwuchs. Bedarf, Angebote und Perspektiven – eine empirische Bestandsaufnahme im Zeitvergleich*. Retrieved from http://www.dzhw.eu/pdf/22/personalentwicklung-fuer-den-wissenschaftlichen-nachwuchs_web.pdf

Krücken, G., Blümel, A., & Kloke, K. (2012). Wissen schafft Management? Konturen der Manageralisierung im Hochschulbereich. In T. Heinze & G. Krücken (Eds.), *Institutionelle Erneuerungsfähigkeit der Forschung* (pp. 219–256). Wiesbaden: VS Verlag für Sozialwissenschaften.

Krücken, G., & Meier, A. (2006). Turning the university into an organizational actor. In G. Drori, J. W. Meyer, & H. Hwang (Eds.), *Globalization and organization: World society and organizational change* (pp. 241–257). Oxford: Oxford University Press.

Lawson, B., & Samson, D. (2001). Developing innovation capability in organisations: A Dynamic capabilities approach. *International Journal of Innovation Management, 5*(3), 377–400.

Mardis, M. A., Hoffman, E. S., & McMartin, F. P. (2012). Toward broader impacts: Making sense of NSF's merit review criteria in the context of the National science digital library. *Journal of the American Society for Information Science and Technology, 63*(9), 1758–1772.

Mayring, P. (2008). *Qualitative Inhaltsanalyse: Grundlagen und Techniken*. Weinheim & Basel: Beltz.

Meier, F. (2009). *Die Universität als Akteur: Zum institutionellen Wandel der Hochschulorganisation*. Wiesbaden: VS Verlag für Sozialwissenschaften.

Meier, F., & Krücken, G. (2011). Wissens- und technologietransfer als neues leitbild? Universitäts-wirtschafts-beziehungen in deutschland. In B. Hölscher & J. Suchanek (Eds.), *Wissenschaft und Hochschulbildung im Kontext von Wirtschaft und Medien* (pp. 91–110). Wiesbaden: VS Verlag für Sozialwissenschaften.

Nickel, S. (2011). Governance als institutionelle Aufgabe von Universitäten oder Fachhochschulen. In T. Brüsemeister & M. Heinrich (Eds.), *Autonomie und Verantwortung. Governance in Schule und Hochschule*. Retrieved from http://www.che.de/downloads/Governance_als_institutionelle_Aufgabe_von_Universitaeten_und_Fachhochschulen.pdf

Paradeise, C., & Thoenig, J. -P. (2013). Academic institutions in search of quality: Local orders and global standards. *Organization Studies, Sage Publications, 34*(2), 189–218.

Pasternack, P. (2007, October–December, 3–6). Hochschulen als wirtschaftsunternehmen. *vhw–*.

Pellert, A., & Widmann, A. (2008). *Personalmanagement in Hochschule und Wissenschaft*. Münster & New York, NY: München & Berlin, Waxmann.

Reichert, S., Winde, M., & Meyer-Guckel, V. (2012). *Jenseits der Fakultäten: Hochschuldifferenzierung durch neue Organisationseinheiten für Forschung und Lehre*. Retrieved from https://www.stifterverband.org/content/jenseits-der-fakult%C3%A4ten

Ringelhan, S., Wollersheim, J., & Welpe, I. M. (2015). Performance management and incentive systems in research organizations: Effects, limits and opportunities. In I. M. Welpe, J. Wollersheim, S. Ringelhan, & M. Osterloh (Eds.), *Incentives and performance: Governance of research organizations* (pp. 83–103). München: Springer.

Roessler, I., Duong, S., & Hachmeister, C. -D. (2015). *Welche Missionen haben Hochschulen? Third Mission als Leistung der Fachhochschulen für die und mit der Gesellschaft* (Arbeitspapier Nr. 182). CHE Centrum für Hochschulentwicklung (Ed.). Retrieved from https://www.che.de/downloads/CHE_AP_182_Third_Mission_an_Fachhochschulen.pdf

Schneidewind, U. (2016). Die „Third Mission" zur „First Mission" machen? *die Hochschule, 25*(1), 14–22.

Smith, M., Busi, M., Ball, P., & Van der Meer, P. (2008). Factors Influencing on organisations ability to manage innovation: A structured literature review and conceptual model. *International Journal of Innovation Management, 12*(4), 655–676.

Statista. (2017). *Anzahl der Hochschulen in Deutschland im Wintersemester 2016/2017 nach Hochschulart*. Retrieved from https://de.statista.com/statistik/daten/studie/247238/umfrage/hochschulen-in-deutschland-nach-hochschulart/

Statistisches Bundesamt. (2007). *Bildung und Kultur: Finanzen der Hochschulen 2005*. Retrieved from https://www.destatis.de/GPStatistik/servlets/MCRFileNodeServlet/DEHeft_derivate_00006889/2110450057004.pdf

Statistisches Bundesamt. (2017a). *Bildung und Kultur: Finanzen der Hochschulen 2015*. Retrieved from https://www.destatis.de/DE/Publikationen/Thematisch/BildungForschungKultur/BildungKulturFinanzen/FinanzenHochschulen2110450157004.pdf?__blob=publicationFile

Statistisches Bundesamt. (2017b). *Bildung und Kultur: Studierende an Hochschulen, Wintersemster 2016/17*. Retrieved from https://www.destatis.de/DE/Publikationen/Thematisch/BildungForschungKultur/Hochschulen/StudierendeHochschulenEndg2110410177004.pdf?__blob=publicationFile

Statistisches Bundesamt. (2017c). *Bildung und Kultur: Personal an Hochschulen 2016*. Retrieved from https://www.destatis.de/DE/Publikationen/Thematisch/BildungForschungKultur/Hochschulen/PersonalHochschulen2110440167004.pdf?__blob=publicationFile

Stern, T., & Jaberg, H. (2010). *Erfolgreiches Innovationsmanagement: Erfolgsfaktoren, Grundmuster, Fallbeispiele* (4th ed.). Wiesbaden: Gabler.

Stifterverband. (Ed.). (2014). *Wie Hochschulen mit Unternehmen kooperieren: Lage und Entwicklung der Hochschulen aus Sicht ihrer Leitungen 2013*. Retrieved from https://www.stifterverband.org/download/file/fid/544

Teece, D. J. (2007). Explicating dynamic capabilities: The nature and microfoundations of (sustainable) enterprise performance. *Strategic Management Journal, 28*(13), 1319–1350.

Teece, D. J., Pisano, G., & Shuen, A. (1997). Dynamic capabilities and strategic management. *Strategic Management Journal, 18*(7), 509–533.

Tertiary Education Commission. (Ed.). (2016). *Performance-based research fund: Guidelines for the 2018 quality evaluation assessment process*. Retrieved from http://www.tec.govt.nz/assets/Forms-templates-and-guides/PBRF-assessment-guide.pdf

Thoenig J. -C., & Paradeise, C. (2016). Strategic capacity and organizational capability: A challenge for universities, *Minerva, 54*, 293–324.

Toole, A. A. (2012). The impact of public basic research on industrial innovation: Evidence from the pharmaceutical industry. *Research Policy, 41*(1), 1–12.

Vega, R. B., & Krücken, G. (2014). Hochschulführung und die dritte Mission: Herausforderungen an akademische Führungskräfte in der unternehmerischen Hochschule. In T. Kliewe & T. Kesting (Eds.), *Moderne Konzepte des organisationalen Marketings* (pp. 127–144). Wiesbaden: Gabler.

Vroom, V. H. (1964). *Work and motivation*. New York, NY: John Wiley & Sons.

Wagner, K., Slama, A., Rogowski, T., & Bannert, M. (2007). *Fit für Innovationen: Untersuchung von Erfolgsfaktoren und Indikatoren zur Steigerung der Innovationsfähigkeit anhand von sechs innovativen Fallbeispielen produzierender KMU*. Stuttgart: Fraunhofer IAO.

Yin, R. K. (2009). *Case study research: design and methods* (4th ed.). Los Angeles, CA: Sage Publications.

MARIA J. MANATOS, SÓNIA CARDOSO, MARIA J. ROSA
AND TERESA CARVALHO

10. INTERNAL QUALITY ASSURANCE

A Political Process Challenging Academics' Professionalism?

INTRODUCTION

Concerns with quality in higher education are not new, however it has been mainly since the late 1980s that they have become more visible and relevant for higher education institutions (HEIs), the government and society as a whole, at least at the European level. The demands for economic efficiency given resource constraints, the increasing role of market regulation, the erosion of trust in institutions associated with managerialism and the new public management, and the massification of higher education led to the need for HEIs to justify the expenditure of public funds and to demonstrate value for money (Deem, 1998; Massy, 2003; Rosa & Amaral, 2007). Similarly "academics are encouraged 'to do more with less' and be more accountable for scarce resources" (Becket & Brookes, 2008, p. 46). Pressures come from both outside and inside institutions. Externally the pressures are exerted by funding bodies and external quality assurance (QA) agencies. Internally, the pressures on academics and non-academic staff are exerted by institutional managers and administrators (Deem, 1998).

After the Bologna Declaration (1999) and the first conferences of European ministers responsible for higher education (Bergen Communiqué, 2005; Berlin Communiqué, 2003; Prague Communiqué, 2001), standards and guidelines for external and internal QA – the Standards and Guidelines for Quality Assurance in the European Higher Education Area (ESG) – were drafted in order to be developed and implemented nationally and institutionally (ENQA, 2015). At a national level, supra-institutional QA schemes have been developed and implemented, once QA agencies started to require them, and accreditation has arisen as a mechanism par excellence for the assessment and assurance of higher education quality (Westerheijden, Hulpiaub, & Waeytens, 2007).

More recently, the emphasis has been put on the development by institutions of internal QA systems (or on the formalisation of the existing internal QA practices) and on ensuring that both the accreditation of the study programmes and the certification of the internal QA systems is achieved (Westerheijden et al., 2007). Moreover, there has been a focus on quality enhancement, giving the responsibility for their quality back to HEIs, as well as other QA procedures less focused on accreditation, such as institutional evaluation.

The increasing establishment of the logic of accountability and of the QA idea in HEIs has led to different degrees of acceptance and support by academics, which largely depend on how they perceive QA in higher education (Cardoso, Rosa, & Santos, 2013; Newton, 2002; Westerheijden et al., 2007).

Academics' resistance to quality seems to be mostly linked with perceptions of it and its assurance as: compliance with requirements as priority and enhancement as secondary (Newton, 2002); an "administrative and cost burden" (Laughton, 2003, p. 309); a culture of getting by where front-line academics, constrained by lack of time, deal with confusing demands (Newton, 2002); a "manifestation of managerialist control" (Harvey, 2006, p. 290), monitoring and controlling the academic work and weakening the academic autonomy; a philosophy that is in "contradiction to the core values of academic culture, and ultimately as a subversion of academic identity" (Laughton, 2003, p. 318); reductionist and incapable of grasping the essence of the educational process and not entirely reliable (Cardoso et al., 2013; Laughton, 2003); emphasising processes rather than outcomes, which seems to be related to a gap between rhetoric and reality regarding QA (Lomas, 2007).

QA seems to somehow fail in matching its more inherent purposes with its practical undesirable implications, which tend to stress its political and more controversial nature. Thus, QA can be seen as a political process of surveillance and regulation of academics and, to this extent, able to challenge the academic profession by subverting the academic identity and work and weakening academic autonomy (Carvalho & Santiago, 2015; Laughton, 2003; Morley, 2003; Newton, 2002; Worthington & Hodgson, 2005).

Subsequently, the general research question leading the study is: to what extent is internal QA being perceived by academics as a political process and, as such, able to challenge their professionalism? The aim is to understand 'how' political are academics perceiving internal QA drivers, cultures and effects, and whether academics' perceptions differ according to some of their characteristics. Moreover, the study intends to understand whether a greater political perception of internal QA is related with a greater perception of a challenge to academic autonomy and professionalism.

QUALITY ASSURANCE IN HIGHER EDUCATION: AN INHERENT POLITICAL PROCESS

QA processes can be seen on a continuum in regard to the relative prominence of political dimensions, meaning that the political extension of QA may vary from almost non-existent to extremely present (Skolnik, 2010).

QA as a political process is mostly coupled with the power relationships in academia in relation to the prevalent notion and processes of QA (Morley, 2003; Skolnik, 2010).

Usually QA processes follow a top-down implementation, implying that academics in top institutional positions play a more important role in this implementation than those at the bottom institutional positions (Salter & Tapper, 2000). This power 'differential' is often reflected in divergences between institutions' management and academic staff over the notion of quality and its assurance, which may contribute to academics resistance to QA and to their perception of it as a philosophy that subverts academic identity, controls academics' work and weakens academic autonomy (Anderson, 2006; Cheng, 2010; Laughton, 2003; Newton, 2002; Skolnik, 2010).

Academics indeed tend to perceive QA as an essentially managerial tool that influences professional autonomy (Hoecht, 2006; Newton, 2002) and makes them feel that they are "less trusted and more controlled" (Hoecht, 2006, p. 556). Therefore, academics' acceptance of QA activities depends, to a great extent, on the level of control they have over it and on the level of academic autonomy QA enables. "Academics in general see self-evaluation and QA as means to administer their everyday life as long as academics' autonomy to their own work is cherished and controlling mechanisms are avoided" (Huusko & Ursin, 2010, p. 868).

In this sense, QA can exercise its power by challenging academic professionalism, either by clashing with the professional values and the ethics of the academic profession, subverting them to a logic of institutional performance, or by changing the power relations in academia, as academic work is assessed and controlled by imposed bureaucratic processes and not by peers.

According to Freidson (1988, p. 72) "professions are deliberately granted autonomy, including the exclusive right to determine who can legitimately do its work and how the work should be done". Only the profession has the recognised right to evaluate the work of professionals and consequently "outside" evaluation is "illegitimate and intolerable". Hence, the "normative" and the "evaluative" dimension seem to constitute, in the words of Larson (1977, p. x), two of the three dimensions of the ideal-type of profession, which lacks a simple and easy definition (Nelson, 1991). While the normative dimension covers the service orientation and ethics of professionals, which justifies the privilege of self-regulation, the evaluative dimension underscores the autonomy and prestige of the profession. Despite the inexistence of clear boundaries of professionalism, the distinctiveness of the professions appears to be found on the combination of the "normative", the "evaluative" and also the "cognitive" and knowledge based dimension of professions (Larson, 1977).

It is argued that academics are being "deprofessionalised" and "proletarianised" by bureaucratic institutions, which are influencing the privilege of self-regulation and the autonomy of academic professionals by increasingly monitoring and regulating their work through QA activities and academic audit (Ball, 2016; Collyer, 2015; Farrugia, 1996; Hoecht, 2006; Joseph & Burnaford, 1994). Therefore, the ethos of "traditional professionalism" seems to no longer be trusted "to deliver what is required, increasing profitability and international competitiveness" (Hanlon, 1998, p. 52) and appears to have been replaced by a "new commercialised professionalism" which is driven by "a commercial rather than a technical logic" (Hanlon, 1998, p. 54). Nevertheless, academics still associate academic autonomy and freedom as one of the core values of their profession (Carvalho & Santiago, 2010, 2015).

Despite the arguments highlighting the damaging, controlling nature of QA and the erosion of academic professionalism, there are also arguments suggesting that the introduction of QA in HEIs is accompanied by a legitimising discourse referring to the principles of accountability, transparency and good service which may not only be used to disguise the controlling nature of the quality regime. The question is whether QA can provide the required accountability and transparency (Hoecht, 2006).

Farrugia (1996) also presents two arguments which bring into question an actual loss of academic autonomy. First, although academics are employed by bureaucratic institutions, and although their work may be greatly influenced and evaluated by bureaucratic processes and not by peers, university culture still values individual autonomy. Second, even when the autonomy is influenced, other valuable professional characteristics are not necessarily lost, since when adopted with the "right intentions", QA can only reinforce the professional standing of competent academics (Farrugia, 1996).

What the literature seems to show is that there is an unbalance and a mismatch between, on the one hand, these "right intentions" of QA and the desirable transparent QA process in place in the majority of the HEIs and, on the other hand, its practical consequences and implications, namely for academic professionalism.

QUALITY ASSURANCE IN PORTUGAL

The new public management and the new managerialism context boosted the deep process of change of QA in Portuguese higher education. In the mid-1990s concerns with quality led to the emergence of a QA system, mostly controlled by HEIs and based on a quality improvement perspective.

However, it was only in 2007 that QA in Portuguese higher education witnessed substantive developments, setting up the conditions, structures and organisation of a more rigorous system of evaluation for higher education, complying with the European exigencies, namely the ESG (Rosa & Sarrico, 2012). Those developments comprise: the legal regulations for degrees and diplomas and the establishment of the general principles of accreditation for HEIs and their study programmes (Decree-Law 74/2006); a new legal framework for all HEIs (Law 62/2007, known by RJIES); the new legal regulations for the quality assessment in higher education, establishing a new QA system (Law 38/2007); and the creation of the Agency for Assessment and Accreditation of Higher Education – A3ES, as the coordination structure of the QA system (Decree-Law 369/2007).

A3ES has started by assessing and accrediting the study programmes and, in a second stage, greatly influenced by the European developments, it has initiated the audit and certification of the internal QA systems. The aim was to support

INTERNAL QUALITY ASSURANCE

"the implementation of internal QA systems in institutions" while upholding "the principle that the institutions must play a fundamental role in the reorganization, improvement and rationalization of their offer of study programmes" (A3ES, 2009, p. 3), since the first responsibility for QA lies with the institutions themselves, as outlined by the ESG (ENQA, 2009).

It is in this context that Portuguese HEIs have started to develop and to implement their internal QA systems, influenced by the guidelines provided by A3ES, which, in their turn, are based on the ESG (ENQA, 2015) and on three additional standards, related to research and development, external relations, and internationalisation (Santos, 2011).

A3ES has been promoting the development of internal systems and their certification, not only by providing the necessary guidelines, but also by pledging "to implement simplified accreditation procedures for those institutions that promote the implementation of internal systems and have performance indicators well above the minimum requirements" (A3ES, 2010, p. 7). Some HEIs have already seen their internal QA systems certified by A3ES and others are preparing for the certification, expecting a lighter touch assessment of their study programmes (Rosa & Amaral, 2014).

METHODOLOGY

The study resorts to the analysis of data from a survey with academics from all Portuguese HEIs. The survey was part of a broader research project, which has studied the changes occurring in recent years in Portuguese HEIs over a comprehensive set of dimensions – internal QA, professionals, performance management and governance – and has aimed to understand the Portuguese academics' perceptions on these changes. The data was gathered through an online survey distributed in the academic year 2014/2015, with a return of 1661 valid answers. The majority of the academics who answered the survey are male, from the public higher education sector, equally distributed among the university and the polytechnic subsystems and mainly without tenure. Furthermore, the majority of the academics have already performed managerial roles, although their involvement in decision making processes is rather low (see Table 10.1).

For this particular research, only the questions related to academics' perceptions about both internal QA – main drivers, culture promoted by its implementation, and its effects – and academic autonomy and professionalism were analysed. The aim was to understand whether the way academics perceive the drivers for the implementation of QA practices, the cultures promoted by it and its effects denotes a view of internal QA as a more or less political process. Furthermore, the research intended to understand to what extent there is a correlation between academics' views on internal QA as a political process and the way they perceive the current autonomy and professionalism of their careers.

Concerning the drivers for QA, the academics were asked about *the importance of different factors for the development of internal QA practices in their institutions*,

Table 10.1. Sample's characterisation

		N	% (valid answers)
Gender	Male	850	53,4
	Female	742	46,4
	Total	1592	100
Sector	Public	1246	77,5
	Private	361	22,5
	Total	1607	100
Subsystem	University	807	50,2
	Polytechnic	800	49,8
	Total	1607	100
Managerial roles	With	859	53,1
	Without	758	46,9
	Total	1617	100
Tenure/Non-tenure	Tenure	298	20,4
	Non-tenure	1165	79,6
	Total	1463	100
Involvement in decision making	Low	884	54,2
	Medium	540	33,1
	High	207	12,7
Total		1631	100

which they rated on a five-point 'Likert' scale (1 – None; 2 – Few; 3 – Medium; 4 – Great; 5 – Extreme).

With regard to the culture promoted by internal QA, academics were asked *what the consequences of the implementation of internal QA practices were, with respect to the culture which is being promoted*, and they had to rate those consequences on a five-point 'Likert' scale (1 – Nothing; 2 – Few; 3 – Medium; 4 – Great; 5 – Extreme).

As far as the effects of QA are concerned, academics were asked to rate on a five-point 'Likert' scale (1 – Strongly disagree; 2 – Disagree; 3 – Neither agree nor disagree; 4 – Agree; 5 – Strongly agree) their agreement with *statements related with the effects of the implementation of internal QA practices.*

Finally, regarding academic autonomy and professionalism, academics were asked to rate on a five-point 'Likert' scale (1 – Strongly disagree; 2 – Disagree; 3 – Neither agree nor disagree; 4 – Agree; 5 – Strongly agree) their agreement with *different statements associated with their academic work*, reflecting different levels of autonomy and professionalism.

Data was statistically analysed resorting in a first phase to descriptive statistics, with the goal of uncovering how far academics perceive internal QA as a more or less political process (taking into account the questions concerning QA drivers, culture and effects) able to challenge their autonomy and professionalism. Then, non-parametric hypothesis tests (Mann-Whitney and Kruskal-Wallis tests for a 0.05 significant level) were run in order to understand whether there were differences according to the characterisation variables thought to challenge academics perceptions on QA: gender, sector (private or public), subsystem (university or polytechnic), tenure/non-tenure, performance of managerial roles (yes/no) and involvement in decision making processes (low/medium/high). Finally, a non-parametric correlations analysis was conducted (Spearman Correlation Coefficients) to understand whether there was a correlation between academics' perceptions of internal QA drivers, cultures and effects on the one hand, and autonomy and professionalism on the other hand. The aim was to find out if a greater political view of internal QA correlates with a view of academic autonomy and professionalism as being influenced.

RESULTS

Academics Perceptions on Internal QA Drivers, Culture and Effects: How Political Are They?

When considering the drivers for the creation or edification of internal QA practices (Figure 10.1) and the quality culture promoted by them (Figure 10.2), academics highlight the importance of the legal requirements and demands from A3ES

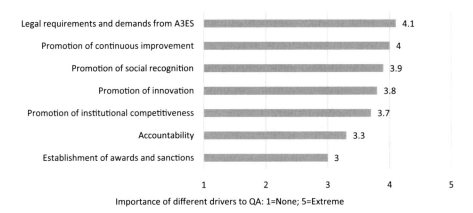

Figure 10.1. Perceptions of academics regarding the drivers for the creation or edification of internal QA practices

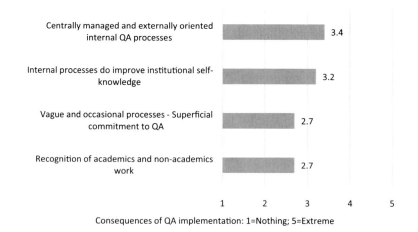

Figure 10.2. Perceptions of academics regarding the cultures promoted by internal QA

(mean score of 4.1) and the institutions' continuous quality improvement as very important drivers (mean score of 4.0), while considering that the establishment of a system of rewards and penalties was not such a relevant driver (mean score of 3.0). Furthermore, academics consider that the QA practices implemented do not contribute to promoting appraisal systems that take into account the individual performance of academics and non-academics (mean score of 2.7), but rather to develop internal processes to improve self-knowledge and self-reflection in the institution (mean score of 3.4).

In general, while some drivers for the implementation of internal QA evidence internal QA as a political process more than others, the cultures being promoted by it do not seem to highly evidence the political nature of QA.

When questioned about the effects of QA practices (Figure 10.3), academics tend to agree with statements that reflect the idea of QA as inducing greater monitoring of academic work (average score of 3.7) as well as a higher tension between management and academics (average score of 3.3). Moreover, they highlight the formalisation of procedures (average score of 4.2) and the time-consuming non-academic activities where QA is included (average score of 4.0). Hence, the implications of the implementation of internal QA seem to highlight a greater political dimension of QA and reveal, to some extent, the rise of practices clashing with academics' values as professionals, since they are not interpreted as improving the monitoring of internal processes, but instead, as an instrument of control over academics' work, as the literature has shown (Laughton, 2003; Lomas, 2007; Newton, 2002). This seems to contrast with a lower political nature of QA purposes, which seems to be in line with the argument of Farrugia (1996) concerning the "right intentions" of QA.

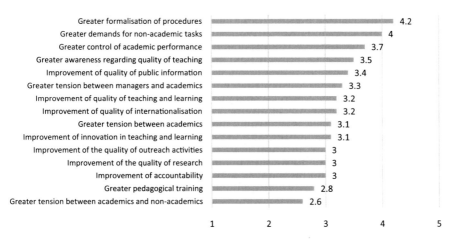

Figure 10.3. Academics' perceptions regarding internal QA effects

Different Academics, Different Perceptions?

In order to understand if there are differences between different groups of academics concerning the way they perceive internal QA as a political process, non-parametric hypothesis tests were run. The results obtained show that there are indeed differences in academics' answers regarding internal QA drivers, cultures promoted and its effects, which are in line with previous studies (Cardoso, Rosa, & Santos, 2013; Manatos, Sarrico, & Rosa, 2015; Stensaker, Langfeldt, Harvey, Huisman, & Westerheijden, 2011; Tavares, Sin, Videira, & Amaral, 2016).

Gender has a significant effect on academics' perceptions of the drivers and effects of QA and of the cultures promoted by it (Table 10.2). In general, findings show that women tend to agree more with the different statements whether they indicate a more or a less political extension of internal QA.

The university sector (private or public) also results in differences in academics' perceptions (Table 10.3). Overall, academics from the private sector tend to agree more with the items under analysis, except for the case of those reflecting a greater political view of QA. This view tends to collect higher agreement from the public sector academics (mean scores higher for the following items: *vague and occasional processes – superficial commitment to QA; greater tension between academics and non-academics; greater tension between academics; greater tension between managers and academics*).

The higher education subsystem (university or polytechnic) does not account for any significant differences in academics' responses (results of Mann-Whitney tests for a significant level of 0.05).

Table 10.2. Academics' perceptions of internal QA according to gender (results of Mann-Whitney tests)

Gender	Male		Female		p-value
	Mean	Median	Mean	Median	
Drivers for the creation or edification of internal quality assurance practices					
Promotion of institutional competitiveness	3.58	4.00	3.73	4.00	.017
Promotion of innovation	3.65	4.00	4.00	4.00	.000
Promotion of social recognition	3.71	4.00	3.99	4.00	.000
Promotion of continuous improvement	3.92	4.00	4.16	4.00	.000
Legal requirements and demands from A3ES	4.04	4.00	4.17	4.00	.010
Culture promoted by quality assurance practices					
Vague and occasional processes – Superficial commitment to QA	2.74	3.00	2.59	2.00	.018
Centrally managed and externally oriented internal QA processes	3.36	3.00	3.50	4.00	.015
Quality assurance effects					
Improvement of the quality of outreach activities	2.96	3.00	2.98	3.00	.016
Greater awareness regarding quality of teaching	3.46	4.00	3.60	4.00	.013
Improvement of the quality of public information	3.30	4.00	3.42	4.00	.045
Greater demands for non-academic tasks	3.87	4.00	4.04	4.00	.000
Greater formalisation of procedures	4.06	4.00	4.30	4.00	.000

The performance of management functions was only significant in explaining differences concerning three QA effects (Table 10.4). Academics performing management functions tend to agree more with the *formalisation of procedures* and with the *demands to perform non-academic tasks*, which seems to indicate that these academics recognise a political dimension in internal QA.

The dichotomy of tenure/non-tenure was also only relevant in explaining differences in the perceptions of internal QA regarding two of its effects (Table 10.5). Academics with tenure positions tend to agree more with statements stressing that QA drives to greater demands for non-academic tasks and to greater formalisation of procedures, which indicate the political character of QA.

The performance of management functions and the tenure status only challenge academics' perceptions on internal QA marginally. On the contrary, the involvement in decision making processes seems to explain a significant number of differences in

Table 10.3. *Academics' perceptions of QA according to the higher education sector (results of Mann-Whitney tests)*

Sector	Public Mean	Public Median	Private Mean	Private Median	p-value
Drivers for the creation or edification of internal quality assurance practices					
Establishment of awards and sanctions	2.94	3.00	3.13	3.00	.022
Promotion of institutional competitiveness	3.61	4.00	3.77	4.00	.010
Promotion of innovation	3.79	4.00	3.91	4.00	.045
Promotion of social recognition	3.80	4.00	4.00	4.00	.002
Promotion of continuous improvement	3.99	4.00	4.21	4.00	.000
Legal requirements and demands from A3ES	4.06	4.00	4.21	4.00	.005
Culture promoted by quality assurance practices					
Vague and occasional processes – Superficial commitment to QA	2.73	3.00	2.44	2.00	.001
Recognition of academics and non-academics work	2.65	3.00	3.05	3.00	.000
Internal processes to improve institutional self-knowledge	3.05	3.00	3.50	4.00	.000
Centrally managed and externally oriented internal QA processes	3.40	3.00	3.53	4.00	.026
Quality assurance effects					
Greater tension between academics and non-academics	2.67	3.00	2.37	2.00	.000
Greater pedagogical training	2.70	3.00	3.30	4.00	.000
Improvement of the quality of outreach activities	2.87	3.00	3.32	3.00	.000
Improvement of the quality of research	2.93	3.00	3.30	3.00	.000
Improvement of accountability	2.98	3.00	3.23	3.00	.001
Greater tension between academics	3.17	3.00	2.61	2.00	.000
Improvement of innovation in teaching and learning	2.99	3.00	3.57	4.00	.000
Improvement of quality of teaching and learning	3.07	3.00	3.63	4.00	.000
Improvement of the quality of internationalisation	3.13	3.00	3.53	4.00	.000
Greater tension between managers and academics	3.38	4.00	2.85	3.00	.000
Greater awareness regarding quality of teaching	3.45	4.00	3.79	4.00	.000
Improvement of the quality of public information	3.30	4.00	3.57	4.00	.000

Table 10.4. *Academics' perceptions of QA according to the performance of management functions (results of Mann-Whitney tests)*

Performance of management functions	With		Without		p-value
	Mean	Median	Mean	Median	
Quality assurance effects					
Greater pedagogical training	2.78	3.00	3.83	4.00	.037
Greater demands for non-academic tasks	4.05	4.00	3.79	4.00	.000
Greater formalisation of procedures	4.23	4.00	4.09	4.00	.001

Table 10.5. *Academics' perceptions of QA according to tenure/non-tenure (results of Mann-Whitney tests)*

Tenure/Non-tenure	Tenure		Non-tenure		p-value
	Mean	Median	Mean	Median	
Quality assurance effects					
Improvement of the quality of research	3.17	3.00	2.95	3.00	.000
Improvement of the quality of internationalisation	3.35	4.00	3.17	3.00	.000

academics' perceptions, mainly those regarding QA effects (Table 10.6). In general, a higher involvement in decision making processes leads to higher agreement with the statements on internal QA drivers, cultures and effects, independent of their greater or lower political character. Interestingly, for three of the internal QA effects denoting its greater political extension (*greater tension between academics and non-academics; greater tension between academics; greater tension between managers and academics*) it is the academics with lower involvement in decision making that seem to have a more political view of internal QA.

Academics' Perceptions on Autonomy and Professionalism: Do They Relate with Academics' Perceptions on Internal QA as a Political Process?

As previously mentioned, this study aims to understand if a greater political view of internal QA is related with a view of academic autonomy and professionalism as being influenced.

Concerning autonomy and professionalism (Figure 10.4), academics seem to be still connected to the values of professionalism, namely *accountability and assessment according to their scientific area* (average score of 4.0). Notwithstanding, academics also tend to agree with the *primacy of managerial values over academic* (average score of 3.7), with an increasing focus on *accountability and evaluation*

Table 10.6. *Academics' perceptions of internal QA according to involvement in decision making processes (results of Kruskal-Wallis tests)*

Involvement in decision making processes	Lower Mean	Lower Median	Medium Mean	Medium Median	Higher Mean	Higher Median	p-value
Drivers for the creation or edification of internal quality assurance practices							
Accountability towards society	3.16	3.00	3.31	3.00	3.52	4.00	.001
Promotion of institutional competitiveness	3.58	4.00	3.65	4.00	3.85	4.00	.006
Promotion of social recognition	3.75	4.00	3.88	4.00	4.08	4.00	.000
Promotion of continuous improvement	3.92	4.00	4.10	4.00	4.27	4.00	.000
Legal requirements and demands from A3ES	4.02	4.00	4.13	4.00	4.27	4.00	.002
Culture promoted by quality assurance practices							
Vague and occasional processes – Superficial commitment to QA	2.82	3.00	2.62	3.00	2.34	2.00	.000
Recognition of academics and non-academics work	2.59	3.00	2.83	3.00	2.99	3.00	.000
Internal processes to improve institutional self-knowledge	2.93	3.00	3.25	3.00	3.63	4.00	.000
QA effects							
Greater tension between academics and non-academics	2.68	3.00	2.57	2.00	2.47	2.00	.038
Greater pedagogical training	2.67	3.00	2.93	3.00	3.13	3.00	.000
Improvement of the quality of outreach activities	2.78	3.00	3.06	3.00	3.33	3.00	.000
Improvement of the quality of research	2.83	3.00	3.10	3.00	3.41	4.00	.000
Improvement of accountability	2.80	3.00	3.18	3.00	3.34	3.00	.000
Greater tension between academics	3.14	3.00	2.96	3.00	2.99	3.00	.019
Improvement of innovation in teaching and learning	2.94	3.00	3.22	3.00	3.45	4.00	.000
Improvement of the quality of teaching and learning	3.00	3.00	3.30	3.00	3.61	4.00	.000
Improvement of the quality of internationalisation	3.05	3.00	3.31	3.00	3.53	4.00	.000
Greater tension between managers and academics	3.36	4.00	3.20	3.00	3.14	3.00	.012
Greater awareness regarding quality of teaching	3.36	4.00	3.63	4.00	3.85	4.00	.000

(cont.)

Table 10.6. Academics' perceptions of internal QA according to involvement in decision making processes (results of Kruskal-Wallis tests) (cont.)

Involvement in decision making processes	Lower Mean	Lower Median	Medium Mean	Medium Median	Higher Mean	Higher Median	p-value
Improvement of the quality of public information	3.13	3.00	3.48	4.00	3.77	4.00	.000
Greater control of academic performance	3.66	4.00	3.71	4.00	3.99	4.00	.000
Greater demands for non-academic tasks	3.90	4.00	3.98	4.00	4.10	4.00	.033
Greater formalisation of procedures	4.13	4.00	4.17	4.00	4.33	4.00	.006

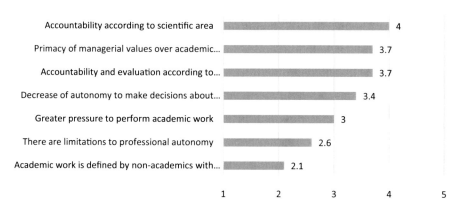

Figure 10.4. Academics perceptions regarding autonomy and professionalism

according to the institutional strategy (average scores of 3.7) and with a *decrease in the autonomy to decide on their own work* (average score of 3.4), which is also in line with previous research (Harvey, 2006; Hoecht, 2006; Newton, 2002).

When exploring the correlations between academics' perceptions of QA drivers, cultures and effects on the one hand, and academics' perceptions of academic autonomy and professionalism on the other, interesting results come out.

QA drivers and cultures which seem to have a less intense political character tend to be negatively correlated with the variables reflecting a decrease of autonomy and professionalism (see Tables 10.7 and 10.8). In fact, and generically, the more academics agree with the importance of the drivers to the implementation of internal QA systems, the less they agree with the statements reflecting a decrease of autonomy and professionalism (*academic work defined by non-academics with responsibility in the area; decrease of autonomy; primacy of managerial values; greater pressure to perform work; and limitations to professional autonomy*). The only exception seems to be the statement about *accountability and evaluation according to the institutional strategy* which positively correlates with all the drivers for internal QA implementation, even when those drivers do not reflect a great political character of internal QA. Furthermore, the more academics agree with the drivers, the more they tend to agree with the idea of *accountability according to the scientific area*, which clearly is in line with academic professionalism. This means that agreeing with internal QA drivers does not seem to be related to the feeling of a challenge to academic autonomy and professionalism (Table 10.7).

The cultures being promoted by internal QA also seem to be negatively related to academics' views about possible influences on academic autonomy and professionalism (Table 10.8). In fact, the more academics agree with the implementation of these cultures, particularly a culture of internal processes to improve institutional self-knowledge and a culture of recognition of academic and non-academic work, the less they tend to agree with the statements *decrease of autonomy to make decisions about academic work; primacy of managerial values over academic profession; greater pressure to perform academic work*; and *limitations to professional autonomy*. Furthermore, the more they agree with these cultures, the more they also tend to agree with the idea of *accountability according to the scientific area*. As for the drivers, academics' opinions on the statement about *accountability and evaluation according to the institutional strategy* positively correlate to three of the cultures, despite that fact these do not hold a greater political character. Overall, it is possible to claim that, with the exception of the internal QA culture characterised by vague and occasional processes and a superficial commitment to quality (which curiously is considered to be the least implemented – see Figure 10.2), the more academics agree with the different QA cultures being promoted, the less they agree with statements suggesting a decrease of autonomy and professionalism.

Nevertheless, the correlations between internal QA effects and academic autonomy and professionalism tell a somehow different story (Table 10.9). Statements indicating a decrease of autonomy and professionalism are positively correlated with internal QA effects, such as: *tension between academics and non-academics, between managers and academics and between academics, greater demand for non-academic tasks* and *greater formalisation of procedures*. It seems that internal QA effects which indicate a more intense political extension of QA are positively correlated with a greater impact on academic autonomy and professionalism, except for the case of the effect *greater control of academic performance* (for which the correlations are negative). It is also interesting to notice that, in general, internal QA effects mainly related with the improvement of the quality of different activities and considered, as such, to have a less political emphasis, are negatively correlated with statements which clearly indicate a decrease of autonomy and professionalism, such as: *decrease of autonomy to make decisions about academic work, primacy of*

Table 10.7. Correlations between QA drivers and the variables reflecting autonomy and professionalism (Spearman correlation coefficients)

Drivers vs. Autonomy and Professionalism	Legal requirements and demands from A3ES demands	Promotion of continuous improvement	Establishment of awards and sanctions	Accountability	Promotion of competitiveness	Promotion of social recognition	Promotion of innovation
Academic work defined by non-academics with responsibility in the area	−0.043	0.100*	0.010	−0.027	−0.057	−0.093*	0.047
Accountability and evaluation according to institutional strategy	0.163*	0.200*	0.175*	0.200*	0.193*	0.179*	0.132*
Accountability according to the scientific area	0.183*	0.177*	0.144*	0.139*	0.108*	0.126*	0.111*
Decrease of autonomy to make decisions about academic work	−0.084*	−0.145*	−0.005	−0.019	−0.112*	−0.110*	−0.090*
Primacy of managerial values over academic profession	−0.036	−0.119	−0.041	−0.055	−0.113*	−0.092*	−0.084*
Greater pressure to perform academic work	−0.024	−0.062*	−0.029	−0.074*	−0.078*	−0.066*	−0.250
Limitations to professional autonomy	−0.082*	−0.155*	−0.076*	−0.044	−0.148*	−0.152*	−0.108*

*Significant correlations for a level of significance of 0.05

Table 10.8. *Correlations between QA cultures and the variables reflecting autonomy and professionalism (Spearman correlation coefficients)*

QA Cultures vs. Autonomy and Professionalism	Internal processes to improve institutional self-knowledge	Centrally managed and externally oriented internal QA processes	Vague and occasional processes – Superficial commitment to QA	Recognition of academic and non-academic work
Academic work defined by non-academics with responsibility in the area	−0.170	0.220	0.076*	0.028
Accountability and evaluation according to institutional strategy	0.175*	0.089*	−0.470	0.153*
Accountability according to the scientific area	0.068*	0.073*	0.140	0.078*
Decrease of autonomy to make decisions about academic work	−0.235*	−0.030	0.189*	−0.190*
Primacy of managerial values over academic profession	−0.258*	−0.020	0.167*	−0.265*
Greater pressure to perform academic work	−0.117*	−0.009	0.047	−0.077*
Limitations to professional autonomy	−0.281*	−0.070*	−0.181*	−0.205*

*Significant correlations for a level of significance of 0.05

managerial values over academic profession, greater pressure to perform academic work and *limitations to professional autonomy*. Another interesting result is the fact that all effects, independent of reflecting QA's greater or lower political character, correlate positively with statements indicating, respectively, a preservation and a limitation to autonomy and professionalism, i.e., *accountability according to the scientific area* and *accountability and evaluation according to institutional strategy*.

Table 10.9. Correlations between QA effects and the variables reflecting autonomy and professionalism (Spearman correlation coefficients)

QA Effects vs Autonomy and Professionalism	Academic work defined by non-academics with responsibility in the area	Accountability and evaluation according to institutional strategy	Accountability according to the scientific area	Decrease of autonomy to make decisions about academic work	Primacy of managerial values over academic profession	Greater pressure to perform academic work	Limitations to professional autonomy
Greater tension between academics	0.090*	0.111	0.028	0.302*	0.302*	0.305	0.294*
Greater tension between managers and academics	0.045	0.035	0.065*	0.325*	0.365*	0.312*	0.317*
Greater tension between academics and non-academics	0.184*	−0.034	−0.042	0.252*	0.199*	0.252*	0.269*
Greater control of academic performance	0.000	−0.174*	0.188*	−0.060*	−0.078*	−0.047	−0.085*
Greater demands for non-academic tasks	0.019	0.044	0.103*	0.148*	0.237*	0.159*	0.082*
Greater formalisation of procedures	0.011	0.074*	0.106*	0.155*	0.251*	0.110*	0.058
Greater awareness regarding quality of teaching	−0.004	0.188*	0.129*	−0.223*	−0.276*	−0.062*	−0.217*
Improvement of innovation in teaching and learning	0.040	0.138*	0.071*	−0.305*	−0.357*	−0.088*	−0.271*
Greater pedagogical training	0.084*	0.142*	0.068*	−0.208*	−0.284*	−0.071*	−0.211*
Improvement of quality of teaching	0.022	0.191*	0.104*	−0.283*	−0.345*	−0.090*	−0.274*

(cont.)

Table 10.9. Correlations between QA effects and the variables reflecting autonomy and professionalism (Spearman correlation coefficients) (cont.)

QA Effects vs Autonomy and Professionalism	Academic work defined by non-academics with responsibility in the area	Accountability and evaluation according to institutional strategy	Accountability according to the scientific area	Decrease of autonomy to make decisions about academic work	Primacy of managerial values over academic profession	Greater pressure to perform academic work	Limitations to professional autonomy
Improvement of quality of research	0.020	0.186*	0.082*	0.237*	−0.320*	−0.068*	−0.249*
Improvement of quality of outreach activities	−0.510	0.165*	0.086*	0.253*	−0.312*	−0.063*	−0.219*
Improvement of quality of internationalisation	0.037	0.185*	0.090*	−0.188*	−0.227*	−0.004	−0.170*
Improvement of public information	−0.024	0.168*	0.119*	−0.234*	−0.247*	−0.044	−0.254*
Improvement of Accountability	0.016	0.167*	0.103*	−0.229*	0.236*	−0.036	−0.190*

* Significant correlations for a level of significance of 0.05

This seems to indicate the presence of an ambiguous perception at this level, adding to the discussion about QA leading (or not) to an actual loss of academic autonomy and professionalism.

CONCLUSIONS

The research presented in this chapter aims to understand how QA, in regard to its drivers, cultures and effects, is being perceived by academics as a more or less political process. Furthermore, the research explores whether a greater political perception of QA is correlated with a greater perception of a challenge to academic autonomy and professionalism. The literature demonstrates that QA has a political nature, involving different perceptions, roles and power relations amongst the different institutions' stakeholders (Harvey & Newton, 2004; Skolnik, 2010). In addition, a glance at the research on QA as well as on academic professionalism and academic autonomy seems to evidence that internal QA processes are having unwanted and controversial implications, namely for academics as professionals (Ball, 2016; Morley, 2003; Worthington & Hodgson, 2005).

The research concludes that QA as a political process seems to be less evident in academics' perceptions on QA drivers and cultures and more evident when it refers to QA internal effects. It seems that when it comes to the 'idea' of QA – i.e., the reasons leading to its implementation – QA emerges as less political and academics tend to agree more with it; but, when what is at stake are the practical consequences of QA – its more political character – academics' agreement tends to weaken.

Furthermore, when analysing the differences between groups of academics regarding the perceptions of a more or less political nature of QA, it is interesting to observe that academics from public universities and academics involved in decision making processes agree more with internal QA effects demonstrating a more intense political nature of QA.

Moreover, while in regard to QA drivers and cultures, a less intense political character of QA is correlated with a lower impact on academic autonomy and professionalism; in regard to QA effects, a more intense political character of QA is correlated with a higher impact on academic autonomy and professionalism, which seems to be in line with previous literature (Morley, 2003; Newton, 2002; Worthington & Hodgson, 2005).

It seems that academics consider that the purpose of the development and implementation of internal QA is less political, mostly serving to improve HEIs and their activities. However, when reflecting on the implications and outcomes of QA practices' implementation, academics perceive them as more political, as serving a certain cause, which derives power from them and shapes their behaviour in a certain way. In this context, our conclusions suggest a sort of 'malfunctioning' between the purpose of QA and its unwanted implications (more political) which must be solved and overcome.

Academic freedom and autonomy has always been an essential value for developing academics' practices and it is still a dominant value nowadays (Carvalho & Santiago, 2010, 2015). The association of QA effects with political purposes is associated with a loss of academics' control over their work.

The literature underlines that the healthiest way to deal with the political nature of QA is to recognise it and "to accept the diversity of views and interests of all stakeholders and work toward the reconciliation of those diverse views and interests", as well as to emphasise "inclusiveness and transparency of the quality assurance process" (Skolnik, 2010, pp. 17, 18). Moreover, QA and professional autonomy do not have to be polar opposites. QA can be tailored to promote learning and innovation rather than bureaucratic control without undermining professional autonomy. As the results of our research show, academics seem to agree with the idea of internal QA as inducing both accountability and evaluation according to institutional strategy – assumed as more likely to challenge autonomy and professionalism – and accountability according to the scientific area – more in line with the values of professionalism and autonomy. Hence, it "is high time for a proper debate between higher education policy-makers and academics on how to achieve quality in higher education teaching and learning while maintaining trust and professional autonomy – on how to maintain both the trust of the public in the quality of university teaching and the perception of academics of being trusted and of having their professional autonomy preserved or reinstated" (Hoecht, 2006, p. 556).

This research contributes to a better understanding of QA as a political process and of its relationships with academic autonomy. Despite its limitations, it tries to add to the discussion on the consequences of QA for academic professionalism. The acknowledgement of potential 'unwanted' consequences of QA, namely for academic professionalism, can help to overcome them.

Overall, it is possible to conclude that internal QA is indeed a political process at least in some of its dimensions; furthermore, it seems that whenever this political character emerges as more evidenced, academics' autonomy and professionalism seem also to be influenced.

However, our research presents limitations, particularly concerning the data. Since the available data is part of a broader project with different research questions and goals, it would be useful to develop further work with specific questions concerning QA and professionalism, in order to better understand if a loss of professionalism and autonomy in academia can indeed be a direct consequence of internal QA implementation.

REFERENCES

A3ES. (2010). *Activity plan for 2010*. Lisbon: A3ES.
Anderson, G. (2006). Assuring quality/resisting quality assurance: Academics' responses to 'quality' in some Australian universities. *Quality in Higher Education, 12*(2), 161–173.

Ball, S. (2016). Neoliberal education? Confronting the slouching beast. *Policy Futures in Education 14*(8), 1046–1059.

Becket, N., & Brookes, M. (2008). Quality management practice in higher education – What quality are we actually enhancing? *Journal of Hospitality, Leisure, Sport and Tourism Education, 7*(1), 40–54.

Bergen Communiqué. (2005). *The European higher education area: Achieving the goals*. Bergen: Conference of European Ministers Responsible for Higher Education, Bergen.

Berlin Communiqué. (2003). *Realising the European higher education area*. Berlin: Conference of European Ministers Responsible for Higher Education, Bergen.

Bologna Declaration. (1999). *The Bologna declaration. Joint declaration of the European ministers of education*. Bologna: The European Higher Education Area.

Cardoso, S., Rosa, M., & Santos, C. (2013). Different academics' characteristics, different perceptions on quality assessment? *Quality Assurance in Education, 21*(1), 96–117.

Carvalho, T., & Santiago, R. (2010). Still academics after all …… . . *Higher Education Policy, 23*(3), 397–411.

Carvalho, T., & Santiago, R. (2015). Professional autonomy in a comparative perspective: Academics, doctors and nurses. In T. Carvalho & R. Santiago (Eds.), *Professionalism, managerialism and reform in higher education and the health services: The European welfare state and rise of the knowledge society* (pp. 30–63). Basingstoke: Palgrave Macmillan.

Cheng, M. (2010). Audit cultures and quality assurance mechanisms in England: A study of their perceived impact on the work of academics. *Teaching in Higher Education, 15*(3), 259–271.

Collyer, F. (2015). Practices of conformity and resistance in the marketisation of the academy: Bourdieu, professionalism and academic capitalism. *Critical Studies in Education, 56*(3), 315–331.

Deem, R. (1998). 'New managerialism' and higher education: The management of performances and cultures in universities in the United Kingdom. *International Studies in Sociology of Education, 8*(1), 47–70.

ENQA. (2009). *Standards and guidelines for quality assurance in the European higher education area* (3rd ed.). Helsinki: European Association for Quality Assurance in Higher Education.

ENQA. (2015). *Standards and guidelines for quality assurance in the European higher education area (ESG)* (Revised ESG approved by the Ministerial conference in Yerevan, on 14 –15 May 2015). Yerevan: European Association for Quality Assurance in Higher Education.

Farrugia, C. (1996). A continuing professional development model for quality assurance in higher education. *Quality Assurance in Education, 4*(2), 28–34.

Freidson, E. (1988). *Profession of medicine: A study of sociology of applied knowledge*. Chicago, IL: The University of Chicago Press.

Hanlon, G. (1998). Professionalism as enterprise: Service class politics and the redefinition of professionalism. *Sociology, 32*(1), 43–63.

Harvey, L. (2006). Impact of quality assurance: Overview of a discussion between representatives of external quality assurance agencies. *Quality in Higher Education, 12*(3), 287–290.

Harvey, L., & Newton, J. (2004). Transforming quality evaluation. *Quality in Higher Educational, 10*(2), 149–165.

Hoecht, A. (2006). Quality assurance in UK higher education: Issues of trust, control, professional autonomy and accountability. *Higher Education, 51*(4), 541–563.

Huusko, M., & Ursin, J. (2010). Why (not) assess? Views from the academic departments of Finnish universities. *Assessment and Evaluation in Higher Education, 35*(7), 859–869.

Joseph, P. B., & Burnaford, G. E. (1994). *Images of school teachers in twentieth-century America*. New York, NY: St Martin's Press.

Larson, M. (1977). *The rise of professionalism: A sociological analysis*. California, CA: University of California Press.

Laughton, D. (2003). Why was the QAA approach to teaching quality assessment rejected by academics in UK HE? *Assessment & Evaluation in Higher Education, 28*(3), 309–321.

Lomas, L. (2007). Zen, motorcycle maintenance and quality in higher education. *Quality Assurance in Education, 14*(4), 402–412.

Manatos, M., Sarrico, C. S., & Rosa, M. (2015). The importance and degree of implementation of the European standards and guidelines for internal quality assurance in universities: The views of Portuguese academics. *Tertiary Education and Management, 21*(3), 245–261.

Massy, W. (2003). *Honoring the trust. Quality and cost containment in higher education.* Bolton, MA: Anker Publishing Company, Inc.

Morley, L. (2003). *Quality and power in higher education.* Berkshire: Society for Research into Higher Education & Open University Press.

Nelson, M. (1991). Academic professionals. *Medical Teacher, 13*(4), 323–332.

Newton, J. (2002). View from below: Academics coping with quality. *Quality in Higher Education, 8*(1), 39–61.

Prague Communiqué. (2001). *Towards the European higher education area.* Prague: Conference of European Ministers Responsible for Higher Education., Prague.

Rosa, M., & Amaral, A. (2007). A self-assessment of higher education institutions from the perspectives of EFQM model. In D. Westerheijden (Ed.), *Quality assurance in higher education: Trends in regulation, translation and transformation* (pp. 181–207). Dordrecht: Springer.

Rosa, M., & Amaral, A. (2014). The portuguese case: New Public Management reforms and the European Standards and Guidelines. In H. Eggins (Ed.), *Drivers and barriers to achieving quality in higher education* (pp. 153–166). Rotterdam, The Netherlands: Sense Publishers.

Rosa, M., & Sarrico, C. S. (2012). Quality, evaluation and accreditation: From steering, through compliance, on to enhancement and innovation? In A. Amaral & G. Neave (Eds.), *Higher education in Portugal 1974–2009. A nation, a generation* (pp. 249–264). Dordrecht: Springer.

Salter, B., & Tapper, T. (2000). The politics of governance in higher education: The case of quality assurance. *Political Studies, 48*(1), 66–87.

Santos, S. M. (2011). *Comparative analysis of European processes for assessment and certification of internal quality assurance systems.* Lisbon: A3ES Readings.

Skolnik, M. (2010). Quality assurance in higher education as a political process. *Higher Education Management and Policy, 22*(1), 1–20.

Stensaker, B., Langfeldt, L., Harvey, L., Huisman, J., & Westerheijden, D. (2011). An in-depth study on the impact of external quality assurance. *Assessment and Evaluation in Higher Education, 36*(4), 465–478.

Tavares, O., Sin, C., Videira, P., & Amaral, A. (2016). *The impact of internal quality assurance on teaching and learning in academics' perceptions.* Ljubljana: Paper presented at the 11th European Quality Assurance Forum.

Westerheijden, D., Hulpiaub, V., & Waeytens, K. (2007). From design and implementation to impact of quality assurance: An overview of some studies into what impacts improvement. *Tertiary Education and Management, 13*(4), 295–312.

Worthington, F., & Hodgson, J. (2005). Academic labour and the politics of quality in higher education: A critical evaluation of the conditions of possibility of resistance. *Critical Quarterly, 47*(1–2), 96–110.

PART 5

STUDENTS AND THE EFFECTIVENESS OF LEARNING

MAGNUS STRAND HAUGE

11. GRADES AS A MEASURE OF STUDENTS' LEARNING OUTCOME

INTRODUCTION

In 2003, Norway introduced a new national grading scale in higher education. The scale is similar to the ECTS scale: a five-point scale (A to E) for passing grades, and one failing grade (F). While the ECTS grading scale is a relative scale, where the best 10% receive an A grade, the next 25% receive a B grade etc., the Norwegian grading scale is based on an absolute grading system where the students' work is supposed to be graded based on a set of predefined criteria. This was at least the intention put forward in the Norwegian Government's white paper to the parliament in 2002 (Ot. prp. nr. 40, 2001–2002, pp. 52–53). One of the advantages with the new national grading scale was that it would make comparisons across different subject fields, and between study programmes, easier. It was also supposed to be a useful tool for employers when considering applicants for a job (Det Norske Universitetsråd, 2000, p. 58).

With the growing focus on learning outcomes and accountability in higher education (HE), the relationship between student performance at two different points in time has become an important area for research (Caspersen et al., 2017). After introducing a new grading scale, where the goal is comparability of grades across study programmes, such a relationship should be easy to study, at least if a reliable and valid measure for a student's competence level when entering higher education exists. In a new white paper however, the Government points to several studies that have shown that there are large differences across higher education institutions (HEIs) and subject fields, and between academic degree levels (Meld. St, 16, 2016–2017, p. 57). Although a "value added" quality indicator that measures the increase in the learning outcome among students at a HEI or a study programme could be of great interest, it seems quite difficult to operationalize such an indicator. Attempts have been made, both at developing a HE grade indicator where institutional and subject field biases have been removed (e.g. Strøm et al., 2013), and at developing indicators measuring success in the labour market (Strøm et al., 2016). However, the suggested grade indicator relies on students changing HEIs at some point in their education process (e.g. between academic degrees), while the labour market indicators can only be calculated some years after the students have finished their studies. To use these indicators to measure the value added component (or quality) of an institution or study programme at a certain time, one actually need to wait several years to be able measure it.

In this chapter, an attempt is made to use data from the Norwegian National Student Survey to make an indicator measuring the value added component from a HEI on their students' learning outcome. Using data from this source makes it possible to use new control variables that can potentially remove at least some of the institutional bias in grading. Although learning outcome is often measured by using grades, other indicators should also be considered, especially considering the lack of comparability of grades across institutions and subject fields. Although HE grades as a measure for learning outcome will be the main focus here, the student survey also includes variables on the students' self-reported learning outcomes. These will be used as measures for learning outcome as alternatives to HE grades.

THEORY

Measuring Learning Outcomes in Higher Education

A student's learning outcome can be measured in several ways. The approaches can mainly be divided into two categories: self-reported and test-based measures. Data on self-reported learning outcomes are often survey-based, while grades are a type of test-based measure (Caspersen et al., 2017).

Typically, studies on grades as a measure of learning outcome have often been focused at the reliability of grades as a measure of students' learning outcome (e.g. Bloxham & Boyd, 2012; Strøm et al., 2013). Studies on the institutional contributions to the students' learning outcome (value added) have used grades in upper secondary school or national tests as a control in the assessment of learning outcomes in higher education (e.g. Liu, 2011; Strøm et al., 2013). Several studies on survey-based self-reported learning outcome as a value-added measure have been conducted as well (e.g. Caspersen et al., 2014). Few studies, at least in Norway, have combined the two approaches, which a main reason for pursuing this approach here.

The Comparability of Grades Across Institutions

As noted in the introduction, it is a political goal in Norway that grades should be comparable across the HEIs. However, previous studies have indicated that the relationship between students' grades at upper secondary school and grades received in higher education is weak in Norway (Næss, 2006; Møen & Tjelta, 2010; Strøm et al., 2013). Møen and Tjelta's (2010) study is from the Norwegian School of Economics (NHH). NHH recruits the students with the highest grades from upper secondary school among all HEIs offering degree programmes in economics. However, NHH also admits students, who start their economic programmes at other HEIs, to the last part of its civil economics programme. The authors find that HEIs with few students and HEIs that admit students with poor grades from secondary school, systematically have a more lenient grading practice. Strøm et al. (2013) looked at grading practice in economics, technology and social science, and concluded that the grading practices at the HEIs were so variable that grades provide limited information on the students' learning outcome across institutions. So, why do these differences in grading occur? Strøm et al. (2013, pp. 12–17) have summarized relevant literature. In short, they sort the causes found in the literature into three different categories: competition between HEIs leading to grade inflation, the introduction of result-based financial incentives and relative grading practice.

Yang and Yip (2002) have looked at universities in the USA where there was an increase in average grade from C in the 1980s to B/B- in the 1990s. They found that because students with better grades usually get employed more easily, universities have incentives to give high grades. The competition between the universities leads to grade inflation. They also find that many of the top universities also have succumbed to this practice.

Among the literature on result-based financial incentives, de Paola (2011) found that such incentives led to a more lenient grading practice in study programmes where supply was higher than demand, compared to study programmes with a demand surplus. Bauer and Grave (2011) have looked at the introduction of a result-based financial system in Germany, but have not found any evidence of a change in grading practice.

Relative grading is the practice of grading based on the overall score or result of the class. This is opposed to absolute grading where grades are given based on a set of pre-defined criteria without taking the overall results of the class into consideration. A relative grading practice can lead to either a lenient or a strict grading practice, depending on the skills of the students in the class. This makes comparison between classes difficult, if not impossible. Studies show that a strict grading practice could have positive effect on learning among skilled students (Bonesrønning, 1999; Betts & Groggers, 2003), but could negatively affect less skilled students' motivation because it will be harder for them to achieve better grades (Covington, 2000). On the other hand, a lenient practice might affect skilled students in a negative way because they only have to perform better than the other students in class (Betts, 1995).

Looking more closely at the situation in Norway, there have only been minor changes in the national grade average since the introduction of a new grading system in 2003 (UHR, 2015). In 2003, a new result-based financial system was introduced as well. A study (Frølich and Strøm, 2008) showed that this system to some degree affected the way teachers graded their students, but only in the lower end of the grading scale by giving students the lowest passing grade instead of failing them. Møen and Tjelta's (2010) finding that HEIs with lesser skilled students tend to be more lenient in their grading practice, seems to point to relative grading as the main cause of the variability in grading between HEIs in Norway. This type of practice is not in accordance with the goal that grades should be comparable across the HEIs. However, the existence of relative grading practice does not necessarily mean that it is used deliberately.

METHODS AND RESEARCH QUESTIONS

In prior research on the relationship between grades received in upper secondary school and higher education, it has been common to include control variables such as gender, age and subject fields in regression models where institutions are added as a set of dummy variables intended to measure the value added effects on HE grades for every HEI. Both Strøm et al. (2013) and Møen and Tjelta (2010) have improved on this basic model by exploiting the fact that many students move between institutions after completing their bachelor's degree (Strøm et al.) or their first years of study (Møen and Tjelta). One disadvantage with these two studies is that they can only be conducted years after the students receive their grades.

Here, data from the Norwegian National Student Survey will be used in an attempt to improve the institutional value added model. This approach allows for calculating institutional value added effects while the students are attending their study programme, and makes it possible to add new control variables that have not been previously been used. Because the survey includes self-reported learning outcomes as well, it is also possible to use this as the dependent variable instead of HE grades. The following research questions will be addressed in this chapter:

1. Are there differences in grading between HEIs, and what can explain why these differences occur?
2. Could the introduction of new control variables improve HE grades as a measure of learning outcome?
3. Are self-reported learning outcomes valid and reliable measures of the students' actual learning outcome?

To answer question 2, the new model has to be compared with the common model from previous studies. Several models are therefore calculated here. The models are numbered, and a lower number indicates that the model is nested in the models with higher numbers. However, model 6 and 7 are both full models, meaning that model 6 is not nested in model 7. The relationship between the models are illustrated in Figure 11.1. Letters are used as a suffix to identify the dependent variable ("a" = grades; "b" = self-reported learning outcome).

The Norwegian National Student Survey

In the Norwegian National Student Survey, all second-year bachelor's and master's degree students are invited to participate. In five- or six-year programmes, the questionnaire is also sent to fifth-year students. In the survey conducted in October 2016 nearly 29,000 students answered the questionnaire (45% response rate), representing 46 HEIs and approximately 1,800 study programmes. Here the selection is limited to students attending study programmes that recruit students from upper secondary school. Of these, only students who gave their consent to merge their answers with their individual background data are selected, giving a final sample size of about 10,000 students attending approximately 600 study programmes. For the five- or six-year programmes, both second- and fifth-year students are included.

Dependent Variables

The main dependent variable is the average grade received in higher education. As noted above, the grading scale used in Norway is the same as the ECTS scale. Grades are converted to numbers (A = 5 and F = 0) before an average is calculated for each student. There are two types of HE grades available in the survey data: the average grade on all courses the student has attended at the institution where he or she is enrolled, and the average grade on all courses belonging to the study programme the student is enrolled in. In this study, the average grade from study programme courses is chosen as the dependent grade variable.

The second dependent variable is self-reported learning outcome. In the survey, the students are asked how satisfied they are with their learning outcome so far in the study programme. Ten different types of learning outcomes are listed, and the students are asked to rate all of them on a scale from 1 (least satisfied) to 5 (most satisfied). They also have the option of not answering or choosing "don't know" as an answer to each. These learning outcomes are all related to the Norwegian Qualification Framework (NQF), which is a part of the European Qualification Framework (EQF). All ten are listed in Table 11.1. Using all of them as dependent variables will be too comprehensive however. One possibility is to construct an index of all ten, but statistical analyses have shown that this is not recommended (results from factor analyses are not shown here). Choosing one or two of them is a better option.

Table 11.1. Correlation between different types of learning outcomes and grades in HE

Type of learning outcome	Correlation – HE grades	p-value	N
Theoretical knowledge	0.2375	0.000	11 836
Knowledge of scientific work methods and research	0.0874	0.000	11 287
Experience with research and development work	0.0254	0.009	10 561
Discipline- or profession-specific skills	0.0604	0.000	11 254
Critical thinking and reflection	0.0999	0.000	11 755
Cooperative skills	0.0153	0.098	11 776
Oral communication skills	0.0214	0.021	11 719
Written communication skills	0.1280	0.000	11 778
Innovative thinking	0.0259	0.005	11 699
Ability to work independently	0.1342	0.000	11 851

Even though grading practices vary between institutions, grades are not completely random. They give at least some indication of the learning outcome of the students. With this in mind, one would expect positive correlation between the grades a student receives and self-reported learning outcome. In Table 11.1, correlations between grade and all types of learning outcome are listed. Generally, the correlations are low, indicating that self-reported learning outcomes measure something different than grades. A weak correlation between self-reported learning outcomes and HE grades have been found in other studies as well. Caspersen et al. (2017, p. 25) suggest that self-reported learning outcomes already include the students' consideration of the value added of the HEIs. Caspersen et al. (2014) reached a similar conclusion. They also found differences between academic disciplines, making it difficult to compare self-reported learning outcomes between disciplines. Identifying a type of learning outcome that is important in most subject fields could minimize this discrepancy. As could controlling for subject field in the models.

Looking back at Table 11.1, theoretical knowledge is moderately correlated with grades, and has the highest correlation with grades among all the learning outcome indicators. It also covers a very important aspect in higher education, and it is likely that most students have obtained theoretical knowledge during the first year of study. Among all the types of learning outcomes this seems to be the best choice as a dependent variable.

Independent Variables and Regression Models

In order to measure the value added effect from HEIs on their students' learning outcome, a variable measuring the knowledge and skills a student has when he/she enters higher education is needed. Here, average grade from upper secondary school is used. The grading scale in upper secondary school runs from 1 (lowest) to 6 (highest), with 2 being the lowest passing grade. For every individual, all final grades are averaged. This is the only independent variable in model 1.

In model 2, the following individual background variables are added: age, gender, parents' education level and a dichotomous variable indicating if a student is in his or hers fifth year of study. These variables are included because they have previously been found to affect HE grades (Caspersen et al., 2017, p. 25). Subject fields are added in model 3 and institutions are added in model 4. Both subject fields and institutions are added as dummy variables with political science and the University of Oslo as reference categories. Model 4a resembles the grade model that Strøm et al. (2013) found unreliable, and will be the basic model that the new model presented here will be compared with. In model 5, the following two questions from the National Student Survey are added as variables: I am attending the study programme of my first choice and I am motivated for working on my studies. Students answer the questions on a five point scale from do not agree (1) to fully agree (5). The two questions are included in an attempt to measure the students' intrinsic motivation, which is important for student achievement (see for instance Jeno, 2018). Ryan and Deci (2000, p. 56) define intrinsic motivation "(...) as the doing of an activity for its inherent satisfaction rather than for some separable consequence". This is in contrast with extrinsic motivation where "activity is done in order to attain some separable outcome" (ibid.). Extrinsic motivation is covered by a question in the survey as well. Since HEIs have a role in influencing the students' extrinsic motivation, this question could potentially correlate with the value added effect, and is therefore not included in the model here. For the same reason, variables measuring student satisfaction are not included.

As indicated above, relative grading seems to be one reason for the previously observed variability in grading among Norwegian HEIs. In order to use HE grades as the dependent variable in a value added model, the effect coming from relative

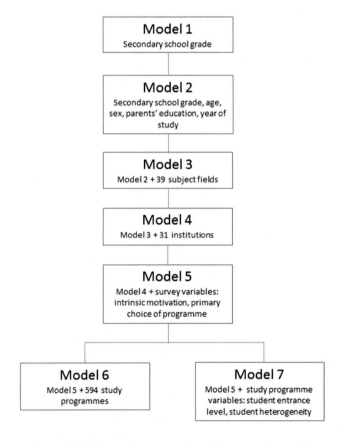

Figure 11.1. Schematic presentation of the regression models

grading must be controlled for. Relative grading is most likely to occur between different academic communities. To simplify, one can look upon each study programme as a separate academic community. Study programmes are included as a set of dummy variables in model 6. The study programme effects include both the effect from relative grading and the value added effect that each study programme has on the students' learning outcome. Measuring the value added effect from each study programme is a comprehensive task however. Because several study programmes have a low number of respondents, the effects will be highly insecure as well. Here, the value added effect will only be calculated at the institutional level, while using subject fields as controls. Including study programmes as dummy variables in such an analysis could remove the relative grading bias, but could potentially remove some of the institutional value added effect as well. To get an indication on the existence and importance of relative grading in the Norwegian higher education system, the model where all study programmes are included as dummy variables were calculated (model 6). The results are, for the reasons explained above, not shown here. Removing some of the effect of relative grading in model 5 can be done by including variables explaining characteristics at the study programme level that is known to correlate with relative grading. Møen and Tjelta (2010) found that average grade from upper secondary school among all students attending a study programme, correlates with the strictness of the grading practice at the study programme. This variable measuring the average initial competence at the study programme level is added in model 7. A negative effect from this variable on HE grades will be in line with the findings of Møen and Tjelta (2010), and is an indication of the existence of relative grading.

The standard deviation of grades from upper secondary school among students in the same the study programme level is included as a variable as well. This is as a measure of initial competence heterogeneity among students within a study programme. In NOKUTs prior in-depth analyses on the data from the National Student Survey it has been found that academic staff often refer to heterogeneity among students as a challenge, both in how they structure their teaching and in grading.[1] The degree of heterogeneity in a study programme could potentially affect the HE grades as well. Although the theoretical explanation for including these variables regard HE grades only, they are included in the self-reported learning outcome models as well. If the results indicate that the model is not improved by adding these two variables, model 7b will be disregarded and in favour of model 5b.

RESULTS

In Table 11.2 the adjusted r^2 of the different models shown in Figure 11.1 are listed. In model 1, upper secondary school grade has a strong effect on, and explains about 12% of the variance in HE grades. It also has a modest effect on the student's self-reported learning outcome, represented here by theoretical knowledge, but only explain about 2% of the variance. The individual background variables increases the explained variance (r^2) in model 2a by about 1%. Age has a modest positive effect on grades while the effect from parents' education, sex and year of study are statistically significant, but weak. In model 2b, where self-reported learning outcome is the dependent variable, the effect from the individual control variables are either weak or insignificant.

The inclusion of subject fields increase the explained variance with almost 4% in model 3a and by 2% in model 3b. This indicates that subject fields influence HE grades more than it influences self-reported learning outcome.

Institutions (model 4) increase the explained variance less than subject fields in both models. This is regardless of the order that subject fields and institutions are included in the models, and is an indication that subject fields explain more of the variation in both dependent variables than institutions. The increase in r^2 is higher in model 4a than in model 4b. Which institution a student attends seems to affect the students' grades more than it affects self-reported learning outcome.

Table 11.2. The adjusted r^2 of the models shown in Figure 11.1

Model number	a) Grades in HE	b) LO – theoretical knowledge
1	0.122	0.020
2	0.131	0.020
3	0.167	0.042
4	0.182	0.048
5	0.218	0.214
6	0.279	0.240
7	0.224	0.214
N	10091	10091

In model 5, intrinsic motivation has a strong effect on both dependent variables. The increase in r^2 in the learning outcome model (5b) is particularly noticeable. Primary choice of study programme has a modest positive effect on self-reported learning outcome and a weak positive effect on HE grades.

In model 6 dummy variables for around 600 study programmes are included. Adjusted r^2 increases considerably in both models, but substantially more in the HE grade model than in the self-reported learning outcome model. Which study programme a student attends seems to explain more of the variance in HE grades than subject fields and institutions combined. This finding supports the choice to add variables describing programme characteristics in the model. Initial competence and heterogeneity among students at the study programme level increase the r^2 in the HE grade model (model 7a is here compared with model 5a). Initial competence has a strong negative effect on grading while study programme heterogeneity has a weak positive effect. Neither of these variables have any effect on self-reported learning outcome. In the discussion below, model 5b is therefore treated as the

Table 11.3. Regression models 4a, 5a, 7a and 5b – results

	Model 4a	Model 5a	Model 7a	Model 5b
Dependent variable	HE grade	HE grade	HE grade	LO – TK
Scale	0-5	0-5	0-5	1-5
Individual variables				
Upper secondary school avg. grade (2-6)	0.657**	0.639**	0.706**	0.068**
Mother's education (1-4)	0.023*	0.022*	0.026*	0.007
Father's education (1-4)	0.043**	0.040**	0.042**	0.004
Female = 1 (dichotomous)	–0.206	–0.050*	–0.056**	–0.004
Age (19-70)	0.016**	0.011**	0.011**	–0.032**
Fifth-year student = 1 (dichotomous)	0.084**	0.116**	0.135**	0.011
National student survey variables				
Primary choice of programme (1-5)	–	0.023*	0.027**	0.129**
Intrinsic motivation (1-5)	–	0.169**	0.168**	0.354**
Study programme variables				
Initial competence (avg. of upper secondary school grade) (3-5.6)	–	–	–0.320*	–
Heterogeneity (sd of upper secondary school grade) (1.3–10)	–	–	0.021**	–
Subject fields (dummy variables)				
(omitted)				
Institutions (dummy variables)				
Oslo School of Architecture and Design	0.219	0.114	–0.040	0.027*
Norwegian School of Theology	0.582**	0.556**	0.370*	–0.001
Queen Maud UC of Early Childhood Education	0.488**	0.445**	0.305**	–0.006
Stord/Haugesund UC	0.279**	0.286**	0.010	–0.008
Bergen UC	0.234**	0.234**	0.154**	–0.024
Hedmark UC	0.450**	0.432**	0.236**	0.002
Lillehammer UC	0.546**	0.490**	0.312**	0.015
Molde UC – Specialized University in Logistics	0.770**	0.748**	0.516**	–0.018
Oslo and Akershus UC of Applied Sciences	0.258**	0.249**	0.157**	–0.017
UC of Southeast Norway	0.305**	0.302**	0.149**	–0.024
Østfold UC	0.367**	0.345**	0.169**	–0.012
Sogn og Fjordane UC	0.390**	0.386**	0.201**	0.013
Volda UC	0.402**	0.386**	0.200**	0.013

(cont.)

Table 11.3. Regression models 4a, 5a, 7a and 5b – results (cont.)

	Model 4a	Model 5a	Model 7a	Model 5b
Diakonova UC	0.352*	0.308	0.189	0.001
Lovisenberg Diaconal UC	0.235*	0.228*	0.181	0.005
NLA UC	0.425*	0.420**	0.301*	0.016
Norwegian Univ. of Science and Technology	0.057	0.046	0.056	0.008
Nord Univ.	0.512**	0.478**	0.312**	−0.017
Norwegian School of Economics	0.299**	0.198*	0.352**	0.020
Norwegian School of Sport Sciences	0.136	0.076	0.075	−0.005
Norwegian Univ. of Life Sciences	0.225**	0.224	0.205**	0.004
Norwegian Police UC	0.308**	0.170*	0.084	−0.036*
UiT – The Artic Univ. of Norway	0.356**	0.340**	0.161**	−0.010
Univ. of Agder	0.272**	0.257**	0.163**	−0.001
Univ. of Bergen	0.128**	0.135**	0.080*	−0.014
Univ. of Stavanger	0.196**	0.178**	0.037	−0.016
VID Specialized Univ.	0.509**	0.504**	0.364**	0.015
Westerdals – WOACT	0.614**	0.593**	0.496**	−0.039**
Univ. of Oslo (ref. cat)	0		0	0
Observations	10164	10164	10164	10164
Adjusted R^2	0.182	0.218	0.224	0.214

* $p < 0.05$, ** $p < 0.01$

full self-reporting learning outcome model. Because model 4a, 5a, 7a and 5b will be discussed in more detail below, the results of these models are presented in Table 11.3.

DISCUSSION

RQ1: Are there differences in grading between HEIs and what can explain why these differences occur?

The results indicate that there is a substantial difference in grading, both between subject fields and between institutions. Since subject fields are treated as control variables here, the effects are omitted from Table 11.3 for space reasons. A quick recount of these effects will be given here. The effects indicate HE grades are lower than expected in civil engineering, law, nursing, engineering and medicine, while they are higher than expected in police studies, pre-school teacher education, art and vocational teacher education. One possible explanation of the observed differences is that upper secondary school grades are not as important in explaining a student's success in some fields compared to others. One example is art studies, where entry examinations are more important than grades as entry requirements. This does not mean that differences in grading practice between subject fields are not problematic, but that they are more difficult to calculate when upper secondary school grades average is used as measure for the students' initial competence level. This shows the importance of controlling for subject fields in he HE grade model.

When comparing model 5a with 4a, it is obvious that intrinsic motivation has a strong effect on grades received in higher education. However, the institutional effects are almost the same in model 5a as in model 4a. Including intrinsic motivation and primary choice of study programme does not affect the differences between the HEIs. The only noticeable difference is at the Norwegian Police Academy where high grades to some degree could be attributed to high intrinsic motivation among students at the institution.

Even after controlling for individual background variables, there are considerable differences between institutions. In model 4a, it is predicted that students at the University of Oslo receive .8 of a grade less than students at the HEI with the highest positive effect on HE grades. This could mean that teachers at some institutions are better at getting students to succeed than at other institutions. An alternative explanation is that grading practices vary between institutions. The last explanation is supported by the negative effect found from average initial competence on the study programme level on HE grades in model 7a. When the average upper secondary school grade among all students in a study programme increases by one grade, the average individual grade in higher education decreases with around 0.3 of a grade. Adding this variable reduces the value added effect from 0.8 to 0.5 at the HEI with the largest effect on HE grades. This supports Mjøen and Tjelta's (2010) findings, and is an indication that relative grading practise exists in the higher education sector in Norway.

Study programme heterogeneity is barely significant in the model, and the effect on grades in higher education is negligible. However, the effect that heterogeneity has on grades in higher education could differ depending on the students' individual grades. A homogenous student group could for instance consist of strong or weak students only. The learning environment will be very different in the two cases. To get a better idea of the effect that heterogeneity has on HE grades, additional models with interaction terms between study programme heterogeneity and individual grade from upper secondary school are calculated. In all models (the results are not shown here), there is a tendency that students with poor grades from secondary school get better grades when the heterogeneity is increased. A student with an upper secondary school grade average of 3 could gain more than 0.5 grade in higher education by entering the study programme with the highest degree of heterogeneity compared to the programme with the lowest degree of heterogeneity. This is an indication that students with weak grades from upper secondary school perform better if they are a part of a student group that is heterogeneous when it comes to grades obtained upper secondary school. However, the average initial competence at the study programme level still negatively affects individual grades in higher education significantly. Although students with weak grades from secondary school seem to benefit from being in a heterogeneous learning environment, they don't actually get better grades than similar students in a homogenous learning environment because they attend study programmes with a higher average initial competence level and are therefore subjected to relative grading. The results could indicate that students with weak grades from upper secondary school get a better than expected learning outcome in a study programme where there also is a large number students with strong grades from upper secondary school, even though this is not apparent by only looking at their actual grades. For students with strong grades from upper secondary school, heterogeneity does not seem to matter much. If there is a trend, it seems to be slightly negative, but the difference is marginal. It is however important to note that the interaction models contains considerable multicollinearity. This weakness makes the interpretation highly insecure. It could nonetheless be worth to look further into this aspect of learning using other quantitative or qualitative approaches.

RQ2: Could the introduction of new control variables improve HE grades as a measure of learning outcome?

The institutional value added effects on HE grades in model 4a and 7a are found in Table 11.3. All institutional effects in model 4a are positive, meaning that a student will get better grades by attending any other HEI in Norway compared to the University of Oslo. The institutional effects are much smaller in model 7a. This means that additional variables added in model 5a and 7a reduce the value added effects for HEIs compared to the University of Oslo. This change has to be attributed to one or more of the added variables. Strøm et al. (2013, pp. 49, 75) found in their study that University of Oslo has a strict grading practice, and it is likely that at least some of the effect can be attributed to this. The alternative explanation is that the effects are reduced because of differences in the students' intrinsic motivation.

When looking at the regression effects in model 7a, it is clear that intrinsic motivation influences students' HE grades more than initial competence and heterogeneity at the study programme level. When comparing the results of model 4a, 5a and 7a in Table 11.3, it is however clear that most of the changes in the institutional value added effects occur when the study programme variables are included in model 7a. Although intrinsic motivation is more important in explaining an individual student's HE grades, it does not affect grading on the institutional level because the differences between institutions in their average score on intrinsic motivation is small. The changes in institutional value added effects seen in model 7a is therefore a result of controlling for the study programme level variables and not the survey variables.

In order to find out if the study programme variables included in model 7a actually control for relative grading, the change in effect between the models are compared with a variable measuring the degree of strictness in institutional grading practice. If institutions that have previously been found to have a strict grading practice improve their value added score in model 7a compared to model 4a, model 7a would be considered a better model because some of the effect that lead to strict or lenient grading practise is removed. Strøm et al. (2013, pp. 49, 75) have calculated how lenient or strict the grading practice is at all public HEIs in Norway that offer at least one of the following subject fields: Business Administration Studies, Technology and Social Sciences. All these institutions are listed in Table 11.4. Here, the effects are standardized and the change in effect between model 4a and 7a is calculated in the right column. The correlation between the change in effect between the models and the variable measuring the grading practice strictness is 0.47.[2] The correlation is

Table 11.4. Institutional effects on HE grades and change in institutional effects from model 4a to model 7a

	Model 4a	Model 7a	Change in effect
Stord/Haugesund UC	0,034	0,012	–0,022
Bergen UC	0,072	0,047	–0,025
Hedmark UC	0,071	0,037	–0,034
Lillehammer UC	0,084	0,048	–0,036
Molde UC – Specialized University in Logistics	0,075	0,050	–0,025
Oslo and Akershus UC of Applied Sciences	0,089	0,054	–0,035
UC of Southeast Norway	0,091	0,044	–0,047
Østfold UC	0,075	0,035	–0,040
Sogn og Fjordane UC	0,062	0,032	–0,030
Volda UC	0,063	0,031	–0,032
Norwegian Univ. of Science and Technology	0,022	0,021	–0,001
Nord Univ.	0,058	0,035	–0,023
Norwegian School of Economics	0,036	0,042	0,006
Norwegian Univ. of Life Sciences	0,040	0,036	–0,004
UiT – The Artic Univ. of Norway	0,093	0,042	–0,051
Univ. of Agder	0,065	0,039	–0,026
Univ. of Bergen	0,039	0,025	–0,009
Univ. of Stavanger	0,051	0,010	–0,041
Univ. of Oslo (ref. cat)	0	0	0
Observations	10164	10164	

Standardized beta coefficients
UC = University College; Univ. = University

statistically significant (p-value 0.043). This indicates that some of the differences in grading practice between institutions are removed in model 7a, and that the model seems to give a more accurate estimation of the institutional value added effects than model 4a. However, the institutional effects found in model 7a are quite different from the institutional effects found by Strøm et al. (2013, p. 56) after they controlled for relative grading. Using the institutional effects as value added indicators on students' learning outcome could lead to misleading conclusions, especially when used without additional information.

RQ3: Are self-reported learning outcomes valid and reliable measures of the students' actual learning outcome?

Students in traditional university fields such as law, physics, mathematics, pharmacy studies and social sciences report a higher degree of theoretical knowledge than other students. So do police students, but this changes once intrinsic motivation is included in the model. Art, architect and teacher education students report a lower degree of theoretical knowledge than students in other fields. This suggests that using theoretical knowledge as a learning outcome variable seems, not surprisingly, to favour more theoretical oriented fields. If self-reported learning outcome is to be used as a measure on learning outcome, it is important to control for subject field affiliation.

While the institutional value added effects were considerable in model 7a, they are almost non-existent in model 5b, even after controlling for subject fields. Some are statistically significant, but this is mostly due to the large number of cases (students) in the regression model. One could argue that asking students to self-report their learning outcome in their second year in a bachelor's degree is too early, and that the validity of the variable would be better if students report their learning outcome later in, or after, their studies. However, the results show that being a fifth year student does not seem to have an impact on the self-reported learning outcome. It could also be argued that using upper secondary school grade as the measure of individual competence level before entering higher education is not a good measure to include as independent variable in a model when self-reported learning outcome as the dependent variable. However, there are no alternatives to this in Norway. Considering self-reported learning outcomes as a value added measure by itself by removing upper secondary school grades completely from the model, does not yield any different results either. As noted above, Caspersen et al. (2014) conclude that self-reported learning outcomes measure different knowledge structures rather than actual learning outcome. The findings here seem to support this conclusion.

CONCLUSION

The Norwegian government has in the last years prioritized the development of new result-based indicators intended to measure the value added component on a student's learning outcome by a HEI and/or study programme. In this chapter, the institutional effects on grades received in higher education and self-reported learning outcome have been analysed to see if these can be used in measuring the value added effect from HEIs.

Prior research has concluded that using HE grades as a measure of student performance should be avoided because there is too much variation in grading practice between institutions. The regression models that these conclusions have been drawn from, have been improved upon here by including variables from the Norwegian National Student Survey and study programme level variables intended to remove the effect that grading practice has on grades. There is no evidence that variables from the National Student Survey improve the HE grade model if objective is to use it as a way to calculate the institutional value added effects on the students' learning outcome. Although it does not explain differences between institutions, it could be argued that intrinsic motivation should be included in these models because it has a strong effect on individual HE grades. Introducing study programme level variables, such as average upper secondary school grades among all students at the study programme, does remove some of the effect of relative grading practice. This has improved the model considerably, but some of the grading bias is still not controlled for. Using the institutional effects calculated by the model as value added effects on the students' learning outcome could potentially lead to misleading conclusions. This does not mean that the model cannot be used at all, but that it needs to be used with care and only in combination with additional information. It could for instance be used to select cases to be studied more closely with qualitative methods, something that could give valuable in-depth knowledge about self-reported learning outcome as measure for learning outcome at the programme level.

The findings indicate that self-reported learning outcomes measure a very different aspect of a student's learning outcome than HE grades. However, it is not found valid as a value added indicator as it seems to measure different knowledge structures rather than actual learning outcome.

NOTES

[1] See for instance Damen et al. (2016), a paper presented at EAIR in Birmingham in 2016.
[2] Standardized coefficients are used here to remove some uncertainty regarding coefficients at HEIs with few responses. The correlation using regular coefficients instead of standardized is .67.

REFERENCES

Bauer, T. K., & Grave, B. S. (2011). *Performance-related funding of universities – Does more competition lead to grade inflation?* Bonn: Ruhr Economic Papers Nr. 288.

Betts, J. R. (1995). Does school quality matter? Evidence from the National Longitudinal Survey of Youth. *The Review of Economics and Statistics, 77*(2), 231–250.

Betts, J. R., & Grogger, J. (2003). The impact of grading standards on students achievement, educational attainment, and entry-level earning. *Economics of Education Review, 22*(4), 343–352.

Bloxham, S., & Boyd, P. (2012). Accountability in grading student work: Securing academic standards in a twenty-first century quality assurance context. *British Educational Research Journal, 38*(4), 615–634.
Bonesrønning, H. (1999). The variation in teachers' grading practices: Causes and consequences. *Economics of Education Review, 18*(1), 89–105.
Caspersen, J., Frølich, N., Karlsen, H., & Aamodt, P. O. (2014). Learning outcomes across disciplines and professions: Measurement and interpretation. *Quality in Higher Education, 20*(2), 195–215.
Caspersen, J., Smeby, J.-C., & Aamodt, P. O. (2017). Measuring learning outcomes. *European Journal of Education, 52*(1), 31–43.
Covington, M. V. (2000). Goal theory, motivation, and school achievement: An inegratuve review. *Annual Review of Psychology, 51*(1), 171–200.
Damen, M. -L., Bakken, P., & Hauge, M. S. (2016). *The influence of faculty expectations on students' workload: Searching for academic challenges.* Paper presented at the 38th EAIR Forum, Birmingham. Retrieved from http://www.nokut.no/Documents/Studiebarometeret/2016/Studiebarometeret_2015_Faculty_expectations_and_Students_workload_3-2016.pdf
De Paola, M. (2011). Easy grading practices and supply-demand factors: Evidence from Italy. *Empirical Economics, 41*(2), 227–246.
Det Norske Universitetsråd. (2000). *Mål med mening.* Retrieved from http://www.uhr.no/documents/M_l_med_mening___utredning.pdf
Frølich, N., & Strøm, B. (2008). Higher education funding and insentives: Evidence from the Norwegian funding reform, *European Journal of Education, 43*(4), 555–576.
Jeno, L. M. (2018). *The antecedents and consequences of students' autonomous motivation* (Doctoral dissertation).
Liu, O. L. (2011). Value-added assessment in higher education: A comparison of two methods. *Higher Education, 61*(4), 445–461.
Meld. St. 16 (2016–2017). *Kultur for kvalitet i høyere utdanning.* Oslo: Kunnskapsdepartementet. Retrieved from https://www.regjeringen.no/no/dokumenter/meld.-st.-16-20162017/id2536007/
Møen, J., & Tjelta, M. (2010). Grading standards, student ability and errors in college admission, *Scandinavian Journal of Educational Research, 54*(3), 221–237.
Næss, T. (2006). *Inntakskvalitet og karakterer i høyere utdanning: Høyere grads kandidater, siviløkonomer og allmennlærere.* NIFU STEP rapport 4-2006.
Ot.prp. nr. 40 (2001–2002). *Om lov om endringer i lov 12. mai 1995 nr. 22 om universiteter og høgskoler og lov 2. juli 1999 nr. 64 om helsepersonell.* Oslo: Utdannings- og forskningsdepartementet.
Ryan, R. M., & Deci, E. L. (2000). Intrinsic and extrinsic motivations: Classic definitions and new directions. *Contemporary Educational Psychology, 25*(1), 54–67.
Strøm, B., Falch, T., Gunnes, T., & Haraldsvik, M. (2013). *Analyse av karakterbruk og kvalitet i høyere utdanning.* SØF-rapport 3/13.
Strøm, B., Falch, T., Iversen, J. M. V., & Nyhus, O. H. (2016). *Kvalitetsindikatorer i universitets- og høgskolesektoren.* Sammen: SØF-rapport 5/16.
UHR. (2015). *Karakterbruk i UH-sektoren 2015.* Retrieved from http://www.uhr.no/documents/Karakterrapport_2015___endelig_versjon.pdf
Yang, H., & Yip, C. S. (2002). *An economic theory of grade inflation* (Working paper). Retrieved from http://econ.ohio-state.edu/hyang/grade-inflation.pdf

GREGORY C. WOLNIAK, CASEY E. GEORGE
AND GLEN R. NELSON

12. THE EMERGING DIFFERENTIAL TUITION ERA AMONG U.S. PUBLIC UNIVERSITES

INTRODUCTION

Few education topics capture more attention and concern than the costs of college, and for good reason, given the substantial resources involved in attaining a college degree and the many benefits that accrue to society's educated class (Mayhew, Rockenbach, Bowman, Seifert, & Wolniak, 2016; McMahon, 2009; Toutkoushian & Paulsen, 2016). In the U.S. context, after decades of tuition increases in excess of inflation (Ma, Baum, Pender, & Welch, 2017), today's students are faced with considerable and historically unprecedented challenges in financing college. Accompanying the challenges associated with college costs, students are also faced with an increasingly complex higher education system (Smerek, 2010; Tierney, 2011; Weisbrod, Ballou, & Asch, 2008) with greater variation in and differentiation between institution types (two-year, four-year, not-for-profit, for-profit, etc.) and degree programs (on-line, hybrid, etc.). Access to clear and accurate information about educational alternatives and their respective costs is ever more essential for student decision-making, especially for low-income and first-generation students who may not have the resources to navigate the complexities of the college application process (Bergerson, 2009; Perna, 2006).

For institutions, particularly public colleges and universities, years of declining state funding has confounded the affordability problem, leading many institutions to seek new tuition-revenue streams. Institutions rely more heavily on tuition and fees to make up for changes in state funding, and tuition increases have been found to correlate with disinvestment from states (Delaney & Doyle, 2011).

In recent years, the implementation of differential tuition (DT) policies by postsecondary institutions has become a prevalent strategy in hopes of increasing revenue or to offset instructional costs in some areas study, and are increasingly the subject of debate at public colleges and universities across the country. DT policies are the purposeful variation in undergraduate tuition by major area of study and/ or year of enrolment (Cornell, 2012; Nelson, 2008; Stange, 2015). While forms of differentiating tuition have a long history in U.S. public higher education in relation to whether or not students attend college in their home state (where "in-state" enrolment accompanies lower tuition and "out-of-state" enrolment accompanies higher tuition), our focus with the present study is on a more recent and more nuanced form of tuition differentiation; that which is based on major area of study and/or year of enrolment, and are increasingly the subject of debate at public colleges and universities in the U.S. and the European contexts.

Notably, DT policies add complexity to understanding college costs, leading the financial burden students face once enrolled to differ from information found in many web-based resources. The most recent issue of the College Board's *Trends in College Pricing* (Ma et al., 2017) acknowledges the definitions of tuition used do not fully incorporate undergraduate differentials, creating challenges for drawing valid cost comparisons between universities. In other words, DT policies may mask from the public the real cost of attendance. For instance, at the University of Illinois, in-state residents first enrolling in 2017–2018 will be charged $12,036 (U.S. dollars) in base tuition, while in-state students majoring in business, chemistry, life sciences, and engineering will face a $17,040 base tuition.

The problematic implications of this stem from studies that have consistently shown students from traditionally underrepresented backgrounds are more sensitive to increases in college costs and less responsive to financial aid, such that tuition increases have a more negative influence on their college enrolment and attendance decisions (Cunningham & Santiago, 2008; Perna, 2006). It therefore stands to reason that underrepresented students may face an even greater challenge navigating complex tuition policies at institutions that have adopted DT policies.

Little is known about the actual prevalence of DT policies or the overall influence on students, particularly those who are underrepresented and often under-resourced. The ability to understand, correctly interpret, and incorporate DT information in decision-making relates to the larger issue of financial literacy; Congressional sub-committees have highlighted the lack of financial literacy in regard to credit cards and purchasing homes, as well as calling for financial literacy to be integrated into K-12 curriculum (U.S. House, 2008; U.S. Senate, 2010). These same concerns should apply to college tuition policies and particularly how higher education institutions communicate their tuition policies to prospective students.

Taken together, pricing fields of study differently may lead to unintended consequences in terms of how differential tuition influences students' higher education decision-making, and may potentially further marginalize disadvantaged groups of college students. Against this backdrop, we sought to take an important step towards improving understandings of DT policies in the U.S. and advancing research on college tuition rates and affordability.

HISTORY AND CONTEXT OF DIFFERENTIAL TUITION

There are roughly 2,800 post-secondary four-year institutions of higher education in the U.S., more than 700 of which are public colleges and universities. The U.S. higher education systems is decentralized; there is no national university, national tuition setting process, or common process of disseminating accurate tuition and fee information. Today, public higher education institutions serve approximately two-thirds of all students nation-wide (NCES, 2017) and are primarily subject to oversight from state governments. Because of the decentralized nature of public higher education in the U.S., there exists considerable variation in the tuition-setting policies across colleges and universities.

The public higher education sector has experienced years of declining state funding and increasing expenditures. Institutions responded to these influences by seeking new tuition-revenue streams (Mumper, 2001; Paulsen, 2001; Rand Corporation & Council for Aid to Education, 1997; Toutkoushian, 2001; Yanikoski & Wilson, 1984), which has negatively affected the affordability of higher education as institutions rely more heavily on tuition and fees.

Studies have confirmed that tuition increases are directly correlated with declines in state appropriations (Delaney & Doyle, 2011). In fact, Weinberg (1977) postulated four decades ago that higher education administrators would need to offset declines in state support by using differential pricing to increase revenue. Examples of differential pricing included charging more for graduate level courses, courses offered during peak times, courses taken by part-time students, level of student and by department or field of study. DT policies, as defined above, are a particularly salient and increasingly prominent form of varying tuition, and the focus of our study.

There are several reasons why educators, policymakers, and social scientists should be concerned about DT policies, particularly at public institutions. The debate over the "fairness" of a uniform tuition policy versus implementing differential pricing has occurred for over forty years. For example, Responsibility Centered Budgeting (Whalen, 1991) and other cost-based models poplar among higher education institutions tend to support charging different levels of tuition for different fields of study. Conversely, charging a uniform tuition level has been argued in terms of equity, in order to spread institutional costs equally across all students (Southern Regional Education Board, 1976).

DT policies also call into question whether institutions have abandoned the basic tenants of public higher education in the U.S., which stemmed from the Morrill Acts 1862 and 1890, and were grounded in notions of access for all citizens (McPherson, 2015). Prior to the 1970s, public university tuition policy in the U.S. generally reflected the principle of affordability, with the majority of the cost of instruction provided by state funding (Toutkoushian, 2001). During that time-period it was easy to determine the cost of a college education, with tuition consisting of one rate for all students who were residents of an institution's home state, regardless of academic field of study or degree objective (baccalaureate, post-graduate, etc.). Ultimately, the increasing prevalence of DT policies marks an increase in privatization and market-based influences in public higher education.

Looking to the European context, we see similar trends. Amidst increasing privatization and market influences on higher education, there is increasing concern and attention among researchers to study the effects of new and evolving tuition practices (e.g., Bruckmeier, Fischer, & Wigger, 2015; Burge, Kim, Rohr, Frearson, & Guerin, 2014; Johnes, 2007). For example, student choice and participation were examined in the wake of the 2012 tuition cap increase in the United Kingdom (Burge, Kim, Rohr, Frearson, & Guerin, 2014; Wyness, 2015) and potential conflicts between DT policies and the Higher Education Funding Council's funding model (Johnes, 2007). In addition, during the nine-year period, from 2005–2014, when German universities were allowed to charge tuition, researchers noted students' time to degree completion was shortened (Bruckmeier, Fischer, & Wigger, 2015). Despite inherent differences between the European and the U.S. higher education systems (Ward & Douglas, 2005), an improved understanding of the tuition/pricing policies may transcend the differences and may inform decision-making across national contexts.

REVIEW OF PAST RESEARCH

A large body of research has examined student's enrolment decisions and choice of academic major in relation to price sensitivity (Hemelt & Marcotte, 2011; Cunningham & Santiago, 2008; Perna, 2006; Heller, 1997), perceived future earnings (Arcidiacono, 2004, 2012; Rothstein & Rouse, 2011; Steinbrickner & Steinbrickner, 2011; Wiswall & Zafar, 2012; Wolniak & Engberg, 2015; Wolniak, Seifert, Reed, & Pascarella, 2008), and receipt of financial aid (Bettinger, 2004; Desjardins & McCall, 2012). In general, these studies draw on the law of demand to explain the anticipated negative relationship between price and enrolment (i.e., quantity demand) caused by students opting for less costly alternatives, all else equal (Toutkoushian & Pausen, 2016). The prevailing assumption is that students behave rationally in making their postsecondary choices by taking into account anticipated long-term benefits (both monetary and non-monetary) and costs (direct and indirect) of attaining a degree. While studies have consistently indicated a negative relationship between costs and enrolment patterns, research is inconclusive in terms of the magnitude of students' responsiveness to changes in higher education pricing (Toutkoushian & Paulsen, 2016). Both theory and empirical evidence point to the notion that, all else equal, as price increases, enrolment declines.

Studies that have specifically considered DT in relation to students' educational decisions are few in number. The handful studies that have examined DT policies suggest a negative influence on persistence and graduation within particular fields of study. For example, Stange (2015) identified that higher tuition in engineering significantly reduced the fraction of engineering degrees awarded, and that a similar though less pronounced relationship appeared in business. Importantly, Stange noted disproportionately larger effects among women and minority students relative to their male and white counterparts. Stange further reasoned that higher prices of certain majors will discourage students from entering (decrease quantity demand for) the affected majors, while noting that if an institution accompanies a major-specific price increase with improvements in the quality of education provided, then demand for a given program of study could actually increase amidst rising prices.

All else equal, higher prices of certain majors will decrease quantity demanded of (discourage students from entering) the affected majors, which may be most pronounced among traditionally underrepresented students. Higher program costs may be initially offset with increases in financial aid, yet as aid diminishes over time, low-income students in higher-tuition programs such as engineering may be burdened with higher overall costs of attending college (George-Jackson, Rincon & Garcia, 2012).

One reason for the lack of research on DT policies is the lack of data. An overview of early versions of such policies was published in 1977, listing various categories of DT based upon student classification such as summer school students, part-time students, continuing education, and on campus or off campus instruction (Weinberg, 1977). More recently, Nelson (2008) identified the programs and levels of undergraduate differentials by major at 74 of 165 public, Research-1 institutions. A similar study was completed in 2011, which found the number of institutions with such policies has steadily increased over the last three decades (Cornell, 2012). Two additional studies were recently completed, gathering DT data at a small number of institutions (University of Washington, 2011; University Leadership Council, 2009).

The lack of comprehensive understandings of the prevalence and potential effects of DT policies motivates the present study. Given trends in college costs and state higher education appropriations, and the appearance of increasing policy rhetoric surrounding tuition differentials at public universities, there is a need to understand the prevalence of and conditions surrounding DT policies.

RESEARCH QUESTIONS

The purpose of the study is to uncover institutional DT policies, its prevalence, and the institutional characteristics associated with the decision to adopt DT policies. We focus on a subsample of public four-year institutions given they enrol a large majority of all postsecondary students, as well as first-time and underrepresented students of color (NCES, 2015). Our study focuses on public four-year research universities classified within the U.S. as having the highest levels of research activity. These 165 institutions enrol approximately half of the public four-year student population (NCES, 2017). Private institutions are not included in our study because their pricing responds to market forces without regard to access and affordability mandates.

By describing the prevalence of DT policies and the extent to which they have increased in recent years, as well as the kinds of institutions that rely on DT, we take an important step towards illuminating this under-researched but increasingly prominent practice. We have designed our analyses to address the following research questions:

- Q1: What is the prevalence of DT policies and how has this changed over time?
- Q2: What institutional factors are associated with the adoption and diffusion of DT policies?

The study is largely descriptive, including statistical tests for association between institutional characteristics and DT status. The study does not seek to identify the effect of DT policies on undergraduate students' enrolment decisions. It does, however, provide important new data on which to drive forward critical conversations surrounding an emerging tuition-setting practice.

CONCEPTUAL FRAMEWORK

The study examines the emergence of an institutional tuition-setting policy. We have therefore grounded this work within the conceptual domain of policy innovation and diffusion. In the context of state-level policy research, innovation is conceptualized as adopting any program new to a particular organization, such as a state or local government, and diffusion points to the notion that organizations are more influenced by other organizations that are within close proximity or who share some common characteristic (Baybeck, Berry, & Seigel, 2011; Berry & Berry, 2007; Makse & Volden, 2011).

Based on the formative work of Walker (1969) and extended by Boehmke & Witmer (2004), diffusion policies are defined as those influenced by combinations of neighboring states' actions and group membership (such as political ideology) that unfold through two mechanisms – learning and economic competition. Policies diffuse by way of learning when an example is provided by the actions of others, which provides a viable strategy to solve an existing problem. Additionally, policies may diffuse by way of market-based economic factors, whereby competitive pressure prompts an organization or state to adopt a policy to defend against the loss of revenue or market position, or in an attempt to preemptively strengthen one's market position (Baybeck et al., 2011). For examples of these frameworks applied to higher education research, see Doyle (2006), Hearn and Griswold (1994), Li (2017), and McLendon, Hearn, and Deaton (2006).

Applied to the present study, it holds that institutional adoption of DT policies occurs over time, such that institutions become similar to one-another in terms of tuition-setting strategies, and that combinations of factors based on learning (e.g., neighbor and group-membership characteristics) and market-based competition (e.g., enrolment demand and pricing characteristics). We have designed our analytic models and hypotheses according to this conceptual framework.

METHODS

Data

The study merges information from three sources. First, new primary data on current DT practises was gathered among all 165 institutions classified in the 2015–16 United States Department of Education's Integrated Postsecondary Education Data System (IPEDS) as public four-year, research-intensive institutions that offer undergraduate degree programs (i.e., Carnegie Classifications of 'high research activity' and 'very high research activity'). Importantly, focussing on this subset of institutions enabled us to examine trends in DT policies, once merged with our second data source. Specifically, our second source of data came from Nelson's (2008) study – the only known national data on institutional DT policies – containing information from the 1991–92, 1999–2000 and 2007–08 academic years. Adding an additional time point from 2015–16 allowed us to examine trends and measure change. Our third source of data was institutional records obtained from the publically-accessible IPEDS Data Center for each of the four time points (1991–92, 1999–2000, 2007–08, and 2015–16), containing an array of institutional characteristics over these years.

Primary data collection occurred between February and March 2016, organized around the following steps. First, the full list of institutions and their website URLs was downloaded from IPEDS. Second, all members of the research team (consisting of three principal investigators and six research assistants) were formally trained to review publically accessible information available on the websites of each institution to determine the existence of DT policies among published 2015–16 tuition rates. Using a targeted and systematic set of procedures, the researchers reviewed information available on the web from each institution to capture if DT policies were included in their 2015–2016 tuition rates. Each case was then flagged as *Yes/No/Cannot determine*.

To enhance validity, three different members of the research team independently entered data for each institutional case. Once all data were entered, the study's principal investigators examined the agreement across all three entries for each institution. Discrepancies were resolved through an iterative discussion process.

The final analytic dataset consisted of a balanced panel containing 660 institution-years. Specifically, the data consisted of 165 public research-intensive universities across four years (1991–92, 1999–2000, 2007–08, and 2015–16). Our institutional sample ranged in enrolment size form under 5,000 students to over 20,000, the majority (62.7%) of institutions in the "20,000 and above" category. The sample also represented every region of the continental U.S. and included five (3%) Historically Black Colleges and Universities.

Analysis

Our analysis plan utilized descriptive and multivariate techniques to address the research questions. First, our descriptive analysis allowed us to identify the prevalence of DT policies over time, based on frequencies of cases of DT stemming from our data collection efforts in 2015–16, in combination with information merged from years 1991–92, 1999–2000 and 2007–08. Second, we examined a host of institutional characteristics within each year, based on mean values in total, for institutions that had adopted DT policies, and for institutions that had not adopted DT policies. We tested for mean differences between DT-adopting institutions and non-DT institutions based on *Chi-sq* statistics for categorical variables and *t*-statistics for continuous variables.

Our multivariate analysis was designed to examine the effects of theory-based measures of institutional learning (group-membership and neighbour variables) and market-based factors on the adoption of DT for a given institution, within a given year, defined as follows:

$$DT_{i,t} = b_1 \text{LEARNING-FACTORS}_{i,t} + b_2 \text{TUITION\&FEES}_{i,t} + b_3 \text{ENROLMENT}_{i,t} + b_4 \text{PROFILE}_{i,t} + \text{YEAR}_{i,t}$$

where $DT_{i,t}$ is the adoption of DT policies in year t for institution i; LEARNING-FACTORS is a vector of three variables representing aspects through which an institution may learn of a policy innovation, including group membership and neighbour-related factors. Specifically, these measures included the number of institutions within the same state that had adopted DT policies, the number of institutions in a neighbouring state that had adopted DT policies, and whether an institution originated as a Land Grant institution (resulting from the Morrill Acts of 1862 and 1890, chartered around a focus on agricultural research, engineering sciences, and community extension); TUITION&FEES included in-state, yearly undergraduate tuition and fees, broken into bivariate measures based on quartiles within each year to represent the relative position of an institution to other public four-year research universities within the same year; ENROLMENT is a vector of three measures, one being the total number of undergraduates enrolled at a given institution (also coded into bivariate indicators based on quartiles), another being the share (percentage) of undergraduates who are enrolled on a full-time basis, and another based on the share (percentage) of undergraduates who were from outside of the institution's home state. Finally, PROFILE was captured based on the 75th percentile average entering admissions test score (combined SAT scores or converted ACT scores for missing SAT scores) which we standardized ($Mean=1$, $SD=0$) and coded into bivariate indicators based on quartiles indicating an institution's position relative to other institutions within a given year. The tuition, enrolment, and profile measures conceptually represent market-based institutional characteristics.

Through our analyses, we tested two hypotheses:

Hypothesis 1: Institutions will be more likely to adopt DT policies if they have other institutions within the same state or neighbouring states who have adopted DT policies. Similarly, institutional group-membership, such as Land Grant status, will predict the likelihood of DT adoption, with the direction of the influence being grounded in historical patterns.

Hypothesis 2: Institutions with stronger relative market positions will be more likely to adopt DT policies. Market position is signalled according to supply and demand factors, including relative tuition, overall enrolment, popularity among out-of-state students, and the academic profile of entering students.

Estimation strategy. Our estimation strategy was tailored to the panel structure of the data, the fact that our outcome variable was dichotomous (DT=1,0), and the limitation that the variables available through IPEDS changed over the years we examined such that the full set of measures described above were only present in the most recent two out four time points. Studies of policy adoption often employ event history or survival modelling to estimate the time until an event occurs for a particular subject (Box-Steffensmeier & Jones, 2004; DesJardins, 2003; Long, 1997). For the present study we were limited by only having two time points for certain variables and therefore employed a more general, logistic regression approach with time fixed effects for the four-year model (1991–92, 1999–2000, 2007–08, 2015–16) and the fully-specified two-year model (2007–08, 2015–16). In addition, to account for time-dependence of the episode of interest (DT), we estimated a Cox Proportional Hazard Model to more formally assess the effects of time-varying covariates. The hazard model estimates served as a sensitivity analysis of the logistic estimates under a different set of statistical assumptions regarding the role of time.

Our models took the following simplified forms, where $x\beta$ represents the array of independent variables listed above, where equations 1 and 2 signify the logistic and hazard models, respectively.

$$\pi_i/(1-\pi_i) = e^{x\beta} \tag{1}$$

$$h_i(t) = h_0(t)e^{x\beta} \tag{2}$$

Equation (1) represents the underlying probability of DT policies for institution i (π_i), controlling for year effects and exponentiated to reflect the odds of the event occurring. For equation (2), $h_i(t)$ is the hazard rate of adopting DT in institution i, year t, and $h_0(t)$ is the unspecified baseline hazard.

RESULTS

Prevalence and Trends of DT Policies

Based on new 2015–16 data indicating DT policies, in combination with data previously gathered for 1991–92, 1999–2000 and 2007–08 (Nelson, 2008), we found nearly a ten-fold increase in DT policies among our sample of 165 public, four-year research universities. Specifically, in 1991–92 DT policies were identified among 9 institutions. Looking to the most recent year, 2015–16, DT was evident among 86 institutions, representing an increase from 5% to 52% of all public, four-year, research universities. In the intermediate years, we found DT policies present in 30 institutions (18%) in 1999–2000 and 67 (41%) in 2007–08. Figure 12.1 maps the patterns of institutional DT adoption across this timespan. Evident in the patterns across years is the clustering of DT policies among institutions in the middle and eastern regions of the U.S. For additional detail, Table 12.1 displays the full list of institutions adopting DT policies by year.

Table 12.1. Institutions adopting DT policies by year

Year	Institutions adopting DT policies	Number new DT adopters	Cumulative number
1991	Rutgers University-New Brunswick Temple University University of Colorado-Boulder University of Colorado-Denver/Anschutz Medical Campus University of Illinois-Chicago University of Michigan-Ann Arbor University of Mississippi University of New Hampshire-Main Campus Wichita State University	9	9
1999	Missouri University of Science and Technology North Dakota State University-Main Campus Oregon State University Portland State University Purdue University-Main Campus Rutgers University-Newark University of Texas-El Paso University of Alabama-Birmingham University of Arkansas University of Idaho University of Illinois-Urbana-Champaign University of Kansas University of Minnesota-Twin Cities University of Missouri-Columbia University of Missouri-Kansas City University of Missouri-St Louis University of North Dakota University of Oregon University of Rhode Island University of South Carolina-Columbia University of Toledo	21	30

(cont.)

Table 12.1. Institutions Adopting DT policies by year (cont.)

Year	Institutions adopting DT policies	Number new DT adopters	Cumulative number
2007	Arizona State University-Tempe Clemson University Colorado State University-Fort Collins Indiana University-Bloomington Indiana University-Purdue University-Indianapolis Iowa State University Kansas State University Louisiana Tech University Miami University-Oxford Michigan Technological University Montana State University Ohio State University-Main Campus Oklahoma State University-Main Campus Pennsylvania State University-Main Campus South Dakota State University University of Montana University of Tennessee-Knoxville University of Texas-Arlington University of Texas-Austin University of Texas-Dallas University of Arizona University of Georgia University of Hawaii-Manoa University of Houston University of Iowa University of Kentucky University of Memphis University of Nebraska-Lincoln University of South Alabama University of South Dakota University of Utah University of Wisconsin-Madison University of Wisconsin-Milwaukee Utah State University Virginia Commonwealth University Virginia Polytechnic Institute and State University West Virginia University	37	67

(cont.)

Table 12.1. Institutions Adopting DT policies by year (cont.)

Year	Institutions adopting DT policies	Number new DT adopters	Cumulative number
2015	Auburn University Ball State University Cleveland State University College of William and Mary Kent State University-Kent Michigan State University Ohio University-Main Campus Southern Illinois University-Carbondale Texas A & M University-College Station University of Akron-Main Campus University of Cincinnati-Main Campus University of Maine University of Maryland-College Park University of Massachusetts-Lowell University of Nevada-Reno University of New Mexico-Main Campus University of Oklahoma-Norman Campus University of Pittsburgh-Pittsburgh Campus University of Virginia-Main Campus Wayne State University Western Michigan University	21	88

Notes: The cumulative number does not reflect cases where an institution had adopted DT in one year but discontinued the policy in a subsequent year. Two such cases exist: Missouri University of Science and Technology, and University of Oregon had DT policies in 2007–08 but not in 2015–16
Source: Nelson (2008); Primary Data

Institutional Characteristics of DT Adopters

Turning to our examination of institutional characteristics associated with DT status, we conducted descriptive and multivariate analyses. First, we examined institutional mean values across an array of variables within each year, and flagged those variables that were statistically different for institutions that had adopted DT policies versus those that had not adopted DT policies. Second, our multivariate analysis examined the likelihood of institutional adoption of DT policies in relation to institutional characteristics, over time.

Descriptive results. Presented in Table 12.2, our analysis of sample means point to several findings. First, it appears that DT policies are more prominent among land grant institutions within the two most recent years we measured (2007–08 and 2015–16). It may be that institutions that share a historic mission centred on research and application in the agriculture, science, and engineering fields are more likely to turn to DT policies to either generate revenue, incentivize students to enter specific fields, or some combination of those rationale. In addition, we found at least some descriptive evidence to suggest that DT policies are more common among institutions if there exists other institutions within the same state that have adopted DT policies; we found evidence of this in both 1999–2000 and 2015–16. The most recent year also provided indication that a similar trend occurs in terms of the presence of DT policies among institutions within neighbouring states.

In terms of tuition and fees, not only does the table demonstrate the striking amount by which in-state tuition and fees have increased over a 15 year time period, it also suggests that institutions adopting DT policies have, on average, higher tuition and fees compared to institutions without DT policies ($10,598.94 vs. $9,580.68 in 2015–16). Furthermore, in the more recent years (2007–08 and 2015–16), it appears that DT policies are more prominent for institutions that have higher enrolments (21,558.19 vs. 17,528.49 in 2015–16).

Reflecting the strength of an institution's market position that would accompany stronger demand from out-of-state students and students who are academically more competitive based on average college admissions tests, we found significant differences by institutional DT status. For both of these measures, though only available in 2007–08 and 2015–16, it appears that DT practicing institutions have, on average, larger shares of out-of-state students and a higher academic profile of enrolling students.

Multivariate results. Results from the logistic and hazard models are presented in Tables 12.3 and 12.4. Our analyses reveal a set of findings that largely, though not entirely, support our hypotheses, as follows.

First, across the full set of results and net of all other factors in the models, it appears that being a Land Grant institution significantly and positively influences the adoption of DT policies. This finding supports Hypothesis 1, based on the notion that the historical, mission-drive context of an institution creates a peer-group of similar institutions from which policymakers learn from and ultimately mimic tuition-setting strategies. Similarly, we found partial evidence of policy diffusion in the results of our logistic regression estimates, where the larger the number of other DT adopters among institutions within a given state, and to a lesser extent neighbouring states, the more likely an institution is to adopt DT policies. However, the finding was not supported by our hazard model estimates, suggesting that while other DT adopters within the same state or neighbouring states increases the odds of institutional adoption, controlling for the year-effects on adoption (as estimated by the logistic model), these variables appear not to significantly influence the time-to-DT adoption (as estimated by the hazard model).

Figure 12.1. Patterns of institutional adoption of differential tuition policies, 1991–92 to 2015–16

Table 12.2. Sample means by institutional differential tuition status,
1991–92 to 2015–16

	1991–92	1999–2000	2007–08	2015–16
Land Grant Institution (%)				
M_{Total}	0.33	0.33	0.33	0.33
$M_{DT=0}$	0.33	0.32	0.24	0.23
$M_{DT=1}$	0.22	0.37	0.45	0.42
$Sig. (_{DT=1\ vs\ DT=0})_t$	***	***		
Number of Institution with DT within Same State				
M_{Total}	0.16	0.53	1.32	1.94
$M_{DT=0}$	0.15	0.44	1.28	1.65
$M_{DT=1}$	0.22	0.93	1.37	2.21
$Sig. (_{DT=1\ vs\ DT=0})_t$	***	*		
Number of Institution with DT in Neighbouring State				
M_{Total}	0.73	2.61	6.22	8.14
$M_{DT=0}$	0.75	2.65	6.00	7.13
$M_{DT=1}$	0.44	2.40	6.55	9.07
$Sig. (_{DT=1\ vs\ DT=0})_t$	**			
Tuition & Fees: In-state ($)				
M_{Total}	2,275.44	3,544.30	6,683.51	10,121.24
$M_{DT=0}$	2,224.96	3,427.34	6,434.52	9,580.68
$M_{DT=1}$	3,144.78	4,055.00	7,036.55	10,598.94
$Sig. (_{DT=1\ vs\ DT=0})_t$	***	***	*	**
Enrolment: Total Undergraduates				
M_{Total}	15,470.92	15,490.81	17,366.66	19,641.62
$M_{DT=0}$	15,427.78	15,576.66	16,330.01	17,528.49
$M_{DT=1}$	16,213.89	15,107.37	18,867.49	21,558.19
$Sig. (_{DT=1\ vs\ DT=0})_t$	*	***		
Enrolment: Percentage Full-Time (%)				
M_{Total}	0.79	0.81	0.84	0.84
$M_{DT=0}$	0.79	0.81	0.84	0.84
$M_{DT=1}$	0.79	0.79	0.84	0.84
$Sig. (_{DT=1\ vs\ DT=0})_t$				
Enrolment: Percentage out-of-state (%)				
M_{Total}	0.18	0.23		

(cont.)

Table 12.2. Sample means by institutional differential tuition status,
1991–92 to 2015–16 (cont.)

	1991–92	1999–2000	2007–08	2015–16
$M_{DT=0}$	–	–	0.15	0.19
$M_{DT=1}$	–	–	0.23	0.27
$Sig. (_{DT=1 \text{ vs } DT=0})_t$	–	–	***	***
Institutional Profile: Composite SAT/ACT (z-score)				
M_{Total}	–	–	−0.07	−0.01
$M_{DT=0}$	–	–	−0.22	−0.20
$M_{DT=1}$	–	–	0.13	0.15
$Sig. (_{DT=1 \text{ vs } DT=0})_t$	**	**		
$N_{DT=0}$	156	135	98	79
$N_{DT=1}$	9	30	67	86

Notes: – Indicates variables not available for a given year. Statistical significance is shown for within-year differences by DT status (DT=No vs. DT=Yes), based on *Chi-sq* statistics (likelihood ratio test) for categorical variables, *t*-statistics for continuous variables.
*$p<0.10$; **$p<0.05$; ***$p<0.01$
Source: IPEDS (1991, 1999, 2007, 2015); Primary Data

Second, DT adoption appears driven by the relative level of an institution's tuition and fees. Our results point to a consistent pattern whereby, when compared to institutions with the lowest quartile of tuition and fees, those in each subsequently higher quartile were significantly more likely to adopt DT policies. This finding was less evident in the two-year hazard model, likely due to less variation in the variable when measured across only two time points.

Third, looking at the effects of the enrolment variables, the results provide mixed evidence to suggest that institutions in the largest enrolment quartile were more likely to have adopted DT policies than those institutions in the lowest enrolment quartile. This finding was not replicated by the hazard models. Alternatively, an institution's share of full-time (versus part-time) enrolees, and the share of enrolled out-of-state students significantly predicted DT adoption (note that out-of-state enrolment was only available in the two most recent time periods captured by the data). These measures point to the strength of an institution's market position in relation to DT adoption.

Our final set of findings indicate the influence of the academic profile of an institution, as defined by students' average admissions test scores. While this measures was only available within our two most recent years of data, the results indicate that the relative position of an institution's academic profile, compared to the other institutions in the sample, significantly predicts DT adoption. Divided into quartiles and tested against institutions in the lowest quartile, we found higher profile

Table 12.3. Estimated odds ratios of differential tuition adoption

	1991–92 to 2015–16		2007–08 to 2015–17	
	Exp(B)	SE	Exp(B)	SE
LEARNING FACTORS				
Land Grant Institution	2.436***	0.228	2.414***	0.309
DT adopters, Same State	1.171**	0.072	1.265***	0.088
DT adopters, Neighbouring State	1.061**	0.026	1.091***	0.031
Tuition & Fees				
In-state TF: Q2	2.213***	0.302	2.330**	0.389
In-state TF: Q3	1.998**	0.320	2.116*	0.427
In-state TF: Q4	3.396***	0.311	2.113*	0.432
Enrolment				
Total UG: Q2	1.610	0.291	2.120*	0.390
Total UG: Q3	1.281	0.300	1.749	0.394
Total UG: Q4	1.723*	0.297	2.664**	0.410
Percent Full-Time	0.087***	0.894	0.002***	1.604
Percent Out-of-State			129.149***	1.030
Profile				
Entering Admissions Test: Q2			2.770***	0.372
Entering Admissions Test: Q3			2.137*	0.404
Entering Admissions Test: Q4			2.797**	0.434
Model Chi-sq (d.f.)	48.236 (d.f.=10)***		82.421 (d.f.=14)***	

Notes: Included in the models but not shown in the table are year fixed effects. For each set of bivariate quartile measures (labelled with "Q"), the excluded comparison group is quartile 1 (Q1). *p<0.10; **p<0.05; ***p<0.01

Source: IPEDS (1991, 1999, 2007, 2015); Primary Data

institutions were more likely to have adopted DT policies than their counterparts in the lowest quartile.

The finding related to effects on DT adoption of tuition and fees, enrolment, and profile largely support Hypothesis 2, whereby an institution's market position is determined based on some combination of supply (e.g., courses offered, seats available, etc.) and demand (e.g., admissible students willing and able to pay). The results indicate that these factors significantly affect the adoption of DT policies. For example, all else equal, higher tuition signals greater quantity demand for the institution, whereas higher total enrolments point to some combination of supply and demand. Percentages of out-of-state students also points to the strength of an institution's market position, specifically the demand among this one segment

Table 12.4. Estimated hazard rate of differential tuition adoption

	1991–92 to 2015–16		2007–08 to 2015–17	
	Exp(B)	SE	Exp(B)	SE
LEARNING FACTORS				
Land Grant Institution	1.574**	0.170	1.499**	0.196
DT adopters, Same State	0.991	0.045	1.037	0.049
DT adopters, Neighbouring State	0.986	0.016	1.009	0.017
Tuition & Fees				
In-state TF: Q2	1.903***	0.241	1.563*	0.262
In-state TF: Q3	1.830**	0.259	1.481	0.284
In-state TF: Q4	2.273***	0.251	1.443	0.292
Enrolment				
Total UG: Q2	1.336	0.230	1.251	0.270
Total UG: Q3	1.333	0.236	1.351	0.273
Total UG: Q4	1.442	0.232	1.375	0.275
Percent Full-Time	0.127***	0.655	0.104**	0.891
Percent Out-of-State			3.199**	0.575
Profile				
Entering Admissions Test: Q2			1.666**	0.253
Entering Admissions Test: Q3			1.509	0.274
Entering Admissions Test: Q4			1.620*	0.288
Model Chi-sq (d.f.)	26.83 (d.f.=10)		26.78 (d.f.=14)	

Notes: For each set of bivariate quartile measures (labelled with "Q"), the excluded comparison group is quartile 1 (Q1). $*p<0.10$; $**p<0.05$; $***p<0.01$
Source: IPEDS (1991, 1999, 2007, 2015); Primary Data

of students. Similarly, the academic profile of entering students is driven by the institutions applicant pool, which also reflects demand for the institution. Simply put, the stronger an institution's market position, the more likely the institution will have adopted DT policies.

DISCUSSION AND IMPLICAITONS

The purpose of the study was to shed new light on institutional DT policies, their prevalence and the institutional characteristics associated with their adoption. Conceptualizing DT policies to be a heretofore-unexamined function of organizational learning factors and market conditions, we focussed our analyses on a subsample of public four-year institutions for whom we had historic data dating back to the 1991–92 academic year. Our results addressed two research questions.

Our first question focused on the prevalence of DT policies and the extent that this has changed over time. Indeed, the adoption of DT policies by higher education institutions has become an increasingly prevalent strategy, such that over half of all public research universities in the U.S. have implemented some form of DT practices. Our findings reinforce and update the small handful of previous studies that have sought to identify DT policies at public universities (Cornell, 2012; Nelson, 2008, and Weinberg, 1977). The data presented here confirm an upward trend in terms of DT policy adoption, which is expected to continue given the identified pattern and the continued challenges in higher education funding within the United States.

Our second research question asked about the factors associated with the adoption and diffusion of DT policies. Here we found strong support that institutional characteristics that signal the institution's market position, as well as historical group membership, significantly affect the adoption of DT policies. We also uncovered mixed evidence to suggest that neighbour effects, or the influence on DT policy adoption of having other institutions with DT policies within the same or a neighbouring state. Here our results indicate that DT adoption among other nearby institutions may increase the likelihood of adopting DT policies in general, but does not affect the time to adoption. It may be that DT policy adoption occurs more from institutions learning from other institutions within an existing group (e.g., Land Grant status), than from institutions within closer geographical proximity. Altogether, our results suggest that market-based, economic conditions and group membership have greater influence than regional or geographic proximity. This finding is somewhat surprising given that much of the tuition-setting policies at public universities is determined at the state level and may signal that specific DT practices within a given institution are strategies that fall outside the scope of state policymakers.

While our findings do not formally suggest institutional rationale for implementing DT policies, it is useful to interpret our results against a backdrop marked by increasing public debate that suggests state-level pressure on institutions to adopt DT policies. For example, following lower than expected state education appropriations for 2016–17, the presidents of all three Iowa public universities were asked by their governing board to present options to increase student tuition and fees through the use of differentials (Charis-Carlson, 2016). In another example, the University of Nebraska (Abourezk, 2011) and the University of Maryland (University of Maryland, 2015) went through similar policy discussions before ultimately implementing DT policies. In these cases it appears that DT policies represent a revenue-generating innovation that institutions are compelled to adopt when faced with declining appropriations from their state. However, in other cases, DT policies have been promoted for very different reasons. Specifically, in Kentucky and Florida, each state's governor sited workforce development concerns as the basis for proposing tuition reductions in areas of study deemed most important to the local economy (such as nursing and STEM fields) in hopes of incentivizing students to pursue those fields (Dorfman, 2016; Wessman, 2012).

The unfortunate implication of such motivations is that a tuition reduction in some fields of study makes leads to other fields, notably the arts and humanities, being relatively more expensive and therefore less accessible to students with fewer financial resources (Hora, Benbow, and Oleson, 2016). Perhaps most interesting is the fact that these two different motivations for DT policies move tuition in opposite directions – some leading to increased tuition within a field of study, while others lead to decreased tuition in a field of study.

Finally, an important extension and unanticipated finding that stemmed from our data collection efforts was the extent that our research team – despite having established a systematic protocol for data collection and conducted training sessions for all members of the research team – encountered high frequencies of researcher disagreement pertaining to institutions' DT status. Recall that three researchers collected DT information on each institutional case for the 2015–2016 academic year. Interestingly, three-way agreement across researchers was present in fewer than half of the cases. This required the principal investigators to adjudicate a large number of cases and suggests that locating and entering institutional tuition data is often imprecise and varied across individuals, even among trained researchers. This finding is notable, as it suggests stakeholders, particularly prospective students and families who would not have undergone the same procedural training as our research team and who likely do not bring the same familiarity with college and university practices, will experience considerable difficulty obtaining accurate college tuition information. Institutions should be prompted by this finding to take a fresh look at their websites, for the purpose of improving their communication strategies and the transparency of tuition information.

Ultimately, with public colleges and universities increasingly looking to DT policies to address revenue, enrolment, workforce, or political challenges, there may be a handful of unintended, negative consequences. Given the lack of data on DT policies and the knowledge that DT information is not always reflected on institutions' publically available cost calculators, DT policies impede the ability of researchers, policymakers, and prospective students to make accurate determinations on the costs of attending a particular institution or choosing a particular major field of study. DT policies appear to be a symptom of a larger transparency problem. In fact, as the U.S. Education and Workforce Committee recently observed: "Despite repeated attempts to enhance transparency in the higher education system, students and families still struggle to access important information that will assist in their search for the right college or university" (U.S. House of Representatives, 2014). To respond to demands for greater transparency and accountability in university pricing, national datasets and resources must move beyond a simplistic focus on average or base tuition to a more accurate reporting of tuition differentials. Admittedly, due to the complexity of DT policies and their variations by institution, by field, and by year of study, capturing such information will be a much more challenging task than simply reporting a single tuition figure. However, without doing so, our collective understandings of postsecondary tuition in the United States will remain limited. Given that DT policies have increased over time and are likely to continue doing so in the coming decades – in the U.S. as well as in European higher education systems – we must also focus attention on how DT is communicated to prospective students and their families. In practice, while institutional autonomy allows for variability in how all tuition, fees, and cost information is displayed, institutions that have DT policies should work toward increased transparency and ease of accessibility communicating those policies to individuals. In terms of research, we encourage the incorporation of DT information in IPEDS reporting to support affordability studies as well as reports on the *true* tuition amounts charged by colleges. Future studies should build on the data we collected to examine the effects of DT adoption on student enrolment and to design experiments that lead to recommendations for presenting accurate and transparent cost information by way of institutional websites. It is our hope that the findings and underlying data resulting from this study will drive forward critical conversations surrounding DT policies and, more generally, the transparency by which higher education institutions convey to the public their tuition policies.

ACKNOWLEDGEMENTS

This research was supported in part by the Spencer Foundation (Grant #201600165). Research assistance for the project was provided by: Michael Moramarco (Arizona State University); Jarrod Druery (University of Louisville); Cassie Kwon (New York University; Emily Zuccaro (University of Louisville); Megan George (Arizona State University); and Tiffani Williams (New York University). All expressed views and empirical conclusions are solely those of the authors.

REFERENCES

Abourezk, K. (2011). UNL chancellor to propose increasing tuition for some classes. *Lincoln Journal Star*. Retrived April 28, 2011 from http://journalstar.com/news/local/education/unl-chancellor-to-propose-increasing-tuition-for-some-classes/article_870bd03c-97e9-5f9b-9b48-620df9173ba5.html

Arcidiacono, P. (2004). Ability sorting and the returns to college major. *Journal of Econometrics, 121* (1–2), 343–375.

Arcidiacono, P., Hotz, J., & Kang, S. (2012). Modeling college major choices using elicited measures of expectations and counterfactuals. *Journal of Econometrics, 166*, 3–16.

Baybeck, B., Berry, W. D., & Siegel, D. A. (2011). A strategic theory of policy diffusion via intergovernmental competition. *Journal of Politics, 73*(1), 232–247.

Bergerson, A. A. (2009). *College choice and access to college: Moving policy, research, and practice to the 21st century* [ASHE Higher Education Report, 35(4)]. San Francisco, CA: Jossey-Bass.

Berry, F. S., & Berry, W. D. (2007). Innovation and diffusion models in policy research. In P. A. Sabatier (Ed.), *Theories of the policy process* (2nd ed., pp. 223–260). Davis, CA: Westview Press.

Bettinger, E. (2004). How financial aid affects persistence. In C. Hoxby (Ed.), *How financial aid affects persistence in college choices: The economics of where to go, when to go, and how to pay for it* (pp. 207–237). Chicago, IL: University of Chicago Press.

Boehmke, F. J., & Witmer, R. (2004). Disentangling diffusion: The effects of social learning and economic competition on state policy innovation and expansion. *Political Research Quarterly, 57*(1), 39–51.

Box-Steffensmeier, J. M., & Jones, B. S. (2004). *Event history modeling: A guide for social scientists.* New York, NY: Cambridge University Press.

Bruckmeier, K., Fischer, G., & Wigger, B. (2015). Tuition fees and the time to graduation: Evidence from a natural experiment. *Journal of Higher Education Policy and Management, 37*(4), 459–471.

Burge, P., Kim, C. W., Rohr, C., Frearson, M., & Guerin, B. (2014). *Understanding the impact of differential university fees in England.* Santa Monica, CA: Rand. Retrieved from https://www.rand.org/content/dam/rand/pubs/research_reports/RR500/RR571/RAND_RR571.pdf

Charis-Carlson, J. (2016, May 1). Iowa university presidents: 'Everything is on the table' for tuition hikes. *Iowa City Press Citizen* . Retrieved from http://www.press-citizen.com/story/news/education/college/2016/04/28/university-iowa-state-northern-regents-tuition-hike-higher-education/83548172/

Cornell Higher Education Research Institute (Cornell). (2012). *2011 Survey of differential tuition at public higher education institutions.* Retrieved from http://www.ilr.cornell.edu/cheri/upload/2011CHERISurveyFinal0212.pdf

Cunningham, A., & Santiago, D. (2008). *Student aversion to borrowing: Who borrows and who doesn't.* Washington, DC: Institute for Higher Education Policy.

Delaney, J. A., & Doyle, W. R. (2011). State spending on higher education: Testing the balance wheel over time. *Journal of Education Finance, 36,* 343–68.

DesJardins, S. L., & McCall, B. (2010). Simulating the effects of financial aid packages on college student stopout, reenrollment spells, and graduation chances. *Review of Higher Education, 33,* 513–541.

DesJardins, S. L. (2003). Event history methods. In J. Smart (Ed.), *Higher education: Handbook of theory and research* (Vol. XVIII, pp. 421–472). London: Kluwer.

Dorfman, J. (2016). States should not choose College Students' majors. *Forbes.* Retrived March 3, 2016, from http://www.forbes.com/sites/jeffreydorfman/2016/03/03/states-should-not-choose-college-students-majors/#251788fd52aa

Doyle, W. R. (2006). Adoption of merit-based student grant programs: An event history analysis. *Educational Evaluation and Policy Analysis, 28*(3), 259–285.

George-Jackson, C. E., Rincon, B., & Garcia, M. (2012). Low-income engineering students: Considering financial aid and differential tuition. *Journal of Student Financial Aid, 42,* 4–24.

Hearn, J. C., & Griswold, C. P. (1994). State-level centralization and policy innovation in U.S. postsecondary education. *Educational Evaluation and Policy Analysis, 16*(2), 161–190.

Hemelt, S. W., & Marcotte, D. E. (2011). The impact of tuition increases on enrollment at public colleges and universities. *Educational Evaluation and Policy Analysis, 33*(4), 435–457.

Hora, M. T., Benbow, R. J., & Oleson, A. K. (2016). *Beyond the skills gap: Preparing college students for life and work.* Cambridge, MA: Harvard University Press.

Johnes, G. (2007). Funding formulae where costs legitimately differ: The case of higher education in England. *Education Economics, 15*(4), 385–404.

Li, A. Y. (2017) Covet Thy Neighbor or "Revers Policy diffusion"? State adoption of performance funding 2.0. *Research in Higher Education, 58,* 746–771.

Long, J. S. (1997). *Regression models for categorical and limited dependent variables.* Thousand Oaks, CA: Sage Publications.

Ma, J., Baum, S., Pender, M., & Welch, M. (2017). *Trends in college pricing 2017.* New York, NY: The College Board.

Makse, T., & Volden, C. (2011). The role of policy attributes in the diffusion of innovations. *Journal of Politics, 73*(1), 108–124.

Mayhew, M. J., Rockenbach, A. N., Bowman, N. A., Seifert, T. A., & Wolniak, G. C. (2016). *How college affects students: 21st century evidence that higher education works* (Vol. 3). San Francisco, CA: Jossey-Bass.

McLendon, M. K., Hearn, J. C., & Deaton, R. (2006). Called to account: Analyzing the origins and spread of state performance-accountability policies for higher education. *Educational Evaluation and Policy Analysis, 28,* 1–24.

McMahon, W. W. (2009). *Higher learning, greater good: The private and social benefits of higher education.* Baltimore, MD: Johns Hopkins University Press.

McPherson, P. (2015). *Celebrating the 125th anniversary of the Morrill Act of 1890 Association of Public Land Grant Universities*. Retrived July 15, 2015, Ffrom http://www.aplu.org/news-and-media/blog/celebrating-the-125th-anniversary-of-the-morrill-act-of-1890

Mumper, M. (2001). State efforts to keep public colleges affordable in the face of fiscal stress. In M. Paulsen (Ed.), *The finance of higher education: Theory, research, policy, and practice* (pp. 321–354). New York, NY: Agathon.

National Center for Education Statistics (NCES). (2015). *IPEDS data center. Pre-defined reports*. Retrieved from https://nces.ed.gov/ipeds/datacenter/login.aspx

National Center for Education Statistics (NCES). (2017). *IPEDS data center. Pre-defined reports*.

Nelson, G. (2008). *Differential tuition by undergraduate major: Its use, amount, and impact on public research universities* (Unpublished doctoral dissertation). University of Nebraska-Lincoln, Lincoln, NE.

Paulsen, M. (2001). Economic perspective on rising college tuition. In M. Paulsen (Ed.), *The finance of higher education: Theory, research, policy, and practice* (pp. 193–263). New York, NY: Agathon.

Perna, L. W. (2006). Studying college access and choice: A proposed conceptual model. In J. C. Smart (Ed.) *Higher education: Handbook of theory and research* (Vol. XXI, pp. 99–157). Dordrecht, The Netherlands: Springer.

Rand Corporation & Council for Aid to Education. (1997). *Breaking the social contract: The fiscal crisis in higher education* (Report No. CAE-100). Santa Monica, CA: California Education Roundtable. (ERIC Document Reproduction Service No. ED 414 806) Retrieved from https://nces.ed.gov/programs/digest/d17/tables/dt17_317.40.asp

Rothstein, J., & Rouse, C. (2011). Constrained after college: Student loans and early-career occupational choices. *Journal of Public Economics, 95*, 149–163.

Smerek, R. E. (2010). Cultural perspectives of academia: Towards a model of cultural complexity. In J. C. Smart (Ed.), *Higher education: Handbook of theory and research* (Vol. XXV, pp. 381–423). Dordrecht, The Netherlands: Springer.

Southern Regional Education Board. (Ed.). (1976). *Tuition policy in public higher education: Financing education, No. 27*. Atlanta, GA: Southern Regional Education Board. (ERIC Document Reproduction Service No. ED131796)

Stange, K. (2015). Differential pricing in undergraduate education: Effects on degree production by field. *Journal of Policy Analysis and Management, 34*(1), 107–135.

Stinebrickner, T., & Stinebrickner, R. (2011). *Math or science? Using longitudinal expectations data to examine the process of choosing a college major* (NBER Working Paper 16869). Cambridge, MA: National Bureau of Economic Research.

Tierney, W. G. (2011). Too big to fail: The role of for-profit colleges and universities in American higher education. *Change, 43*(6), 27–32.

Toutkoushian, R. K. (2001). Trends in revenues and expenditures for public and private higher education. In M. Paulsen (Ed.), *The finance of higher education: Theory, research, policy, and practice* (pp. 11–38). New York, NY: Agathon.

Toutkoushian, R. K., & Paulsen, M. B. (2016). *Economics of higher education: Background, concepts, and applications*. Dordrecht, The Netherlands: Springer.

United States Congress, House. (2008, June 26). *Problem credit card practices affecting students hearing before the Subcommittee on financial institutions and consumer credit of the committee on financial services* (U.S. House of Representatives, One Hundred Tenth Congress, second session). Washington, DC: U.S. G.P.O.

United States Congress, Senate. (2010, May 1). *The more you know, the better buyer you become financial literacy for today's homebuyers: Hearing before the Subcommittee on Economic Policy of the Committee on Banking, Housing, and Urban Affairs* (United States Senate, One Hundred Tenth Congress, second session, on financial literacy and education efforts targeted to both first time homebuyers and existing home owners and to improve accessibility to education programs). Washington, DC: U.S. G.P.O.

University Leadership Council. (2009). *Differential tuition at public universities: Models and implementation strategies, custom research brief*. Washington, DC: The Advisory Board Company.

University of Maryland. (2015). *Differential tuition frequently asked questions.* Retrieved from http://bursar.umd.edu/Differential%20Tuition%20FAQ.pdf

University of Washington Office of Planning and Budgeting. (2011). *Emergence of differential tuition at public universities.* Retrieved from http://opb.washington.edu/sites/default/files/opb/Policy/Differential%20Tuition_Brief.pdf.

Walker, J. L. (1969). The diffusion of innovations among the American states. *American Political Science Review, 63,* 880–899.

Ward, D., & Douglas, J. (2005). *Dynamics of variable fees: Exploring institutional and public policy responses* (Research & Occasional Paper Series: CSHE.5.05). Berkeley, CA: Center for Studies in Higher Education.

Weinberg, I. (1977). *The effects of price discrimination on the elasticity of demand for higher education.* New York, NY: Fordham University. (ERIC Document Reproduction Service No. ED 150907)

Weisbrod, B. A., Ballou, J. P., & Asch, E. D. (2008). *Mission and money: Understanding the university.* New York, NY: Cambridge University Press.

Wessman, J. (2012). Should science majors pay less for college than art majors. *The Atlantic.* Retrived November 5, 2012, from http://www.theatlantic.com/business/archive/2012/11/should-science-majors-pay-less-for-college-than-art-majors/264417/

Whalen, E. (1991). *Responsibility centered budgeting.* Bloomington & Indianapolis, IN: Indiana University Press.

Wolniak, G. C., Seifert, T. A., Reed, E. J., & Pascarella, E. T. (2008). College majors and social mobility. *Research in social stratification and mobility, 26,* 123–139.

Wyness, G. (2015). *Paying for higher education* (Paper No. EA026). London: London School of Economics and Political Science, Centre for Economic Performance. Retrieved from http://cep.lse.ac.uk/pubs/download/ea026.pdf

Yanikoski, R., & Wilson, R. (1984). Differential pricing of undergraduate education. *Journal of Higher Education, 55,* 735–750.

PART 6

THE ROLE OF HIGHER EDUCATION IN REGIONAL INNOVATION

VERENA RADINGER-PEER

13. THE INSTITUTIONAL ENVIRONMENT AND ORGANISATIONAL CHALLENGES OF UNIVERSITIES' REGIONAL ENGAGEMENT

INTRODUCTION

While it is commonly accepted that universities are key repositories of new knowledge and highly qualified graduates, the roles hey are expected to play have changed significantly over the past 30 years. It was in the 1980s when first claims on universities' regional engagement arouse in regional policy. It is though impossible to understand the rise of the engagement mission without contextualising it against a background of wider societal shifts and the impact these had on higher education (Benneworth, 2009). Being aware of the fact, that universities have an increasingly complex array of institutional missions, which must be managed simultaneously (Neave, 2006), the present chapter aims to investigate the organisational challenges and institutional change processes which come along with universities' regional engagement. In this understanding regional engagement is not a self-evident process (Peer & Penker, 2016) but rather a phenomenon which is extrinsically claimed or/and endogenously induced. It is rather a strategic task which universities and their members undertake (Benneworth, 2009) and which necessitates institutional change within the wider organisational field as well as organisational responses within the HEI.

Universities are among the oldest institutions in society, dating back to the 15th century. In this time, they have played a critical role in processes of socio-economic development at the national and sub-national levels (Bender, 1991). They are often referred to as institutions themselves (Diogo et al., 2015) which underwent abrupt or gradual/incremental institutional change (Mahoney and Thelen, 2010) which in turn affected their organisational structure as well as their role in society. The invention of the Humboldtian university in the 19th century by the emperor Wilhelm von Humboldt is referred to as the first academic revolution and states an abrupt, exogenously induced change which brought about radical institutional reconfigurations. Research is introduced as core mission and academic freedom in teaching and research as a core feature. Therewith university gained a certain degree of internal as well as external autonomy from economic as well as political forces. The Humboldtian university prevailed as the model for large-scale research universities till recently. At the same time the land grant university in the US emerged. Although supported with similar means as the Humboldian university (e.g. granting of land) they are expected to provide a public role, especially in advising agriculture and conducting relevant research. Further major changes occurred after World War II: while many universities suffered a brain drain of faculty, they have been expected to contribute to the economic development of their regions and nations. An expansion of foundations of the higher education sector as well as foundations in areas that previously lacked a university are the consequence. The organisational change accompanying these processes were new connections between university and industry, also named "mode 1 of innovation". In this model, the university was more of a knowledge provider than a partner in ongoing technological development (Malecki, 1997). Another major institutional change with organisational consequences was released in many European countries by the '68 revolutions: they claimed for a democratic university system with access for all citizens and an abandonment of education privileges. The consequence were the invention of democratic mass universities (Delanty, 2002), elimination of study costs but also the invention of admission restrictions (e.g. Germany) on the other hand. At the same time national governments began to expand and diversify the size of their higher education system to respond to increasing technological demands of their economies. The institutional shift to a so called knowledge economy and "Mode 2" of knowledge production led to an understanding of innovation as result of interactions of different organisations/actors via new kinds of co-operative and flexible organisational behaviour (Gibbons et al., 1994). At the same time there was an increasing interest in maximising the commercial impact of universities' knowledge base. Among the organisational changes was the invention of Technology Transfer Offices (Klofsten et al., 2000). Colyvas and Powell (2007) revealed in their investigations of the Stanford university, that the federal legislative mandates became instilled in the mission of universities, the biotech industry defined ample opportunities for scientific development and mobility and therewith university administrators and faculty absorbed these field-level transformations by amalgamating prior agendas into these new horizons.

Although Bender (1991) states that universities have always been civically engaged the understanding of university engagement altered. While the concept of the "entrepreneurial university" emphasizes the strategic approach towards promoting different pathways of knowledge transfer as well as their institutionalization (Clark, 2001; Etzkowitz & Leydesdorff, 2000), the "Triple Helix" approach emphasizes universities as catalysts of interactions and negotiations with government and industry (Etzkowitz & Leydesdorff, 2000). Apart from their contribution to regional innovation, attention is increasingly directed towards the wider contribution of universities to regional, cultural and community development, often referred to as the "3rd mission" of HEIs (Arbo & Benneworth, 2007). Laredo (2007) concludes that the notion of "third mission" is highly ambiguous and is itself directly dependent upon three interrelated aspects: (a) the configuration of the specific activities of a given university, (b) its territorial/geographic embeddedness and c) the national institutional framework.

Various concepts, such as "the civic university", "the engaged university" (Chatterton & Goddard, 2000), "the sustainable university" attempt to grasp this broader and more adaptive role of universities in regional development. While several investigations aim towards deriving precise definitions and concepts on universities' regional engagement, thus focusing on the "what" (see e.g. Breznitz and Feldman, 2012), the present chapter aims to contribute to the "how" of universities' regional engagement, therewith enfolding the institutional and organizational challenges and change processes which accompany universities' regional engagement activities. In doing so, the second section describes the theoretical framework the chapter is based on. The third section undertakes a critical reflection of existing conceptual and theoretical approaches on universities' regional engagement like, the "engaged university", "triple helix university", "entrepreneurial university", "Regional Innovations Systems university" and the "sustainable university". The fourth section critically reflects the case study of the Johannes Kepler University Linz, Austria. The section discussion and conclusion, reflects the findings in a broader context and concludes.

THEORETICAL CONSIDERATIONS AND FRAMEWORK

In the debate on organisational and institutional change two, often separately dealt with bodies of literature are taken into account, that is institutional theory on the one hand as well as (organizational) learning theory on the other. In line with Haunschild and Chandler (2008) the author is convinced that they are rather complementary than competing. While much of the literature in institutional analysis emphasizes external influences and exogenous shocks to explain institutional and organizational change, learning theory emphasizes the endogenous nature of these processes.

From an institutional theoretical perspective universities are open systems (Scott, 2001; Pinheiro, 2011) and as such in lively exchange with their surrounding environment ('organizational field') (Jongbloed et al., 2008). Thereby they are prone to various influencing factors of their institutional environment, which may be of regulative, normative or cultural cognitive nature (Scott, 2001). Each of these pillars offers a different rationale for institutional legitimacy, either by being legally sanctioned, morally authorized or culturally supported (Powell, 2007). The regulative pillar emphasizes institutions' rules and constraints such as regulatory processes, monitoring and sanctioning activities (Scott, 2001). The normative pillar includes values, norms and roles which push compliance for social obligations (Diogo et al., 2015). The cultural-cognitive pillar corresponds to the shared conceptions of the cultures that constitute the nature of social reality. These institutional pillars exert three mechanisms of diffusion: coercive, mimetic and normative. Coercive mechanisms involve political pressure, force of the state, control and authority. Normative mechanisms take into account values, as conceptions of the preferred and desirable together as well as norms, as manner how things should be done. Normative mechanisms include also the concept or roles, defined as conception of appropriate goals and activities for particular individuals or specifies social positions. Mimetic forces drew on habitual, taken-for-granted responses to circumstances of uncertainty (Powell, 2007). Research studies revealed that among the most influential institutional agents within the organizational field of HEIs are (a) the government and the regulatory framework, (b) financing and funding programs, (c) regional structure and networks (governance mechanisms) (Trippl, 2015; Fritsch et al., 2015).

Organisational learning theory, on the other hand argues that organisational and institutional changes are the result of an endogenous learning process. Such change might result from three possible sources (Haunschild & Chandler, 2008):

- And institution might evolve deliberately over time, adapting to field level changes in experience affecting values, beliefs and attitudes;
- An institution might be affected by a specific agent of change (institutional entrepreneur) that learned from its own experience or the experience of others and initiated change;
- An institution might undergo unintended change as the result of boundedly rational action, imperfect imitation or ordinary routines that led to unintended outcomes.

In line with Olsen (2001) the publication at hand, classifies universities' regional engagement as institutionalized, if it takes shape as (a) a formal or informal rule, (b) a repertoire of standard operation procedures (routines), (c) structural changes within the organization (technical core or extended periphery), is supported by resources (people, funding, infrastructure). Institutionalization is therewith the result of increased taken-for-grantedness and heightened legitimacy (Colyvas & Powell, 2007).

In line with the conception of Diogo et al. (2015) as well as Reale and Primeri (2015) organizational institutionalism is perceive as a good theoretical ground for the study of HEIs, their behaviour, actors and interactions with the organisational field as well as a clearer understanding of institutionalization processes. It is therefore perceived as apt framework to analyse existing concepts of universities' regional engagement on the one hand as well as an empirical case study on the other.

MATERIAL AND METHODS

Due to the focus on a "how" research question, the case study method is applied (Yin, 2003). Case study methodologies have gained significance in the social and economic sciences throughout the last years and are characterized on the one hand by the fact that the object of research is surveyed in its real context and on the other hand that they are dependent on multiple sources of data and information which are combined via triangulation. The empirical data gathering is divided into three streams: (a) comprehensive literature review on universities' regional engagement (b) qualitative data gathering through in-depth interviews with key stakeholders at the university and in the region and (c) analysis of policy documents, strategies, federal governmental programmes etc. Through archival records as well as current documentation, institutional and organizational changes are traced back until the foundation of the university. Twelve in-depth interviews have been conducted with university members (members of the vice-rectorate for research, institute heads of the Institute for Environmental Law, Institute for Environmental Management in Companies and Regions), representatives from the Chamber of Commerce, the Federation of Austrian industry, the city of Linz (environmental department), an expert on sustainability from the federal government of Upper Austria as well as the managing director of the Linzer Higher Education fund.

As a case study, the Johannes Kepler University (JKU) has been chosen. The JKU has been founded in 1963 as one of the youngest universities in Austria. The JKU has 2,709 employees (2015), out of which about one-half (1,339) are academic personnel. The university is structured into four faculties: the faculty of social and economic sciences, the faculty of law, the faculty of technical and natural sciences and (since 2014) the medical faculty. The structure and focus of the faculties developed due to the prominent role of the federal and city government as well as regional industries in the orientation of the university. This helps to explain, for example, why a faculty of humanities, for example, does not exist. In 2012 the JKU achieved the 41st rank in the Times Higher Education 100 Ranking Under 50. The JKU is the only "young" Austrian university that achieved a ranking in the worldwide best 100 (http://sciencev2.orf.at/stories/1699381/).

Linz, the capital of Upper Austria, has a population of 201,595(2016) and is Austria's third-largest city. At the four Universities (JKU, University of Arts and Industrial Design Linz, the Anton Bruckner Private University for Music, Drama and Dance as well as the Catholic-Theological Private University Linz) 24,500 students are enrolled (winter term 2015/16). In addition, the two teacher training colleges count 2,800 enrolled students and the two Universities of Applied Life Sciences (Fachhochschule OÖ, Fachhochschule Gesundheitsberufe OÖ) amount up to 1,200 students. According to the interview partners more than 50 percent of the students at the JKU have their community of origin in Upper Austria. Linz is at the same time one of the main economic centers of Austria with the highest rate of employment to population. The largest sector is manufacturing, in which 17 percent of all employees work. For several decades Linz had the image as a grey industrial city. Restoration and reutilization projects of former industrial sites (e.g. Tabakfabrik) into culturally interesting locations, an economic program which strived for a diversification of the local economy (supporting tourism and trade), as well as a comprehensive social program oriented to improving have all contributed to changing the image of Linz to a culturally active and economically aspiring city. In 2009 Linz was nominated European Capital of Culture.

ANALYSIS OF CONCEPTS OF UNIVERSITIES REGIONAL ENGAGEMENT FROM AN INSTITUTIONAL AS WELL AS LEARNING THEORETICAL PERSPECTIVE

Due to their prominence in the scientific literature the following concepts have been taken into account in the subsequent analysis, that is "the engaged university", "the entrepreneurial university", "Mode 2 university", "Triple Helix university", Regional innovation system (RIS) university" and "sustainable university". Based on the theoretical framework described in the second section, Table 13.1 presents the findings of the comprehensive literature review on university engagement. The institutional framework as well as mechanisms, the claimed organisational changes as well as indicators for institutionalization of engagement activities are elaborated.

The following lessons can be drawn from the investigation of the literature on university engagement from an institutional theoretical perspective:

- a widespread institutional change towards regional engagement within the university system tackles especially the normative and cultural-cognitive pillar, to a lesser extend the regulative one;
- institutional changes within the political and regional environment towards appreciation for university engagement activities as well as new forms of collaboration, interaction and participation are deemed necessary;
- therewith it becomes evident, that universities' regional engagement is not a self-driven, autonomous process, but highly dependent on and influenced by its institutional environment and regional absorptive capacity;
- the incorporation of regional engagement into the governmental regulatory framework as well as funding and finance legitimizes especially commercialization based activities (entrepreneurial university, RIS, triple helix);
- individual change agents who serve as role models and carriers of normative and cultural-cognitive change within academia are highlighted in all concepts;
- while in commercialization-based concepts institutionalization becomes visible as structural change (foundation of TTOs, incubators etc.) as well as fixed routines (e.g. patent registration) it is more difficult to grasp them in the engaged, mode2 and sustainability university concepts;
- while universities (especially the university management) may experience coercive or mimetic pressure (regulatory and funding framework by the government, concurrence with other HEIs) when it comes to commercialization-based activities, the driving forces of non-commercialization based activities may be different ones;
- it may therefore be assumed that these types of engagement are dependent upon a strong normative and cultural-cognitive bottom-up change process. This may be induced by single highly engaged individuals (management and/or faculty), the participation in international networks (and therewith adaptation to field level changes) or an unintended outcome;
- the various concepts differ when it comes to the role HEIs play in the wider regional context. While they are given a key position in the engaged university, sustainability university and entrepreneurial university concept, they are one out of many actors within the RIS, Triple Helix or Mode2 model.

Apart from this theoretical investigation of the institutional and organizational challenges, the subsequent sections investigate the institutional framework conditions

Table 13.1. Analysis of the institutional framework and mechanisms as well as organisational change processes of selected models of university engagement. (N = normative nature, C-C = cultural cognitive nature, R = regulative nature)

Concept (core of the definition)	Institutional framework/mechanisms	Necessary organisational change	Indicators of Institutionalization of university regional engagement
Engaged university (The regional focus is integrated in all activities of the universities, that is research, teaching and other knowledge exchange activities)	The university, as institutional actor, is expected to contribute to regional innovation networks; (N, C-C) Universities become partners in the elaboration of regional development strategies (N) Universities adapt to regional needs (N, C-C); Public financing takes into account regional engagement activities (R) Regional engagement activities of universities are appreciated in the regional environment (C-C)	Integration of the regional focus into the mission and strategy of the university (N) Integration of the regional focus/perspective into teaching and research (N) Participating in strategic regional networks (N, C-C) Change of the self-perception of the university (C-C) Transdisciplinarity (N, C-C); Institutional entrepreneurs as role model (N)	Regional needs are incorporated into the core activities of research and teaching and have a certain degree of taken-for-grantedness; Engagement activities are supported with resources (people, funding, infrastructure); Engagement activities are perceived as legitimated within the HEI as well as in the HEI institutional environment (e.g. political consideration of university regional engagement in core funding (R))
Entrepreneurial university University applies an economic mission and focuses on the commercialization of knowledge via patents, licenses and spin-off foundations	Commercialization activities of HEIs enter the regulatory framework (R) (e.g. Bay Dole act) Establishment of an entrepreneurial culture within the organisational field (C-C) Interdependencies between the three institutional spheres economy, politics as well as university emerge;	Establishment of transfer units at the interface of the university and the regional environment (structural change) Leadership styles are aligned to those of private companies (N); Internal incentive structures (N, C-C); Normative and cultural-cognitive change towards "entrepreneurial scientists" (N, C-C); Change in the self-perception of the university from a general mission towards an economic mission (C-C, N); Commercialization activities are taken into account in the evaluation (R) Close relationships to companies: cooperation and mixing of personnel.	Supported by infrastructure, personnel, finances (e.g. TTOs); Standardization of certain procedures (patenting, licensing); Commercialization activities have established as new source of financing

(cont.)

Table 13.1. *Analysis of the institutional framework and mechanisms as well as organisational change processes of selected models of university engagement.* (N = normative nature, C-C = cultural cognitive nature, R = regulative nature) (cont.)

Concept (core of the definition)	Institutional framework/mechanisms	Necessary organisational change	Indicators of Institutionalization of university regional engagement
Mode 2 university New form of knowledge production in inter- and transdisciplinary research teams ("context sensitive science")	The academic system as a whole is subjected to wide-ranging transformations due to new forms of knowledge production; Knowledge production is application oriented, transdisciplinary and heterogeneous; Problems are not formulated a-priori but defined together with practitioners and users; At the same time universities experience competition from extramural research institutions; Boundaries between basic and applied research disappear;	New forms of knowledge production as well as working methods (e.g. research question is defined together with respective regional actors) (N, C-C) Transdisciplinarity (N, C-C) Emergence of cooperative and flexible organizational behavior (Gibbons et al. 1994) (N)	Integrating regional stakeholders/experts in the formulation of the research problem becomes taken-for-granted; Standard operating procedures to guarantee transdisciplinary research settings emerge. Social responsibility for research results enfolds (=> new criteria to evaluate the quality of research take root;)
Triple Helix University University – industry – government relations are generated endogenously with overlapping institutional spheres were hybrid organizations emerge at the interface	New mode of science-policy making; the three institutions science – policy – industry interact and interfere with the tasks of each other (e.g. HEIs interfere with the private sector via technology transfer and start-ups); Normative and cognitive change towards transdisciplinarity takes place (N, C-C)	Foundation of hybrid organizations such as knowledge transfer offices, university incubator facilities; New firm foundations/spin offs; Transdisciplinary thinking and working methods (N, C-C)	Investment of resources (TTOs, incubator facilities)

(cont.)

Table 13.1. *Analysis of the institutional framework and mechanisms as well as organisational change processes of selected models of university engagement. (N = normative nature, C-C = cultural cognitive nature, R = regulative nature) (cont.)*

Concept (core of the definition)	Institutional framework/mechanisms	Necessary organisational change	Indicators of Institutionalization of university regional engagement
RIS University At the focal point are collective, interactive learning processes between universities and other actors of the RIS with the aim to generate innovations on the regional level.	Interactive collective learning processes between HEIs and other RIS actors aiming towards a systemic innovation are at the core; Focus of HEIs is on knowledge provision and exchange (whereby it may be refunded or not); The role of the HEI is influenced by the regional environment and the prevailing knowledge base (absorptive capacity); Spatial proximity states an important facilitator;	Expectation towards universities to engage in cluster initiatives as well as other regional networks ("connected university"); Universities are expected to: create spin-offs Offer regionally adapted further education programs make their infrastructure available	Highly qualified graduates, research cooperation, knowledge-spill overs (no compensation) are taken-for-granted
Sustainable/transformative university (sustainability is incorporated as key principle into management practices as well as teaching and research)	Universities are recognized as key institution in the great transformation; Networks to strengthen the sustainability capacity and action are set up (e.g. Copernicus Network, Network is emphasized over single organisations); The function of HEIs as societal role models is emphasized.	Change of management and operational practices towards more sustainable practices or conduction of certifications (e.g. EMAS) Sustainability is taken into account as core principle in teaching and research (N, C-C)	Sustainability diffuses into teaching and research as well as operations of the HEI; e.g. certifications such as EMAS Further education programs with focus on sustainability are set up; Sustainability is a core issue in study programs. Institutes with a strong sustainability focus are implemented. Interdisciplinary platforms on sustainability related topics are institutionalized.

225

as well as organisational challenges of becoming a regionally engaged university on the example of the Johannes Kepler University (JKU) in Linz (Austria). The JKU is well known for its close relationship to the local and federal government as well as the regional industry. Apart from commercialization-based activities, the author has been able to enfold non-commercialization based engagement activities as well.

REFLECTIONS ON THE CHALLENGES OF UNIVERSITIES' REGIONAL ENGAGEMENT FROM THE PERSPECTIVE OF THE JOHANNES KEPLER UNIVERSITY IN LINZ

Recalling the aim of the present chapter, that is to contribute to the understanding of "how" universities become regionally engaged, the empirical evidence from the JKU is structured as follows: first, the institutional environment which influences the regional engagement activities of the JKU is elaborated along the theoretical framework; second, the organisational challenges and change processes going along with these kind of activities are presented. For the JKU the focus will be on two types of engagement activities, that is commercial based ones, defined as university regional engagement activities with a clear impact on technological development and innovation and those with a non-commercial perspective (e.g. consultation for regional problems, further education programmes, contract research for policy makers in the field of sustainability).

There is consensus among all the key informants that the level of the university's commitment to regional engagement is high. The investigation of the development plans and performance agreements of the university as well as the statements from the interview partners indicate an understanding of regional engagement of the JKU consisting of:

- *Research*: basic as well as applied research plays a dominant role at the JKU. Regional companies provide the highest percentage of third-party funding. The JKU is very active in R&D cooperation (COMET Program, CD Labs etc.) with regional industry partners.
- *Teaching*: the study programs are aligned to the regional needs and demands of the regional labour market. But also sustainability related institutes and teaching activities have been set up at the beginning of the 1990s inspired by developments at the city government as well as federal government of Upper Austria.
- *Further education and lifelong learning*: the LIMAK Austrian Business School has been founded in 1989 as cooperation of the regional economy, industry, the public sector as well as the JKU and provides international further education programs. It is the oldest Business School in Austria and among the oldest in Europe.
- *Regional problem solving activities*: policy consultation and contract research in the field of Law, Energy, energy transition, environmental law; participation in regional platforms, initiatives and strategy processes; student projects and master thesis.

The Institutional Framework of Regional Engagement Activities of the JKU

The founding history of the JKU had an enormous impact on all engagement activities of the JKU. The Austrian Ministry for Education had not considered Linz, the capital of the federal country of Upper Austria, as location for a university. The city of Linz as well as the federal government of Upper Austria had thereupon set up the Linzer Hochschulfond (Linz University Funds – LHF). The LHF was organized as a public corporation with the purposes of financing the foundation as well as the operation of the JKU in the early 1960s for a time period of ten years. The focus was on the establishment and operation of the institutes but also the acquisition or rental of property or buildings. The board of trustees of the LHF was split between half of the members from the federal government and half of representatives from the city government. Furthermore, the board of trustees was comprehensively involved in the planning of the faculties and institutes of the JKU, the study programs, research foci, budget planning etc. Due to this Austrian-wide unique instrument of the LHF, there was from the beginning on a strong influence from politics as well as industry. One interview partner brought it to the point "There is no such thing as a regional mission, but the university had from the beginning on a clear mission to serve the industry". Although the relationship between the JKU as well as politics and industry is described as symbiotic, coercive mechanisms can be observed: the industry as well as regional economy in the form of advocacy groups publicly express their expectation towards the JKU. That is, to adapt the study programs to the need of the regional labour market and industry, to engage in research cooperation (such as Christian Doppler Labs) as well as in other economic initiatives such as cluster initiatives (e.g. Clean Teach Cluster). Their claim is substantial in that the majority of the JKUs third party funding comes from the regional industry. While the relationship of the JKU and the regional economy is described as rather informal at the beginning, within the last 15 years a trend towards formalization and institutionalization can be observed, which is mainly induced by the national level. In line with developments in other European Countries the Austrian University Law was drastically revised in 2002 (UG 2002), wherein universities are adjudged greater autonomy and freedom, but are at the same time also given good reasons for acting more entrepreneurially. The UG 2002 had an extensive influence on the general university funding: there was a shift of federal government research support from basic science through the FWF (Austrian Science Fund) to applied research that could increase innovation and productivity in the economy and for individual businesses (FFG – The Austrian Research Promotion Agency). These university internal developments and changes, which also took place in other European countries, can be summarized under New Public Management (NPM). While universities have received more autonomy, they also experienced more competition (for public funding, students etc). Although some interview partners from politics state, that third party funds are not the main motivation to engage in cooperation with industry, university members as well as industry partners perceive them as a main driver. While the influence of the UG 2002 on the amount of engagement activities of the JKU was not as wide-ranging as it was for other Austrian universities (see also Goldstein et al., 2016), the JKU has on the other hand not been able to establish its autonomy to the extent as other universities did. As one interview partner confirms, "The JKU was never as autonomous as other universities and not all cooperation and forms of participation have been voluntary".

Apart from these commercialization-focused engagement activities there have been interesting developments in the institutional environment of non-commercialization based engagement activities, especially in the field of sustainability. A further reason for choosing the city of Linz and the region of Upper Austria as a case is their development from an industrial city and region towards an Austrian-wide leader of transition towards sustainability (Radinger-Peer & Pflitsch, 2017). They have been the first throughout Austria in various sustainability related fields e. g. first to join the ICLEI – Local Governments for Sustainability Initiative, first province with a sustainability concept and strategy, first diocese in Linz powered by 100% green electricity, first province to transform the energy system. The institutional mechanisms promoting sustainable development can be drawn back to the early 1990s. Influenced by international developments (UN conference in Rio 1992), various parallel developments at the level of the city of Linz, the federal country of Upper Austria as well as the JKU have taken place. The federal government took the lead to anchor sustainability in its development plans and strategies. While sustainability was discussed in a holistic way at the beginning of the 1990s, it became more focused on energy related issues (energy transition, energy technology, energy economy) in the year 2000. These developments also influenced the regional engagement activities in this field as will be shown in the subsequent section. In parallel sustainability related research activities have been supported and incentivised on a national level by the Austrian Climate and Energy Fund which was set up by to Austrian ministries in 2007.

Organisational Change Processes at the JKU

Most obvious organisational change processes take shape as structural changes, e.g. the foundation of new institutes and study programmes. In close collaboration with the industry in 1966 study programs in the field of social economy, business administration, national economy as well as law, followed by technical mathematics, technical physics and – for the first time in Austria – computer science in the early 1970s have been introduced. Furthermore, in the 1990s with support of the city of Linz as well as federal government of Upper Austria the Institute for Environmental Law as well as Institute of Environmental Management in Companies and Regions have been founded with the adjunct study programs to promote research and teaching activities in the field of sustainability. Furthermore in 1987 the RISC Research Institute for Symbolic Computation as part of the Software Park Hagenberg was founded as one of the first technology centres close to Linz. In order to support knowledge transfer and commercialization activities the university supported the tech2be incubator together with the University of Applied Life Sciences and founded the Science Park to offer Start-ups adequate facilities. Furthermore, a research support and technology transfer office has been set up as part of the vice-rectorate for research.

Overall there is a strong alignment of the mission statements as well as strategy papers of the JKU to the overall strategies and areas of focus of the federal government. Although there is evidence of a normative change of the university management towards consciousness for sustainable development issues (signing of the Copernicus Charter, signing of the Graz Declaration), sustainability is not consistently anchored in the mission statements and strategy documents of the university.

What becomes evident in all investigated types of engagement activities is the high influence of single highly engaged individuals on normative and cultural-cognitive change. Among these highly influential personalities is the rector, his role in representing the university but also his expertise as individual. Although the university does not have an official role in political decision-making, the rector is regularly invited to participate and to contribute his perspective. The networking capability is outlined as one of his strengths which is attributed as important to get the university connected with politics as well as industry. Furthermore, it is emphasized that those individuals who are very successful in raising third party funds are also those who are visible in the public sphere and therefore approached for various other activities (e.g. lecture/speeches, contract research, consultancy). Especially in the field of sustainability related activities, individual personalities feel the normative obligation to engage in the topics of environmental law, evaluation of local sustainability processes (such as LA21), research in the field of climate change, renewable energy, sustainable technologies and environmental politics. This perceived normative pressure is often aligned to the position they occupy within the university (department head, head of the institute). It has to be mentioned at this point, that within many of these activities bottom up engagement encounters top down support. For example, the federal government Upper Austria approached the institute of environmental management to evaluate the Local Agenda 21 processes in one hundred municipalities in Upper Austria, and thus gave an incentive to the institute to broaden their ecological focus to a more holistic understanding of sustainability. Therewith a development has been triggered which may be characterized as unintended in the beginning which further on resulted in a new research focus of the institute (Local Agenda 21 processes and further on Smart City concepts).

Also the foundation of the Energy Institute was strongly supported by the city of Linz, the regional industry as well as federal government of Upper Austria. Interestingly the Energy Institute, which is an example for the combination of commercialization-based activities and a focus on sustainability, is not a university institute but an association with strong connections to the JKU. Reasons for this organisational decoupling from the universities can be found in the expectations towards the Energy Institute to conduct inter- and transdisciplinary applied research projects in the field of energy law, energy economics as well as energy technology as well as to support politics and the regional economy in energy related issues with scientific evidence. According to the interview partners, the fast growing number of research projects of the institute can be laid back to contract research from regional companies, the government of Upper Austria as well as the high success rate of project proposals submitted to the Austrian Climate and Energy fund. Research projects focus on issues of macro- and microeconomic analysis of energy related areas, technological aspects of biogene fuels, smart grids as well as legal aspects of energy and environment related fields. Two of the three directors of the Energy Institute also hold a position at institutes of the JKU. In 2009 the Energy Institute initiated the Professional Master of Science (PMSc) programme "Energy Management".

Although the high engagement of individual personalities cannot be emphasized enough, it is pointed out that engagement activities are undertaken more on demand than initiated pro-actively. Therewith it also becomes evident that more or less the same number of persons are approached again and again. Especially in the field of sustainability the engagement activities are rather fragmented among three institutes, which are not even informed about each other. It is stressed that the more voluntary an activity is, the less is the interest for engagement of university members.

What regards the institutionalization of regional engagement activities; especially commercialization-based activities are supported with resources (financial, personnel, infrastructure), have established routines (patent applications, F&E cooperation) which led to structural changes (foundation of the science park, technology transfer office). This is not to the same extent the case for university engagement activities in the field of sustainability. While the respective institutes and study programs can be attributed to structural change, the support with resources or the establishment of routines cannot be confirmed. There are certain events, like the "Austrian Days of Environmental Law" which are taking place on an annual basis, but the therewith organisation is highly dependent on single individuals, where it is not yet sure what will happen if they leave the university.

DISCUSSION AND CONCLUSION

Apart from the "what", the book section at hand aimed to investigate on the "how" of regional engagement, therewith shedding light on the processes of institutional and organisational change and the underlying mechanisms. Comparing the insights from the conceptual analysis and the empirical case study of Linz it can be confirmed that engagement is not a self-evident process (Radinger-Peer & Pflitsch 2017; Peer & Penker, 2016). Hence, it is stimulated by the institutional environment on the one hand and supported as well as shaped by the internal organisational learning processes on the other. The JKU shows strong characteristics of an entrepreneurial university, which was imprinted already in the founding idea of the university. Furthermore, the institutionalization as well as therewith organizational structural changes have been triggered by the changes of the University Law 2002. At the same time there are also indications of the engaged university concept. There are numerous activities in the field of regional problem solving where individual university members contribute their expertise, participate in platforms or advisory boards and hence contribute to region-specific solutions. This is also the case for activities to promote the sustainable development of the region. What regards the latter there has again been a strong incentive from the federal government of Upper Austria and its programs and strategies in the field of sustainability. The influence of the institutional environment on the university is on the one hand of a coercive nature as well as normative one. The former refers to the strong support of the regional industry and economy to establish the university in the 1960s and the therewith expectations that she will spur the regional economy. On the other hand the activities in the field of sustainability have a strong normative component, therewith emphasizing the role of universities for a sustainable development of the region and society as such. Although the JKU is perceived as one of the most regionally engaged universities in Austria a widespread normative and cultural-cognitive change towards regional engagement cannot be observed within the university and university system as such.

Single individuals and their awareness are the backbone of commercialization and non-commercialization focused activities. In line with Trippl (2015) as well as Fritsch et al. (2015) it can be confirmed that (a) the government, (b) financing and funding programs and c) the regional structure and networks are strong institutional agents. On the other hand institutional entrepreneurs are crucial to take action and act as role models to induce normative and cultural-cognitive change.

One aspect which became strongly visible in the case of Linz is the historical imprinting of the universities role within their region. While the foundation process with the Linzer Higher Education Fund may be rather unique, it is an interesting example for a path dependent evolution of the university-region interface (Arbo & Benneworth, 2007). The therewith power constellations and governance mechanisms have reached a certain degree of institutionalization and are therefore seen as taken-for-granted and legitimated.

Especially commercialization based engagement activities are often overestimated when it comes to frequency and importance: "open channels" such as informal links, conferences and joint publications are proven to occur most often, followed by consultancy, contract research and recruitment of graduates, with patenting and licensing being of lowest importance (Abreu et al., 2009; Cohen et al., 2002). The respective models (entrepreneurial university, RIS, Triple Helix) apply only to a selected number of academic disciplines with a technological – economic focus. Social, cultural and societal regional needs are often not tackled in the mentioned concepts. Further concerns are raised that (a) scientists often lack interest in commercialization and (b) commercialization-based research activities do not automatically meet the regional needs (Trippl, 2015). Therewith university engagement may be seen as a principal-agent problem (Goldstein et al., 2015), whereby politics as well as university management have a different perception as university researchers.

While commercialization-based activities have entered the regulative framework in Austria (based on the University Law 2002) this is not the case for non-commercial engagement activities. Although the university law refers to the "societal role" of universities, this does not anchor them in the core fields of teaching and research. Often referred to as "third mission" activities, there is not yet a widespread cognitive-cultural as well as normative change within the universities. As they are not yet officially rooted in the core fields of teaching and research, concerns of legitimacy of these kind of activities arise, accompanied by a lack of internal incentive structures (Henke et al., 2016). On the other hand, individual engaged researchers and HEI members lack time resources and internal reward, which may hamper future activities. Furthermore, the high autonomy of individual faculties/departments and researchers makes it difficult for the university management to order regional engagement top down.

What can be learned from the Linz case study is that regional engagement is a multi-faceted activity which is dependent on bottom up engagement and top down support. As the university is a multi-level organisation with a certain degree of autonomy of its members the reasons to engage regionally cannot only be based on personal conviction. There rather needs to be an attractive mix of incentives (e.g. funding, recognition for the academic career, other support) from the side of the public government but also within the university system as such to spur this kind of activities.

The present book section aimed at critically reflecting on existing concepts of universities' regional engagement, therewith supposing that the "what" of regional engagement gives a far too narrow picture of the complex picture of regions and their development processes on the one hand as well as universities and their operations, functions and structure on the other. These stated results confirmed that a dynamic investigation and understanding of the process of university engagement supports the understanding (a) why certain types of engagement (e.g. entrepreneurial university) dominate over others, (b) which organizational and institutional changes accompany the process of universities to become engaged with their regional environment and (c) to understand where and why institutionalization happens. In doing so further investigations could help to consolidate the knowledge on the interplay of institutional environment and organisational change and the therewith type(s) of universities' regional engagement.

REFERENCES

Abreu, M., Grinevich, V., Hughes, A., & Kitson, M. (2009). *Knowledge exchange between academics and the business, public and third sector*. London: UK-Innovation Research Centre, University of Cambridge.

Arbo, P., & Benneworth, P. (2007). *Understanding the regional contribution of higher education institutions: A literature review* (OECD Education Working Papers No. 9). Paris: OECD Publishing.

Bender, T. (1991). *The university and the city: From medieval origins to the present*. Oxford: Oxford University Press.

Benneworth, P. (2009). *Characterising modes of university engagement with wider society. A literature review and survey of best practice*. Newcastle upon Tyne: Newcastle University.

Breznitz, S. M., & Feldman, M. P. (2012). The engaged university. *Journal of Technology transfer, 37*, 139–157.

Chatterton, P., & Goddard, J. (2000). The response of higher education institutions to regional needs. *European Journal of Education, 35*(4), 475–496.

Cohen, W. M., Nelson, R. R., & Walsh, J. P. (2002). Links and impacts: the influence of public research on industrial R&D. *Management Science, 48*, 1–23.

Colyvas, J. A., & Powell, W. (2007). *Institutionalization processes and the commercialization of university research*. Stanford: Stanford University School of Education.

Clark, B. (2001). The entrepreneurial university: New foundations for collegiality, autonomy, and achievement. *Higher Education Management, 13*(2), 9–24.

Delanty, G. (2002). The university and modernity: A history of the present. In K. Robins & F. Webster (Eds.), *The virtual university: Knowledge, markets and management.* Oxford: OUP.

Diogo, S., Carvalho, T., & Amaral, A. (2015). Institutionalism and organizational change. In J. Huisman, H. de Boer, D. Dill, & M. Souto-Otero (Eds.), *The Palgrave international handbook of higher education policy and governance*. London: Palgrave Macmillan.

Etzkowitz, H., & Leydesdorff, L. (2000). The dynamics of innovation: From national systems and "Mode 2" to a Triple Helix of university-industry-government relations. *Research Policy, 29*(2), 109–123.

Fritsch, M., Pasternack, P., & Titze, M. (Eds.). (2015). *Schrumpfende Regionen – dynamische Hochschulen. Hochschulstrategien im demografischen Wandel*. Wiesen: Springer VS.

Gibbons, M., Limoges, C., Nowotny, H., Schwatzman, S., Scott, P., & Trow, M. (1994). *The new production of knowledge*. London: Sage Publications.

Goldstein, H., Peer, V., & Sedlacek, S. (2016). *Pathways and challenges of university engagement: Comparative case studies in Austria* (Working Paper No.7). MODUL University Vienna.

Haunschild, P., & Chandler, D. (2008). Institutional-level learning. In R. Greenwood, C. Oliver, K. Sahlin, & R. Suddaby (Eds.), *The Sage handbook of organizational institutionalism* (pp. 624–649). Thousand Oaks, CA: Sage Publications.

Henke, J., Pasternack, P., & Schmid, S. (2016). *Third Mission bilanzieren. Die dritte Aufgabe der Hochschulen und ihre öffentliche Kommunikation* (HoF-Handreichungen 8). Halle-Wittenberg: Institut für Hochschulforschung (HoF).

Jongbloed, B., Enders, J., & Salerno, C. (2007). Higher education and its communities: interconnections, interdependencies and a research agenda. *Higher Education, 56*(3), 303–324.

Klofsten, M., & Jones-Evans, D. (2000). Comparing academic entrepreneurship in Europe: The case of Sweden and Ireland. *Small Business Economics, 14*(2), 299–309.

Laredo, P. (2007). Revisiting the third mission of universities: Toward a renewed categorization of university activities? *Higher Education Policy, 20*(4), 441–456.

Mahoney, J., & Thelen, K. (2010). A theory of gradual institutional change. In J. Mahoney & K. Thelen (Eds.), *Explaining institutional change. Ambiguity, agency and power*. New York, NY: Cambridge University Press.

Malecki, E. (1997). *Technology and economic development*. London: Longmans.

Neave, G. (2006). Redefining the social contract. *Higher Education Policy, 19*(3), 269–286.

Olsen, J. P. (2001). Garbage cans, new institutionalism, and the study of politics. *American Political Science Review, 95*(1), 191–198.

Peer, V., & Penker, M. (2016). Higher education institutions and regional development – A meta-analysis. *International Regional Science Review, 26*(1), 88–94.

Pinheiro, R. (2011). *In the region, for the region? A comparative study of the institutionalisation of the regional mission of universities* (PhD thesis). Department of Educational Research Faculty of Educational Sciences, University of Oslo, Oslo.

Powell, W. W. (2007). *The new institutionalism. The international encyclopedia of organization studies.* Thousand Oaks, CA: Sage Publications.

Radinger-Peer, V., & Pflitsch, G. (2017). *The role of higher education institutions in regional transition paths towards sustainability. The case of Linz*. Austria: Review of Regional Research. Retrieved from https://doi.org/10.1007/s10037-017-0116-9

Reale, E., & Primeri, R. (2015). Approaches to policy and governance in higher education. In J. Huisman, H. de Boer, D. Dill, & M. Souto-Otero (Eds.), *The Palgrave international handbook of higher education policy and governance.* London: Palgrave Macmillan.

Scott, W. R. (2001). *Institutions and organizations. Ideas, interests and identities.* Stanford: Stanford University.

Trippl, M. (2015). Die Rolle von Hochschulen in der Regionalentwicklung. In M. Fritsch (Ed.), *Schrumpfende Regionen – dynamische Hochschulen. Hochschulstrategien im demografischen Wandel* (pp. 43–58). Wiesen: Springer VS.

Yin, K. R. (2003). *Case study research. Design and methods.* New Delhi & London: Sage Publications.

JÜRGEN JANGER

14. UNIVERSITIES' ROLE IN REGIONAL INNOVATION RECONSIDERED

Looking at the Bottom of the Iceberg

INTRODUCTION

Regional innovation has always been more or less purposefully affected by higher education institutions and more specifically by universities. As an example, public higher education institutions in the 19th century USA benefitted from federal funding to engage in service to their communities, such as faculty consultation with firms and agricultural organisations, conferences open to the public and student internships (Roper & Hirth, 2005). However, policies towards fostering regional innovation have been driven lately particularly by the concept of the entrepreneurial university. This is often tantamount to encouraging universities to directly contribute to economic development through commercialization of their research-based discoveries, e.g. through licensing of patents or supporting academic spin-off firms, rather than indirectly contributing through consultation or collaborative R&D with firms or training workers through further education programmes.

The popularity of these approaches in Europe may be linked to the perception of a European paradox in policy-maker circles (see the EU's High Level Group Report, 2017). According to this paradox, the EU does not manage to turn its excellent knowledge base into commercially successful innovations so that the reform need is perceived as highest in terms of commercializing of research results. Smart specialization strategies or triple helix-inspired policy approaches at the regional level often view the "products" of the third mission of universities, such as patents or spin-offs, as a key contribution of universities (Etzkowitz & Leydesdorff, 2000; EUA, 2014; Goddard, 2011; Goddard et al., 2013; for a critical discussion, see Uyarra, 2010).

However, these conceptual approaches often pay little attention to how well universities can pursue their first two missions, research and teaching, and how research and teaching performance condition the role of universities in regional innovation. Prestigious universities such as the US-based MIT and Stanford University are often cited as an example of successful commercialization strategies in terms of the number of licensing income from patents and of the jobs created through academic spin-offs. What is less often mentioned is the relationship between the budget of MIT (3.3 billion US-Dollar for 11,376 students in 2016) or Stanford (5.9 billion US-Dollar for 16.336 students[1]) and average European universities.

This corresponds, e.g., to approx. 75–130% of the budget for the entire Austrian university system which catered to 309,000 students in 2015.[2] Recent empirical evidence indicates the potential importance of scientific productivity and the quality of teaching for an effective contribution of universities to regional innovation (Abramovsky, Harrison, & Simpson, 2007; Abramovsky & Simpson, 2011; Belderbos et al., 2014; Calderini & Scellato, 2005; Della Malva & Carree, 2013; D'Este et al., 2013; Perkmann, King, & Pavelin, 2011; Suzuki et al., 2017; Van Looy et al., 2011). Conceptual approaches emphasizing the entrepreneurial university also focus less on how pathways besides patents and spin-offs, such as the mobility of graduates, affect regional innovation, bringing the full set of potential university contributions to regional innovation to the attention of policy makers.

This chapter aims at a systematic and a comprehensive picture of the role of universities in regional innovation processes. We first build a conceptual model of the potential contributions of universities to regional innovation processes to establish the various potential ways of engagement or interaction between universities and regional innovation actors, followed by a review of the empirical literature on which university contributions firms actually rely most on. In the third step, we look at the empirical evidence on which factors drive the effectiveness of universities' contributions to regional innovation, with a particular focus on whether research and teaching quality matters. From these three steps, we gain a thorough understanding of the potential and the actual role of the various university outputs in firm innovation processes at the regional level. The results serve as a basis for discussion of whether recent regional innovation initiatives overly stress universities' third mission as a driver of regional innovation performance, neglecting the first and second mission of universities also in terms of funding and hence putting pressure on universities' efforts to increase research and teaching quality.

UNIVERSITY OUTPUTS AND BUSINESS SCIENCE LINKS: A CONCEPTUAL MODEL

What do universities produce of relevance for innovative activities[3] by firms and other organizations? Focusing on innovative activity in firms, a first look at the available literature indicates that at an aggregate level outputs of universities, which are relevant for innovations are the following: knowledge, as well as researchers and graduates as carriers of knowledge, and skills how to create more, absorb or use knowledge and successfully applying it (Gibbons & Johnston, 1974; Kline & Rosenberg, 1986; Martin & Irvine, 1981; Salter & Martin, 2001).

Outputs of Universities: Knowledge

With a view to assess the potential contribution of knowledge originating from universities to innovative activity, we need to differentiate knowledge along two dimensions which are relevant for how university-created knowledge is going to be used in corporate innovative activity. The first is distinguishing between the stock of knowledge, i.e. the accumulated result of research in the past; and flows of new knowledge, resulting from current research. Of course, the former is much bigger and not less relevant for innovative activity than new knowledge, as shown by the often very long time lags between scientific discoveries and their use in commercial application (see Adams, 1990; Kline & Rosenberg, 1986).

Hence the stock of knowledge, the generic knowledge pool (see Salter & Martin, 2001) is usually going to be quantitatively more significant for innovative activity than the flow of new knowledge. However, participating in the creation of new knowledge (e.g. via being involved in research projects) is an important way of learning-by-doing the skills required for carrying out research as well as gaining insights into the most recent developments of current research.

The second distinction concerns tacit vs. codified knowledge, or knowledge which can be accessed in written or formal form vs. "the knowledge of techniques, methods and designs that work in certain ways and with certain consequences, even when one cannot explain exactly why" (Senker, 1995, p. 426, citing Rosenberg, 1982, p. 143).

Outputs of Universities: Skills and Graduates

The main output of universities' core mission teaching, is the dissemination of knowledge and skills through researchers and graduates. Researchers and graduates have been trained in working with knowledge, understanding it, using it, changing and expanding it, they are problem solvers, which is an essential ingredient for innovation and maybe even more important than knowledge itself (see Senker, 1995, for an account of this). As Clark, 1983, p. 12, puts it for the case of university teachers and researchers: "In varying combinations of efforts to discover, conserve, refine, transmit, and apply it, the manipulation of knowledge is what we find in common in the many specific activities of professors and teachers".

University-educated people are experts in working with knowledge, which is at the root of innovative activity. In surveys of graduates asking for the most useful outcomes of their higher education training for their current position in industry, respondents most often cite next to the knowledge they gained skills such as individual initiative, ability to overcome complex problems, communicating effectively, being part of a team etc. (see e.g. Martin & Irvine, 1981).

These knowledge-related skills can be used in two ways by graduates (and researchers moving into industry) to support innovation. First, by creating new knowledge in firms, and/or second, by being able to understand the knowledge created by others, in- and outside of the firm, and to apply it to a given problem (see Cohen & Levinthal, 1989, 1990; Griffith, Redding & Reenen, 2004, on the role of research for both creating new knowledge and absorbing outside knowledge; and the discussion around open innovation). Graduates and researchers from higher education, when moving to industry, enhance both research and absorptive capacity of firms. This clearly shows how participation in higher education develops skills and some of the mechanisms by which they contribute to innovation capacity of firms.

The main outputs of universities relevant for innovation in firms are in summary knowledge, as well as graduates and researchers moving to industry as carriers of knowledge and skills. How do universities interact with firms and other institutions to become relevant for innovative activities? An important determinant of the potential contribution of outputs from universities in all its forms to innovative activities is how they become involved with innovative activity by firms or other organisations. We choose a broader term here than "knowledge or technology transfer", as these terms suggest a linear transferring of university outputs into innovative activity, whereas often innovative activity is based on the interaction of e.g. firm and university researchers, as in joint research.

Ways of Interaction between Universities and Business

There is a lot of literature on the categorization of mainly research (and not teaching) based business-science links, encompassing the traditional "technology transfer" literature. One suggestion consists in distinguishing academic relational engagement with industry (such as through collaborative R&D, contract research and consulting) from commercialization (such as patenting and licensing, spin-off creation) (see Perkmann et al., 2013). Relational academic engagement is usually much more widespread than academic commercialisation as a way for university outputs to become involved in firm innovative activity (see Perkmann, King, & Pavelin, 2011).

Another approach suggests distinguishing by the formality or intensity of the link between science and business, such as between informal contacts and complex collaborative research projects (Hewitt-Dundas, 2012). For instance, knowledge transfer might occur via publications, patenting or licensing of university inventions supported by technology transfer offices, contract research for firms or collaborative research with firms, but also via informal contacts between university researchers and firms. These different ways of interaction between university and business imply different levels of cooperation intensity or formality in terms of the need for formal contracts regulation the interaction.

In these categorizations there is often little attention on the role of mobility of researchers and graduates, and so also on the role of teaching for universities' contribution to regional innovation. Only recently has there been more attention on on the role of graduates for innovation (see e.g. Veugelers & Del Rey, 2014). We suggest a very simple distinction which can include all the ways of interaction between business and universities – flows of knowledge and flows of people. The first does not involve university researchers or graduates leaving the university as an employer to be able to contribute to regional innovation, while the second involves mobility of people between universities and businesses. Table 14.1 summarises the variety of ways of interaction according to these broad types.

Table 14.1. *Various ways of how university outputs can become relevant for regional innovation*

Way of interaction	Type of knowledge involved	University mission
Flows of knowledge		
Collaborative research	Flow of new knowledge	Research and third mission
Contractual research	Flow	Research and third mission
(Informal) Consulting	Stock of existing knowledge	Research and third mission
Invention protection through patents and technology licensing	Flow	Third mission
Reading of university publications, attending of conferences by corporate researchers	Flow of new knowledge	Research
Flows of people		
Spin-offs	Flow	Third mission
Student and graduate Start-ups	Flow and Stock	Third mission
Attraction of firms	Flow and Stock	na
University researchers moving to industry	Flow and Stock	na
University graduates working in corporate research	Flow and Stock	Teaching
University graduates working in non-R&D corporate functions	Stock	Teaching

University Outputs in Models of the Innovation Process in Firms

This broad table shows that spin-offs and commercialisation of patents are only two specific ways of how university outputs can become relevant for regional innovation. This becomes even clearer when the various interaction ways are related to innovation process models such as the linear model (Balconi, Brusoni, & Orsenigo, 2010), the chain-linked model (Kline, 1985) or various other models (e.g. Klevorick et al., 1995; Micaëlli et al., 2014). These models give different views on which aspects of university "outputs" matter for firms at the regional level. We synthesise this literature to draw a comprehensive model of how various university outputs enter firm innovation processes, not just focusing on spin-offs, science parks, patents and technology licensing, but also looking at labour mobility, publications, informal consulting and the flow of graduates between universities and firms and stressing the differences in how these various channels can enter innovation processes, e.g. in the form of tacit vs codified knowledge. Figure 14.1 is adapted from the chain-link model by Kline (1985). It presents various ways of how university outputs can enter innovation processes at the firm level. We are going to briefly outline some examples, in the process elucidating how the model works.

First, contrary to the view of the linear model which served as a backdrop to Bush's 1945 report to the US Government on the role of science and its funding, it is now widely acknowledged that innovation often starts in firms themselves, often without any direct contact to universities. In Figure 14.1, a potential market idea often – not always – is produced by firms themselves. This does not mean that university knowledge or skills taught by universities play a small role for innovation in firms. In most innovation-active firms, R&D and innovation activities are carried out by university-trained researchers and qualified employees. Moreover, more downstream activities in the innovation process such as developing prototypes, gearing up the production lines for mass production as well as marketing and sales usually also imply activities by university-trained engineers and managers. In a nutshell, university knowledge and skills are embodied in university graduates who work on all stages of the production process.

Second, when the firm has no potential market idea, the firm can generate ideas by screening the available stock of knowledge which is partly university-created (see Klevorick et al., 1995, for an account of how firms tap into the available knowledge pool). This may involve reading publications, attending conferences, consulting university researchers or even licensing technologies from universities, turning university inventions into marketable products. In this case, university outputs are involved on both the firm level (university-trained employees) and the university level (knowledge held in publications, patents, presented at conferences, etc.).

Third, another potential case is that a firm embarks on innovative activity based on a potential market idea, but then encounters technological difficulties which require outside knowledge to be solved. This knowledge may already be existing, in which case we face the same mechanisms as in our second example just above. Or, the creation of new knowledge is necessary, in which case the firm will enter collaborative R&D together with university researchers, or it may just give a research contract to university researchers.

Fourth, a special case consists in university research discoveries being commercialised by the university researchers themselves through creating an academic spin-off, i.e. setting up a firm which commercialises new university knowledge.

Of course, Figure 14.1 presents a highly stylized model of a firm's innovation processes and the potential role of university outputs in it. Firms will also get ideas from other actors, such as customers or suppliers, and will source knowledge also from other firms (e.g. through strategic alliances) or technical research institutions outside universities. However, in spite of its stylised nature, it highlights that university patents and spin-offs are just two ways of many in which university outputs can impact regional innovation.

UNIVERSITIES' ROLE IN REGIONAL INNOVATION

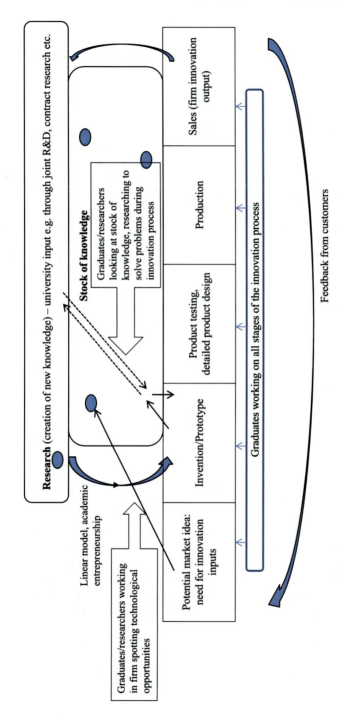

Figure 14.1. A conceptual model for the role of universities in innovative activity. (Adapted from the chain-link model, Kline, 1985)

HORSES FOR COURSES: EMPIRICAL EVIDENCE ON WAYS OF INTERACTION

In the next step, we survey the empirical evidence on which university outputs are used most frequently by firms and what their relative advantages are. Are firms mostly using informal contacts with university researchers, patents granted to universities, do they mostly read publications or is it mainly the flow of skilled graduates which brings most value to them?

Although the transfer of knowledge and skills via the mobility of graduates and researchers is less explored, an Expert Group commissioned by the European Commission highlights besides indicators related to co-operation and commercialization also those indicators related to people (Expert Group on Knowledge Transfer Indicators, 2011). Graduates as a pathway of interaction between universities and businesses have one big advantage over other forms of interaction: tacit knowledge cannot be transferred by reading publications which contain codified knowledge, but must be embodied in researchers or graduates. This is one reason why J.R. Oppenheimer states (as cited in Stephan, 2007, p. 71): "The best way to send information is to wrap it up in a person". OECD evidence shows that tacit knowledge is actually gaining importance in the innovation processes of firms (OECD, 2015).

Empirical evidence furthermore indicates that the hiring of graduates is one of the three preponderant ways of "knowledge transfer" besides informal contacts and publications (see Arundel, van de Paal & Soete, 1995; and Veugelers & Del Rey, 2014, for a survey). In the US, publications, conferences and the mobility of PhD graduates seems to matter more than university prototypes, patents and licenses (Cohen, Nelson, & Walsh, 2002).

Overall, income from licensing technologies to firms (based on university patents) or from participations in spin-offs is on average very small and heavily skewed towards the top US research universities (Veugelers & del Rey, 2014). This picture contrasts with the focus of the triple helix- and entrepreneurial university literatures, which often stress the impact of universities through licensing of patents and spin-offs based on examples such as MIT and Stanford University (see, e.g., Hsu et al., 2007, Kenney & Goe, 2004; Etzkowitz et al., 2000). Focusing on the 3rd mission of universities in terms of technology transfer, on research, implies focusing on only a small fraction of the total potential contribution of universities to regional innovation. Spin-offs and patents are both conceptually and empirically only one small way of how university outputs can become relevant for regional innovation.

By way of contrast, the twin function of graduates, but also of researchers moving to industry, as carriers of the stock of both codified and tacit knowledge and as skilled in problem-solving, in knowing how to create or absorb new knowledge, leads some authors to state that graduates are possibly the most important contribution of universities to innovative activity (Salter & Martin, 2001; Veugelers & del Rey, 2014). Leten, Landoni, and Van Looy (2014) investigate industry differences with respect to the impact of university graduates and research and find that while graduates have a positive impact on technological firm performance in all the sectors examined, university research only has a positive impact in more science-based sectors such as electronics and pharmaceuticals. This means that the impact of university patents and spin-offs is likely to be more sectorally specific than the impact of university graduates.

Furthermore, indirect support for the importance of graduates comes from investigating barriers to innovation. This allows in principle for a more focused view: rather than trying to single out one factor among a myriad of different ones driving innovation, firms are asked which barriers to innovation are most impeding their innovative activity. The available evidence shows that in countries close to the technological frontier, the lack of qualified employees is the barrier most likely to be perceived by firms (Hölzl & Janger, 2014). This kind of evidence is often based on the Community Innovation Survey, which does not differentiate the lack of employees by level of education, so that no precise information can be gained about the specific role of higher education.

All in all, it is surprising that the importance of graduates as a way to get university outputs involved into innovative activity does not figure more prominently in both the academic literature and in regional innovation strategies, compared with the importance attached to disembodied knowledge outputs of academic research (such as patents) or commercializing research discoveries through spin-offs. This is all the more surprising as frequently firms lament the lack of qualified employees, as well as of science and technology graduates, but to the best of the author's knowledge, they seldom complain about a lack of university-generated patents or spin-offs (see, e.g., Milne, 2013).

DETERMINANTS OF THE EFFECTIVENESS OF WAYS OF INTERACTION BETWEEN UNIVERSITIES AND FIRMS

In the third step, we look at the empirical evidence on which factors affect the effectiveness of universities' contributions to regional innovation, with a particular focus on whether research and teaching quality matters for the impact of universities on regional innovation. There is widespread evidence that research and teaching quality matter for the impact of universities on innovation and economic performance. E.g.,

- R&D intensive firms locate close to high quality universities (Abramovsky et al., 2007; Belderbos et al., 2009)
- Star scientists boost firm entry and start-up creation (Zucker & Darby, 2007, p. 4) "geographic distribution of new science-based industry can be mostly derived from geographic distribution of human capital embodying the breakthrough discovery upon which it is based"; also Di Gregorio and Shane, 2003, find correlation of scientific productivity with start-up creation
- Technology transfer activity is more successful in high productivity-universities (Conti & Gaule, 2011)

- Top research universities attract top (foreign) (PhD)-students, which e.g. in the US contribute disproportionately to innovation performance (Van Bouwel & Veugelers, 2012, 2013; Hunt & Gauthier-Loiselle, 2008)

In a systematic review of how academic engagement (relational academia-industry links such as joint R&D) differs from academic commercialisation (university spin-offs, or licensing of university patents), Perkmann et al. (2013) find a clear picture that at the individual level, scientific productivity is positively associated with both forms of research-based university contributions to innovative activity, engagement and commercialisation. Top-publishing university researchers also feature high levels of patenting and academic entrepreneurship. However, at the organisational level (department or university level), academic engagement is negatively associated with research quality in some studies and uncorrelated in other studies, whereas commercialization is also positively related to research quality at the organizational level. Perkmann et al. (2013) hypothesize that that may be due to highly motivated individuals not necessarily affiliated to higher quality research institutions who see academic engagement as a resource producing device at lower ranked institutions, where fewer resources are available.

In other words, R&D co-operations and contract research are to be found more frequently also in universities with lower scientific productivity, while commercialization based on patents and spin-offs is more likely to be found in universities with higher scientific productivity. Our review clearly shows that research quality – and being at the top in scientific productivity, at both the individual and the organizational level – matters for the performance in patents and spin-offs (in the "commercialization"-arm of university-industry ways of interaction). Of course, also differences in universities' internal organizational set-up will play a role for the effectiveness of universities' contribution to regional innovation. This concerns both the organization of research and teaching and the organization of third-mission related activities. As an example, the organization of academic working units of universities as departments or chairs may lead to different links with their regional environment. Departmental structures are usually more diversified than chair-based structures, potentially allowing for a wider range of links. A large literature analyses the determinants of effectiveness of technology transfer offices in terms of contractual licensing arrangements, incentive pay, local development objectives, staff experience, etc., usually finding significant effects of organizational differences on regional innovation performance (see, e.g., Conti & Gaule, 2011).

Overall, narrowly focusing on fostering patents and spin-offs through, e.g., incentives and support infrastructures (science parks) may be ineffective, both because it may fail to stimulate academic commercialization without underlying research prowess, and because the much bigger contributions of universities to regional innovation such as graduates, informal consulting and collaborative research are being overlooked. The focus in the academic literature, but also from policy makers, on commercialization through patents and spin-offs can be viewed

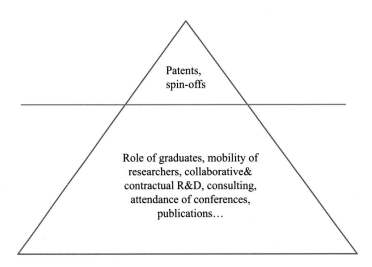

Figure 14.2. An iceberg model of universities' impact on regional innovation

as an "iceberg" model of universities' impact on regional innovation, as the most important ways of contribution seem to be less in the focus.

CONCLUSIONS

While universities have always played a role for innovation activities, recent conceptualizations of this role have led to a policy focus on improving the impact of universities on regional innovation through commercialization activities such as licensing technologies and setting up spin-offs based on university inventions. Frequent ways of implementations of such a focus can be seen, e.g., in funding for science parks and dedicated IPR commercialisation offices. In particular the Triple Helix and entrepreneurial universities literature often take top US research universities as examples for the entrepreneurial role of universities in regional innovative activities, which have large budgets and excellent teaching and research faculty, managing to attract the best researchers and students from all over the world. Also the national innovation systems literature leads to a focus on cooperation and the linkages of universities with business, without stressing the conditions of effectiveness of such linkages. Further strands of the academic innovation literature have focused on academic patenting and licensing, as well as on other forms of interaction mainly involving research (rather than the stock of knowledge available), such as publications, joint research, spin-offs etc.

The point of the present contribution is not to say that this literature is wrong, but that it misses important parts of the story, both in terms of the other pathways through which university outputs can impact on (and always have impacted on) regional innovation and in terms of the conditions of effectiveness for commercialization strategies, namely research excellence. We aimed at stressing the much larger role of universities in regional innovation, based on both a conceptual model of university-industry interaction and a review of the empirical evidence. Both elements or missions of universities – research producing knowledge and teaching producing graduates as carriers and able manipulators of knowledge – are of high importance for the innovation system of a region and its capacity to provide new technologies and support innovation in general. As we have tried to say, the first two missions research and teaching are at least as important for regional innovation as the third mission. Higher education graduates are one of the main carriers disseminating knowledge and skills from higher education institutions to firms (and the rest of the society), helping both to access the stock of knowledge and to create new knowledge in firms. Moreover, this contribution has stressed that in particular research quality and excellence is an important pre-condition for successful commercialization, as licensing income and spin-off dynamics are heavily skewed towards the top research universities.

At the same time, higher education institutions are sometimes criticized as ivory towers for their lack of producing patents and spin-offs. A focus on fostering commercialization of academic research only, without at the same time strengthening the core missions of research and teaching, carries hence the danger that additional funding is only provided for narrow aspects of university activities, limiting the contribution of universities to regional innovation. Teaching is already mostly overlooked by international university rankings, giving usually more weight to research excellence. When regional innovation policies also underestimate the importance of teaching for regional innovation, the teaching mission of universities may face more pressure, in terms of e.g. the allocation of public funding. It is noteworthy that the EU-initiative Innovation Union (European Commission, 2010) focuses on the transfer of research results through technology transfer offices, rather than on graduate mobility as a strong vehicle for making higher education institutions a valuable input for innovative activity.

To make that point to policy makers more clearly, there needs to be more evidence as to which way of interaction matters most to firms and other organizations, able to guide public policies and higher education institutions. Resource allocation and priority setting with a view to fostering the contribution of universities to regional innovation need more evidence in particular for teaching. For the improvement of a firm's capacity to innovate, it matters to understand not only the relevance of academic research, but also other significant factors such as human capital, skills development, "intrapreneurship", organizational capacity and entrepreneurship, factors that are rather produced by the teaching side of higher education institutions, that should be recognized by education and innovation policies. In fact, one corollary of our analysis is certainly that often, education policy is also innovation policy. Too often, the two are separate, with budgets unable to focus on cross-cutting priorities such as skills for innovation. One suggestion which can be investigated further, as an example, are regional study programmes tailored to regional firms' needs. When

UNIVERSITIES' ROLE IN REGIONAL INNOVATION

budgets are constrained, too much energy and funding flowing into setting up science parks and fostering spin-offs – using the research side of the third mission – rather than thinking about tailored graduate programmes for regional firms (developing the "teaching" side of the third mission!) may be ineffective. To take up the general theme of this book, with a view to their contribution to regional innovation, higher education institutions are definitely under a lot of pressure to cope with multiple challenges.

NOTES

[1] See http://web.mit.edu/facts/financial.html, and http://facts.stanford.edu/administration/finances
[2] See uni:data, the Austrian information system on universities.
[3] Defined in the Oslo Manual, p. 18, as "Innovation activities include all scientific, technological, organisational, financial and commercial steps which actually lead, or are intended to lead, to the implementation of innovations" (OECE -- Eurostat, 2005).

REFERENCES

Abramovsky, L., Harrison, R., & Simpson, H. (2007). University research and the location of business R&D*. *The Economic Journal, 117*(519), C114–C141.

Abramovsky, L., & Simpson, H. (2011). Geographic proximity and firm-university innovation linkages: Evidence from Great Britain. *Journal of Economic Geography, 11*(6), 949–977.

Adams, J. D. (1990). Fundamental stocks of knowledge and productivity growth. *Journal of Political Economy, 98*(4), 673–702.

Arundel, A., van de Paal, G., & Soete, L. (1995). *PACE report: Innovation strategies of Europe's largest industrial firms: Results of the PACE survey for information sources, public research, protection of innovations and government programmes: Final report*. Brussels: MERIT.

Balconi, M., Brusoni, S., & Orsenigo, L. (2010). In defence of the linear model: An essay. *Research Policy, 39*(1), 1–13.

Belderbos, R., Van Roy, V., Leten, B., & Thijs, B. (2014). Academic research strengths and multinational firms' foreign R&D location decisions: Evidence from foreign R&D projects in European regions. *Environment and Planning A 46(4), Nr. 4*, 920–42.

Bush, V. (1945). *Science, the endless frontier: A report to the president*. Washington, DC: US Government Printing Office. Retrieved from http://www.nsf.gov/od/lpa/nsf50/vbush1945.htm

Calderini, M., & Scellato, G. (2005). Academic research, technological specialization and the innovation performance in European regions: An empirical analysis in the wireless sector. *Industrial and Corporate* Change, *14*(2), 279–305.

Clark, B. R. (1983). *The higher education system: Academic organization in cross-national perspective* (94720). Berkeley, CA: University of California Press.

Cohen, W. M. & Levinthal, D. A. (1989). Innovation and learning: The two faces of R & D. *The Economic Journal, 99*(397), 569–596.

Cohen, W. M., & Levinthal, D. A. (1990). Absorptive capacity: A new perspective on learning and innovation. *Administrative Science Quarterly, 35,* 128–152.

Cohen, W. M., Nelson, R. R., & Walsh, J. P. (2002). Links and impacts: The influence of public research on industrial R&D. *Management Science*, 48(1), 1–23.

Conti, A., & Gaule, P. (2011). Is the US outperforming Europe in university technology licensing? A new perspective on the European Paradox. *Research Policy, 40*(1), 123–135.

D'Este, P., Tang, P., Mahdi, S., Neely, A., & Sánchez-Barrioluengo, M. (2013). The pursuit of academic excellence and business engagement: Is it irreconcilable? *Scientometrics, 95*, 1–22.

Della Malva, A., & Carree, M. (2013). The spatial distribution of innovation: Evidence on the role of academic quality for seven European countries. *Economics of Innovation and New Technology*, 22(5–6), 601–618.

Di Gregorio, D., & Shane, S. (2003). Why do some universities generate more start-ups than others? *Research Policy, 32*(2), Nr. 2, 209–227. doi:10.1016/S0048-7333(02)00097-5

Etzkowitz, H., & Leydesdorff, L. (2000). The dynamics of innovation: From National Systems and and "'Mode 2'" to a Triple Helix of university–industry–government relations. *Research Policy, 29*(2), 109–123.

Etzkowitz, H., Webster, A., Gebhardt, C., & Terra, B. R. C. (2000). The future of the university and the university of the future: Evolution of ivory tower to entrepreneurial paradigm. *Research Policy, 29*(2), 313–330.

EUA. (2014). *The role of universities in Smart Specialisation Strategies.* Brussels: EUA.

European Commission. (2010). *Europe 2020 Flagship Initiative Innovation Union 2010.* SEC.

Expert Group on Knowledge Transfer Indicators. (2011). *A composite indicator for knowledge transfer.*

Gibbons, M., & Johnston, R. (1974). The roles of science in technological innovation. *Research Policy, 3*(3), 220–242.

Goddard, J. (2011). *Connecting universities to regional growth: A practical guide, Commissioned by DG Regional Policy, European Commission, 2011.* Retrieved from http://ec.europa.eu/regional_policy/activity/research/publications_en.cfm

Goddard, J., Kempton, L., & Vallance, P. (2013). Universities and smart specialisation: Challenges, tensions and opportunities for the innovation strategies of European regions. *Ekonomiaz, 83*(2), 83–102.

Griffith, R., Redding, S., & Reenen, J. (2004). Mapping the two faces of R&D: Productivity growth in a panel of OECD industries. *Review of Economics and Statistics, 86*(4), 883–895.

Hewitt-Dundas, N. (2012). Research intensity and knowledge transfer activity in UK universities. *Research Policy, 41*(2), 262–275.

High Level Group. (2017). *Maximizing the impact of EU Research & Innovation Programmes, Lab-Fab-App, investing in the European future we want.* European Commission, DG Research and Innovation.

Hsu, D. H., Roberts, E. B., & Eesley, C. E. (2007). Entrepreneurs from technology-based universities: Evidence from MIT. *Research Policy, 36*(5), 768–788.

Hunt, J., & Gauthier-Loiselle, M. (2008). *How much does immigration boost innovation?* (Working Paper Series, No. 14312). National Bureau of Economic Research. Retrieved http://www.nber.org/papers/w14312

Kenney, M., & Goe, W. R. (2004). The role of social embeddedness in professorial entrepreneurship: A comparison of electrical engineering and computer science at UC Berkeley and Stanford. *Research Policy, 33*(5), 691–707.

Klevorick, A. K., Levin, R. C., Nelson, R. R., & Winter, S. G. (1985). On the sources and significance of interindustry differences in technological opportunities. *Research Policy, 24*(2), 185–205.

Kline, S. J. (1985). Innovation is not a linear process. *Research Management, 28*(4), 36–45.

Kline, S. J., & Rosenberg, N. (1986). An overview of innovation. In R. Landau & N. Rosenberg (Eds.), *Positive sum strategy: Harnessing technology for economic growth* (pp. 275–305). Washington, DC: National Academy Press.

Leten, B., Landoni, P., & Van Looy, B. (2014). Science or graduates: How do firms benefit from the proximity of universities? *Research Policy, 43*(8), 1398–1412.

Micaëlli, J.-P., Forest, J., Coatanéa, E., Medyna, G. (2014). How to improve Kline and Rosenberg's chain-linked model of innovation: Building blocks and diagram-based languages. *Journal of Innovation Economics, 15*(3), 59–77.

Milne, R. (2013). Alarm over skills shortage in Europe. *Financial Times.* Retrieved from http://www.ft.com/intl/cms/s/0/51dc6cca-c145-11e2-b93b-00144feab7de.html#axzz2ehsBtaoW.

OECD. (2015). *The future of productivity.* Paris: OECD.

OECD, Eurostat. (2005). "Oslo Manual. Guidelines for collecting and interpreting innovation data." A joint publication of OECD and Eurostat. Paris: OECD.

Perkmann, M., King, Z., & Pavelin, S. (2011). Engaging excellence? Effects of faculty quality on university engagement with industry. *Research Policy, 40*(4), 539–552.

Perkmann, M., Tartari, V., McKelvey, M., Autio, E., Broström, A., D'Este, P., Fini, R., ... Sobrero, M. (2013). Academic engagement and commercialisation: A review of the literature on university–industry relations. *Research Policy, 42*(2), 423–442.

Roper, C. D., & Hirth, A. (2005). A history of change in the third mission of higher education: The evolution of one-way service to interactive engagement. *Journal of Higher Education Outreach and Engagement 10*(3), Nr. 3, 3–21.

Salter, A. J., & Martin, B. R. (2001). The economic benefits of publicly funded basic research: A critical review. *Research Policy, 30*(3), 509–532.

Senker, J. (1995). Tacit knowledge and models of innovation. *Industrial and Corporate* Change, *4*(2), 425–447.

Stephan, P. (2007). Wrapping it up in a person: The mobility patterns of new PhDs. *Innovation* Policy *and the Economy, 7*, 71–98. Retrieved from http://www.nber.org/chapters/c0034.pdf

Suzuki, S., Belderbos, R., & Kwon, H. U. (2017). The location of multinational firms' R&D activities abroad: Host country university research, university–industry collaboration, and R&D heterogeneity. *Advances in Strategic Management*, 125–159.

Uyarra, E. (2010). Conceptualizing the regional roles of universities, implications and contradictions. *European Planning Studies, 18*(8), 1227–1246.

Van Bouwel, L., & Veugelers, R. (2012). An "Elite Brain Drain": Are foreign top PhDs more likely to stay in the US? (SSRN 2109278). Retrieved from http://papers.ssrn.com/sol3/papers.cfm?abstract_id=2109278

Van Bouwel, L., & Veugelers, R. (2013). The determinants of student mobility in Europe: The quality dimension. *European Journal of Higher Education, 3*(2), 172–190.

Van Looy, B., Landoni, P., Callaert, J., van Pottelsberghe, B., Sapsalis, E., & Debackere, K. (2011). Entrepreneurial effectiveness of European universities: An empirical assessment of antecedents and trade-offs. *Research Policy, 40*(4), 553–564.

Veugelers, R., & Del Rey, E. (2014). *The contribution of universities to innovation, (regional) growth and employment* (EENEE Analytical Report No. 18).

Zucker, L. G., & Darby, M. R. (2007). *Star scientists, innovation and regional and national immigration* (NBER Working Paper 13547).

Printed in the United States
By Bookmasters